French Fiction Today

Warren Motte

FRENCH FICTION TODAY

DALKEY ARCHIVE PRESS

First Dalkey Archive edition, 2017.

Library of Congress Cataloging-in-Publication Data
Names: Motte, Warren F., author.
Title: French fiction today / by Warren Motte.
Description: First Dalkey Archive edition. | Victoria TX : Dalkey Archive, 2017. | Includes bibliographical references.
Identifiers: LCCN 2017006132 | ISBN 9781943150168 (pbk. : alk. paper)
Subjects: LCSH: French fiction--21st century--History and criticism. | Meaning (Philosophy) in literature. | Literature--Philosophy.
Classification: LCC PQ681 .M686 2017 | DDC 843/.9209--dc23
LC record available at https://lccn.loc.gov/2017006132

www.dalkeyarchive.com
Victoria, TX / McLean, IL / Dublin

Dalkey Archive Press publications are, in part, made possible through the support of the University of Houston-Victoria and its programs in creative writing, publishing, and translation.

Printed on permanent/durable acid-free paper

For Gerald Prince

Contents

Introduction 3

Marie NDiaye's Greening 7

Jean Rolin's Explosion 29

Christine Montalbetti's Engaging Narrations 49

Antoine Volodine's Crossings 77

Marie Cosnay's Roman-Fleuve 101

Patrick Deville's Novelty 121

Gérard Gavarry's Ceremony 141

Lydie Salvayre's Voices 156

Tanguy Viel's American Novel 178

Pierre Bayard's Wormholes 197

Notes 218

Bibliography 236

Introduction

Among the many pleasures that fiction puts on offer, the opportunity to lose oneself in mild abstraction is by no means the least; and I imagine that all of us have availed ourselves of that opportunity, whether sparingly or in a more insouciant manner. For my part, I am intrigued by the way literary texts invite us to enjoy moments such as that, through gestures that are sometimes overt, and at other times a bit more subtle. There is a passage in Jean-Philippe Toussaint's first novel, *La Salle de bain* [*The Bathroom*] that puts such an invitation on offer, in a manner that is particularly eloquent. It occurs when his narrator is gazing out of his window into a rainswept Parisian street:

> It was raining. The street was wet, the sidewalks dark. Cars were parking. Other cars, already parked, were covered with rain. People were crossing the street quickly, going in and out of the post office in the modern building across from me. A little vapor began to cover my windowpane. Behind the thin coat of mist, I observed the passersby sending their letters. The rain gave them a conspiratorial air: stopping in front of the mailbox, they would draw an envelope from their coat and thrust it through the slot very quickly so as not to get it wet, meanwhile pulling up their collars against the rain. I put my face close to the window and, eyes against the glass, suddenly had the impression that all these people were inside an aquarium. Perhaps they were afraid? The aquarium was slowly filling. (*The Bathroom* 20)

Many things could be said about this textual moment. I am

chiefly interested, however, in the way that the narrator imagines his own situation with regard to the world around him. On the one hand, he is clearly *inside* his apartment, looking *out* at the street and at the people hurrying along it. On the other hand, as soon as he imagines that those people are in an aquarium, his position shifts to that of someone on the *outside* looking *in*. That outside-inness is more than passingly uncanny; and yet it seems to me perfectly exemplary of the kind of site that we inhabit when we read fiction.

For clearly, reading is a real-world activity. By that I mean that it takes place in the world of phenomena, a behavior that is conditioned (and sometimes constrained) by real-world considerations. We sit upright in our favorite chair or sprawl flat out on our sofa; the dogs are barking or they are silent; the telephone rings or it does not; our gimpy right knee is bothering us or it feels okay; we have made our mortgage payment on time or we are badly in arrears. Yet when we read fiction, we also dwell in the fictional world. Therein, we partake of the heady fruit of the lotus and lose ourselves. We gaze aghast upon the tortured souls in the eighth circle of Hell; we listen as a peer of the realm sounds his horn too late; we test the keen edge of a harpoon honed by a tattooed Kokovokoan; we detect the very particular aromas emanating from the kitchen as a middle-aged Irishman prepares to dine on the inner organs of beasts and fowls; we taste a perfectly prepared martini cocktail, shaken, not stirred. In other terms, we are always divided when we read fiction. We are *outside*, but we are also *inside*; we are *here*, but we are also *there*—and vice versa, as it were.

Seen in long focus, what is surprising about our behavior as readers is how easily we migrate from the phenomenal world to the fictional world, and back again. Indeed, that migration is so fluid and so constant that it may be more useful to imagine the reader as inhabiting both worlds simultaneously. In that latter light, we can view the real world and the fictional world in an isotopical and mutually implicative fashion, rather than in a hierarchical manner where one is always subordinated to the other. That may in turn provide us with a more lucid vision of our behavior as readers, engaging in a series of gestures that are sharpened, intensified, and refined by the immersive power of fiction. Without a doubt, such a dynamic demands significant agility on our part; and I am convinced that any readerly agility we may muster originates in the exercise of our critical faculties. In arguing that point, I do not mean to suggest that our readings are condemned to a joyless and dour sobriety of purpose. Quite to the contrary, I believe that it is when we put our critical powers *in play* that we truly come into our own as readers.

It also helps to recognize that we can immerse ourselves up to our necks in fiction, while never abdicating our critical faculties, that the one gesture does not debilitate the other. To the contrary, immersion actuates our critical sense, and our critical sense stokes our desire to inhabit the fictional world. If such were not the case, Jean-Philippe Toussaint's protagonist would see nothing more than a rainy street when he gazes out the window. And gazing upon *him*, we would see no more than random scribblings on a page. Such a perspective does not bear contemplation for long. Its very bleakness urges us toward another position, I think. One that we can occupy at our leisure, and wherein we are no longer obliged to choose between subject and object, self and other, inside and out.

That is the spirit in which I would like to approach the novels I will shortly be discussing. Each of these texts wagers insistently upon our willingness to speculate about literature and its uses, in an age when the value of literature is no longer taken as axiomatic. Each of these texts may be thought of as a *critical novel*, a form that calls upon us to engage with it in a critical manner, promising that meaning will arise in the articulation of writing and reading. Each of these authors participates in a debate about what the novel is as a cultural form in our present—and about what it may become, in a future that begins right *now.*

Some of these essays have appeared as articles in professional journals. I thank the editors for permission to use them here, in revised form. I have translated my quotations from the French originals, and I have translated the titles of French works, except those whose meaning seems self-evident (italics denote a published English translation). All translations are mine, unless otherwise noted.

Marie NDiaye's Greening

THE EXTRAORDINARY PROMISE evinced in Marie NDiaye's first writings, such as *Quant au riche avenir* [As to the rich future] (1985) and *Comédie classique* (1987), which were published while she was still in her teens, has by now been abundantly confirmed. NDiaye's talent is well beyond dispute, and the literary prizes she has been awarded—most notably a Prix Femina for *Rosie Carpe* (2001) and a Prix Goncourt for *Trois Femmes puissantes* [*Three Strong Women*] (2009)—suggest that her work appeals not merely to a small cadre of sophisticates, but to a broader, more general readership as well. There is something about her writing that masterfully resists recuperation and institutionalization, however, and that quality of her work has not escaped her critics. Perhaps it is bound up in the way NDiaye puts the very notion of marginality into play in her work, turning it this way and that, examining it from a variety of perspectives.[1] Conceivably it stems, in part at least, from the way she couches the fantastic in the fabric of the quotidian, in a dynamic of mutual interrogation.[2] Maybe it results from her desire to rethink literary convention, to question and to innovate.[3] The three major, obsessional themes that Lydie Moudileno has identified in NDiaye's writing, "fault, anxiety, and mediocrity" ("L'Excellent Français" 28), undoubtedly heighten the strangeness of her texts and thus bolster their resistance to easy normalization. And recently, Shirley Jordan has argued that ineffability, undecidability, and a ghostly quality characterize NDiaye's work, rendering it opaque and resistant to interpretation.[4]

It is that very opacity and that very resistance which interest me most closely in NDiaye's writings, for I am convinced that those phenomena are conscious constructions. They are elaborated, I believe, with a great deal of deliberation by a writer who wishes above all to claim an independence that is utterly particular in its terms. Among Marie NDiaye's texts to date, it is *Autoportrait en vert* [*Self-Portrait in Green*] (2005) which puts those traits on offer most insistently. Published twenty years after NDiaye's first book, with a dozen well-received works preceding it, her *Autoportrait* stands apart from her other texts, and calls the idea of the "oeuvre" into question. Readers have been quick to register the hybridity of the text,[5] granted that it mixes prose narration and photographic illustrations. For my part, I shall concentrate on the former rather than the latter. For one thing, those illustrations have been analyzed in detail by Shirley Jordan. For another, according to NDiaye herself, the question of illustration didn't interest her in the slightest, and indeed the photographs were arranged in the text not by her, but rather by her editor (Asibong and Jordan 195–97).

Elliptical, sibylline, dense, and arduous, NDiaye's *Autoportrait en vert* offers a rich field of maneuver for an inquisitive reader, and a textuality that challenges conventional strategies of interpretation, through effects of misdirection. The first and most obvious of those effects is contained in the title, for there is very little material in the text that can be identified as autobiographical, despite certain superficial and thinly anecdotal similarities prevailing between the first-person narrator of *Autoportrait* and NDiaye herself.[6] Readers familiar with Marie NDiaye's writing are used to the way her texts put forward a view of personal identity that is very skeptical. Yet in *Autoportrait en vert* that skepticism is far more pervasive and troubling still, embracing as it does the creation of character, the way the narrator tells her story, and, inevitably, the manner in which the author imagines herself. Instead of a self-portrait, what NDiaye provides in this text might be thought of as a dream of a self-portrait, in the first instance an oneiric fable about a woman dressed in green. Like the narrator, that woman lives near Bordeaux on the banks of the Garonne, itself green and in flood. As those waters rise, they serve to heighten the urgency and the sense of looming disaster that color the text from the very beginning:

> All of us know that the dikes surrounding our village allow the river to rise nine meters above its normal level before it floods us.
>
> We know that. It's the first thing that anyone who decides to move here learns, in this region that has always been subject to the Garonne's flooding. That which we don't know, this evening, is how it will be tonight, or tomorrow morning—if, like last time, ten months ago, the rising water will stop at the very top of the dike, or instead, like twenty-two years ago, it will overflow, drown our streets, rush into the ground floor of our houses, sometimes reach the second story, sometimes engulf the whole house. (*Autoportrait* 7)

That flooding is a canny, literal figure of certain techniques of textual saturation that NDiaye practices on the thematic level, in a work that plays dizzyingly with literary meaning, that spills over familiar conduits of narrative coherence, and that proclaims over and over again its own *greenness.*

The notion of greenness, announced in the title in apposition to the idea of the self-portrait, is yet another sleight of hand, pointing us in a direction that will offer rather little succor. For "green" is not so much a color in this text as it is a mood, or a way of being. As Marie NDiaye causes examples of greenness to multiply before us, one may be tempted to see in that trait something akin to character, or actant, in view of the broad and constantly evolving role that it plays in the textual economy and the importance with which it is invested.

In its first iteration, the idea seems simple enough, when the narrator remarks on a woman in green whom she sees as she takes her children to school and back each day:

> I passed her house four times a day. And I looked at her and never saw her, yet a dark dissatisfaction made me turn my head that way, despite which I never noticed anything other than a pretty and unusual banana tree. I braked in front of the house. I drove very slowly, and not once did my eyes fail to land on the motionless, wary silhouette of the woman in green standing next to the banana tree, far more imposing than herself, I have no doubt whatever about that. Because four times a day my heart was gripped by something unnamable but not absolutely negative, as soon as I had passed the farm with the lone banana tree in its fenced yard; and after that moment, on the way to school, there were many banana trees in many yards that my gaze encountered with the utmost indifference. (9)

As simple as it may seem on the level of event, however, it should be noted that Marie NDiaye takes considerable pains to wrap that encounter in strangeness. Why had the narrator failed to see the woman in green for such a long time? What is the character of the narrator's dissatisfaction, and why should it be "dark"? What is this unnamable thing that tugs at the narrator's heart each time she passes by that house? These are the sorts of questions that NDiaye encourages us to ask, as we try to make sense of the text through a process of readerly inferencing. She coaxes us on in that process through the example of her narrator, who likewise asks herself questions about this woman in green. "That which I don't know: is she waiting for me?" queries the narrator for instance, musing a bit later, "The woman in green is there, every day. Is she still there when I'm no longer there?" (12). Among all of the questions that we might be tempted to ask—and questions do ramify, after all, it's in their very nature—there is one that seems preponderant: how does this woman in green relate to the implicit promise in the text's title? Put another way, given her greenness, how might she be involved in a dynamic of self-portraiture?

It shortly becomes apparent that the latter question will have to be posed on a variety of fronts in *Autoportrait en vert*, for that woman in green is only the first in a series that Marie NDiaye puts on display, one after the other. I would like to rehearse those figures here very briefly, in order eventually to suggest the relationship that prevails among them. Not to put too fine a point on it, that relationship is tensive in character, it seems to me, as NDiaye shuttles between resemblance and difference in her descriptions of these women.

When the narrator reflects on the woman standing next to the banana tree, she is reminded of another woman, one whom she had encountered in her childhood: "The troublesome memory of a woman in green comes back to me, from the time I was in grade school. That big woman, both brutal and massive, promises us we'll go to jail if we eat too slowly, if we get our clothes dirty, if we raise our eyes toward hers. She has green eyes, and she matches them with her checked skirts and her turtleneck sweaters" (15). This woman surges up out of the narrator's distant past, and as such she may have even less claim to objective, phenomenal reality than the woman by the banana tree. Clearly, what brings her into being in the present is a gesture of memory and ideation, and it is interesting to note that her greenness is constructed both on the level of *being* (the color of her eyes) and on that of *appearance* (her skirts, her sweaters).

The next woman in the series is the narrator's new stepmother. She herself figures in yet another series, for the narrator mentions that her father had remarried four or five times (31). This woman dresses only in green, and although she is naturally brown-eyed, her husband's income allows her the luxury of wearing green contact lenses (30). Complicating her relationship with this woman, from the narrator's point of view, is the fact that they are of the same generation, and had been best friends before the narrator's father intervened: "His new wife had been my best friend for twenty years. Would she still be my best friend if she hadn't married my father? She certainly would be" (30). Curiously, this former friend of the narrator had not always been a woman in green, but in fact *became* one after her marriage: "my friend became a woman in green" (34), the narrator mentions, suggesting thereby that such greenness may in some cases be cultivated.

Thereafter appears another woman in green, one who is far more spectral in character, but no less important as a figure in the narrator's personal mythology:

> I never met that other woman in green, the fourth or fifth, whose presence in my personal mythology eclipses by its very light certain women in green in the real world. I'm not even sure that she was dressed in green. Perhaps it doesn't matter. She is nonetheless a pure allegory of a woman in green. Everything that I know about her comes from Jenny. (40)

In her manner of presenting this figure, that narrator shies away from arguments involving demonstrable, phenomenal existence, and instead makes the case for the importance of ideation, arguing that this woman in green, even if only *imagined*, has as much right to membership in this strange sisterhood as any of the others—and indeed perhaps more. In a sense, the narrator must make that gesture, since this woman is distanced from her by two removes. Rather than a character in her own story, she is a character in that of a friend, Jenny; and it is Jenny's reading of her greenness that counts here, in the first instance at least. This woman had married Jenny's childhood love, and as a result her greenness had come into full flower: "Jenny told me, I think, that this woman was always dressed in green" (49). Thereafter, she exercised a curious attraction upon Jenny herself, until the day when Jenny, stopping by for a visit, found that she had hanged herself in the basement. The narrator intimates that there was something about that event that Jenny found impossible to live with, for she herself died by a drug overdose—whether by accident or by design it is unclear—a few years thereafter.

Finally, there is the narrator's own mother. Like her former friend, her mother has remarried, and very unfortunately in her daughter's view. Like her former friend, too, the narrator's mother has become a woman in green, achieving that transformation in the space of an instant: "all of a sudden [she] she changes herself into a *woman in green*" (62–64). Gazing at her mother in her new guise, the narrator wonders how she herself is implicated in such a metamorphosis, what that change presages for her:

> And I discover suddenly, as my gaze lands on my mother's slim calves in their shiny stockings, on her hips swinging sharply, that my mother is a woman in green of a kind that I have not yet encountered—and what is this fate, I ask myself, that makes me meet my mother as a woman in green in order to persuade me that my own destiny lies there? There's no need to see her actually dressed in green—we're well beyond that sort of childishness. (68)

Clearly, the last figure in this catalogue ushers the narrator (and us right along with her) into the realm of the figural once and for all. Greenness accedes here to a status that can be understood only as a matter of ontology; and by virtue of that accession, it becomes for the narrator a question far more harrowing still.

Surveying those women in green, the question of their mutual affinity necessarily arises—and indeed Marie NDiaye takes great care to ensure that it should. The most salient and striking feature they share is that they are all anonymous when the narrator presents them to us.[7] It is as if the narrator had no means of identifying them in a more stable and conventional way. Or perhaps it is their very greenness that defines them, beggaring any other identifying traits before the fact. The narrator herself never reveals her name to us. One can read that as a typical move in contemporary fiction, which puts questions of identity on trial as a matter of course, or one can choose to read it as a more focused gesture in a text that adduces the notion of anonymity as a key term in a broader discourse involving the difficult construction of the self.

Marie-Claire Barnet suggests that the women toward whom the narrator points are linked by their mutual association with the Garonne.[8] Shirley Jordan sees in them an elective (rather than inherited) family, which enables the narrator to sculpt her identity to her own specifications.[9] Though I think those suggestions are useful and productive ones, I see these women in green a bit differently. There is something about each of them, and all of them collectively, that serves to put the narrator very ill at ease—and thereby putting us readers ill at ease, as well. In an effort to suggest what might be at issue in that dynamic, I would like to parse the greenness of those women a bit more closely.

That greenness is colored by a variety of attributes, some of them relatively stable over the course of the text, some of them far more slippery and shifting. One of the more reliable traits of women in green is that they are often unkind, if to different degrees. "Green couldn't be, nevertheless, the only color of cruelty," muses the narrator, "no more than green could be the necessary color of cruelty. But who can deny that cruelty likes to dress in various shades of green?" (15–16). The woman in the nursery school displays that trait in abundance. She is, in the narrator's recollection, a kind of ogress (26) who carries unsuspecting children "along an endless corridor" (15). Her purpose therein is not specified, but it cannot be innocent. She inspires terror and loathing in the narrator, even at many years' remove.

The narrator wonders aloud at one juncture in her story

whether greenness may serve as a kind of virtual contraceptive, protecting the woman who displays it from fertility (36). If such is the case, it is legitimate to associate greenness with a sexuality that is recreational, rather than procreational. It is charged with erotic power, but for reasons that are never made explicit. One woman in green's beauty has increased visibly, the narrator remarks, thanks to the sexual pleasure that she has found in her life (58); another, when offered a green silk scarf as a gift, chooses to wear it around her hips rather than around her neck (72). That eroticism has something telluric about it, and indeed the narrator muses early in her story upon a burgeoning, earthy eroticism that seems to take over her village in the springtime, when the Garonne is in full spate.

That feature of greenness harmonizes nicely, moreover with another attribute that NDiaye sketches on several occasions: its propensity to inspire jealousy in other women. That jealousy may be sexual in character, or it may be more simply affective. The narrator, for instance, cannot bring herself to pardon her former friend, for in her view the latter blithely sacrificed the friendship that they had shared in order to enter into an amorous relationship with the narrator's father. Seeing them together as a couple, now, makes the narrator jealous: "They glow with conjugal happiness, that's undeniable. So much so that they are enviable in their own way—yes, aren't they enviable?" (36). The narrator's friend Jenny is jealous, too, though her jealousy is in some sense more straightforward, granted that the woman in green has married Ivan, Jenny's former fiancé, and thus has usurped a role that Jenny feels to be rightfully hers. That woman nonetheless exerts a strange and powerful attraction over Jenny, who goes to visit her every day when Ivan is not at home. When finally she confesses those visits to Ivan, he too becomes enmeshed in a web of jealousy that is now more broadly distributed, if no better defined: "it's against her, Jenny, that Ivan's jealousy has turned" (59).

Distance and aloofness seem also to define these women in green. Reflecting on the woman her own mother has become, the narrator sketches her thus: "My mother is a woman in green, untouchable, deceiving, infinitely mutable, very cold, knowing how, through her will, to become very beautiful, but also knowing how not to desire it" (72). Her coldness is clearly a closely calculated display, just like her beauty—and indeed perhaps it is calculated to serve the same ends. These women in green have mastered the art of self-presentation; the image that they put on display is a sculpted and properly stony one in which nothing is left to chance, and which no mere event can trouble. That feature puts the women around them (the narrator or Jenny, for instance) very much in the wrong, as if they themselves were rendered weaker and more fragile by virtue of their frequentation of green women. Those latter are authoritative, even imperious in their relations with others. The woman standing by the banana tree whom the narrator sees every day as she takes her children to school, and whom the narrator describes unconditionally as "absolutely a woman in green," is obviously used to being obeyed without question, and she would never think of thanking anyone for a favor rendered (74). The rigid, unbending quality of these women in green must somehow be read, however, through their constant mutability, their quality of being "infinitely mutable," as the narrator puts it.

There are very few things in *Autoportrait en vert* upon which one can rely with certainty. One of those things is the principle of undecidability that colors the text from first page to last, and which makes it very difficult to say anything categorical about it. Certain critics see that feature as one of Marie NDiaye's writerly signatures.[10] Another reliable thing (and one most certainly affiliated with the former) is the principle of mobility upon which NDiaye wagers. It plays out on the level of character most obviously, but it also shapes the presentation of themes and ideas in NDiaye's work. Finally, there is the principle of alterity. Each of these women in green—whatever else she may be—is radically *other*, and her otherness infects the women who come into contact with her, such that they, too, come to feel contingent and out of place.[11] Greenness is a bane and a curse; it's a plague.

It is furthermore (and importantly) uniquely and exclusively feminine. That much at least is clear. Beyond that fundamental consideration however, greenness blurs the question of identity, rather than sharpening it. Throughout *Autoportrait en vert*, the proper name, normally the surest guarantor of identity, is a fragile, undependable thing at best. NDiaye puts that feature of her text into evidence early on, when the narrator wonders what it is about her sightings of the woman standing by the banana tree that disturbs her so: "But I have a taste for names, and, believing that my trouble came from not knowing the names of the inhabitants of the farm, I asked around. I was told: 'Oh, there? Those are the X . . .' And it happened to be a typical name in this area, one designating a lot of families. I got nothing out of it, there was nothing to be learned from a name like that one" (9–10). NDiaye's strategy here is an interesting one. Her narrator learns the woman in green's name, but we do not—or not quite yet at any rate. The narrator's informant patently finds nothing exceptional about the woman in green's family. Moreover, the family name itself is common to the point of banality, and, like the banal itself, it refuses to signify in any meaningful way. It frustrates the interpretive efforts that the narrator brings to bear; it just does not *make sense*.

Of course, our own efforts to make sense of things come hard up against senselessness in this passage too, if for reasons that are somewhat different. Obviously enough, Marie NDiaye is withholding information from us here—or feigning to do so, rather (for that information does not exist prior to its enunciation in a fictional world)—as she plays upon our semiotic desire. For the time being, we must put up with this "X," the very integer of the unknown, instead of the name, banal and meaningless though it may be. Such a tactic figures strongly in the way that NDiaye elaborates the hermeneutic code[12] in her *Autoportrait*, and she exploits it deftly on a couple of other occasions. In an effort to prove to herself that the woman in green by the banana tree actually exists, the narrator one day goes to visit her. Inviting the narrator to have a cup of coffee, the woman in green obligingly introduces herself, mentioning both her family name (which the narrator already knows) and her first name (26). She quite naturally expects the narrator to reciprocate, yet she refuses to do so, choosing instead to withhold that information from the woman in green—and, not incidentally, from us as well. Once again, the narrator keeps back the name, both her own and that of the woman in green, playing a sly game with naming and, more broadly, with the question of identity. When we finally do learn the woman in green's name, NDiaye causes her narrator to sabotage it as a reliable signifier of identity: "I think that the woman in green, who told me her name was Katia Depetiteville, is not Katia Depetiteville" (27). As much as the narrator might like to *know*—and as much as we would like to know, right along with her—such knowledge seems, for the moment at least, well beyond her ken.

Throughout *Autoportrait en vert*, women in green have the vexatious habit of putting the notion of identity squarely on trial. Jenny's rival, for instance, whom Jenny had seen hanged and dead, seems to make a reappearance after Jenny's own death, to the narrator's consternation: "Might it be imaginable that someone other than the woman in green had been buried in her place? But then who was the hanged woman whose knees Jenny had embraced?" (60–61). In a very similar perspective, the narrator wonders where her mother might be, now that she has a new husband and a new daughter. One day, she imagines, she will receive a letter. Not a simple, forthright one certainly, but rather one that serves to put her mother's identity very much in question: "I won't write, and neither will they, until the day perhaps when I will get a letter from an unknown place, with photos of unknown people, people who will prove to be my relatives in different degrees—a letter whose authenticity I will doubt, even if it is signed 'Mommy,' and which I will tuck away somewhere it will never be found" (72). The doubt that clouds the question of her mother's identity quite naturally troubles the narrator, for it vexes the way that she imagines herself. The specter of unreliable identity is vexatious for the reader as well—and all the more so, of course, in a narrative presenting itself as an *autoportrait.*

The manner in which Marie NDiaye subverts the important issue of identity in her text takes its place in a broader pattern of event and theme wherein she invokes the uncanny. NDiaye establishes that topos as a matter of priority, informing us as she does so that things in the world she presents are not as we might expect them to be. Having herself seen the woman in green on several occasions (though not yet having spoken with her), the narrator stops her car in front of that woman's house and asks her four children if they observe anyone standing next to the banana tree. When each of them reports that there is nobody to be seen, the narrator reacts with something that is more than mere perplexity: "A shiver ran up my spine" (11). Clearly, there is something prodigious about the woman in green, something that escapes from the categories we use to understand the phenomenal world, something very troubling indeed. Marie-Claire Barnet speaks of "the feeling of confusion into which NDiaye plunges us" (159),[13] and in this case that sense of confusion is generated by the narrator's feeling that things cannot be explained rationally, a feeling that she projects very largely upon us.

Greenness in this world comes prefurnished with its own uncanniness, then. That difficult lesson is confirmed when the narrator, strolling through her village, comes upon a woman she ought to know: "Just then, I run into Cristina, but as soon as I see her I no longer know if it's her, or Marie-Gabrielle, or Alison—it's not that I can't think of her first name, but rather that I no longer know who this one is" (17). Cristina (or Marie-Gabrielle, or Alison) is wearing shorts with green flowers on a green background, despite the fact that "green is not the usual color of women's shorts" (17). As this encounter develops, the narrator is sucked into a whirlpool of confusion. The woman in the green shorts speaks of her children, but the narrator seems to remember that Cristina is childless; she wonders if she has not seen the "real" Cristina across the street, while chatting with the "unreal" Cristina; after their chat, the narrator is astonished to learn that it has lasted two whole hours. Marie NDiaye is careful to leave that encounter unexplained, never furnishing us with a way to rationalize it, preserving it as something fundamentally strange and aberrant.

The same is true of an incident wherein the narrator's children find an unknown creature in the road near their house. "—It was all black! It ran away, it's quick!" they report to her, asking her to tell them what it might be. Her reply suggests that the creature is not only unnamed, but also unnamable: "—Go back in the house, I say, with a shiver. No, I don't know its name. I think, I say, that it doesn't have a name in our language" (93). Yet again, the *shiver* that she experiences tells us that we are in the presence of something very unnatural indeed. The children are clearly very perturbed by this incident, as is their mother. Beyond that local effect, however, this is a moment when reason breaks down quite irretrievably in the text, an aporetic moment clearly framed as such by NDiaye.

Other such moments are not hard to find in *Autoportrait en vert*. I mentioned that Jenny's rival seems to return after her death; and when she does so, she is resplendent in green, more green than ever as it were, "wrapped in a very elegant green coat with cuffs and collar made of real fur, dyed green" (57). She is not the only ghost that haunts NDiaye's *Autoportrait*.

There is something clearly spectral about Katia Depetiteville, for instance. During one of her early visits to that woman in green, the narrator sees Katia throw herself off the balcony of her house. A moment later, the narrator is sitting in Katia's kitchen, unaware of how she got there, while Katia picks herself up from the ground, explaining that she had not jumped to impress the narrator, but rather to do away with herself. She inquires as to the object of the narrator's visit with a calmness as superb as it is disquieting, granted the circumstances. Obviously shaken, the narrator tries as she may to understand that encounter: "I ask myself: where is the real Katia Depetiteville? When later I mention the woman in green, in the schoolyard or in the village, people reply with astonishment, Katia Depetiteville has been dead for at least ten years. And I won't be surprised, having anticipated that" (27). Plainly enough, those others whom the narrator consults fail utterly to *see* Katia Depetiteville, just as the narrator's own children fail to see her. In the very best tradition of apparitions, in other terms, Katia's appearances are very selective indeed.

A question arises inevitably here: why can the narrator see Katia, where others cannot? If Katia's very greenness designates her as an individual well outside of the ontological norms that we habitually appeal to, does the narrator in some sense share that status—or that curse? Throughout the *Autoportrait*, the narrator ponders the question of her relationship to the women in green, and that of her own position with regard to greenness itself. Is the latter a state of being that awaits her, or is it a contagion that she has already contracted? What kinds of inflections will it have, has it already had, upon her behavior, upon her thinking, upon her self? Those questions and many others of similar stripe circulate freely in the *Autoportrait*, a text that puts on stage elaborate dramas of interpretation wherein the desire to know is played agonistically against the failure to understand. As I mentioned earlier, these are the moments that intrigue me most in this text, for they seem to anticipate and parry in advance the kinds of interpretational gestures that readers are inclined to make. As the narrator struggles to make sense of things, her efforts enfigure ours, sometimes frankly, sometimes ironically.[14] Thus, while we read *Autoportrait en vert*, we inevitably watch ourselves read as well, for such is the way that NDiaye has constructed her text.

"Really, I don't understand that Katia" (75), the narrator complains. One might point out, however, that her failure to understand this first woman in green is the very motor of this story, it is what allows the story to *become*. Furthermore, whatever else she may be (and we don't know much about her in fact, apart from her failure to understand the women in green), the narrator is deeply committed to stories. "All stories interest me" (11), she observes early in her narrative; decidedly, she is a creature of narrative. She looks upon stories with an eye that is not utterly naive. To the contrary, she is aware that certain stories may arise from other stories, or serve to engender further stories, as the case may be. Having listened to the story told by the woman who may or may not be Cristina, the narrator senses that she may have heard it before. "Either someone told me that story, or it's a scene borrowed from a novel that both of us happen to have read," she muses. "Now I'm eager to get home in order to look in my library for the book from which this story was taken" (23). This story demands that she *do* something with it, in other words. She is not content to be a passive consignee of narrative; rather, she is impelled to act upon it in some way, even if her action does not allow her a full understanding of the story's meaning. On one occasion, she frets that she has over-interpreted the letter that Jenny's parents had sent her after Jenny's death (61). On another, she realizes that something crucial about the story her father's new wife has just told her has escaped her: "Ambiguity once again, gropings, questions about all of this green" (31).

If Marie NDiaye causes her narrator to grapple so closely with the problem of interpretation, it is at least in part because she wishes to coax her reader into a meditation on that very problem. It is just when that problem is the thorniest, intriguingly enough, that a message becomes apparent to the narrator—and perhaps to us as well. For even in those moments when the narrator fails most miserably to understand (in the *greenest* moments, so to speak) she senses nonetheless that the stories she hears implicate her in ways that are absolutely unavoidable:

> But for my own part, how can I not see a fatal meaning in all of that? How can I not see, in the apparent coincidence of my father's remarriage and the transformation of my friend into an eternal woman in green, a message addressed to me, transmitted not only by the particular color of this woman, but by the pair of them, a woman in green and a skeletal father? How to read that message, I still don't know. (33)

These stories tell her something about herself. Each woman in green tells her something about herself. Each narrative contains a nugget of truth about herself. Taken together, we might see those stories as different elements in a self-portrait that is simultaneously very hypothetical and very real. Very real, because the narrator (and I am speaking of the *narrator* here, rather than of NDiaye, at least for the time being) tells her own story, such as it is, through those other stories in *Autoportrait en vert*. Very hypothetical, because that self-portrait surely does not seem detailed enough, or coherent enough, or convincing enough for that matter. That this should be the case is hardly surprising, for the narrator is very chary indeed about revealing who she really is, especially when confronted with an audience so patently *green*: "in spite of the woman in green's face, so close that I could raise my hand and touch it, something impalpable, a veil, a glimmering of unreality prevents me from telling her who I am" (26). And in point of fact, is Marie NDiaye's own stance in this book so very different from that of her narrator?

When she is invited to a literary colloquium in Ouagadougou, where her father and his new wife now live, the narrator regards the prospect of seeing her father with a great deal of trepidation. She has never lived with him, and thus her father does not know her at all well. "Moreover this man, my father, this concerned, intelligent man, so thin, prides himself on never reading a novel. Consequently I know that he has never read me, and that he prefers to ignore the existence of my books, out of respect for me as it were, because he considers literature as something so vile" (80). Behold a father's judgment in its crudest form, unnuanced, unswayed by circumstance, and quite beyond appeal. Yet it is just in such a moment that the narrator reveals something fundamental about herself: she is not merely a recipient of stories, she is also a maker of stories. And if the lesson she has learned about the stories she hears—that there is always a message therein addressed to her—is a valid one, perhaps the same holds true for the stories she tells. Except that in the latter case, stories being as transitive as they are, the message is addressed to someone else. In certain instances, it is perhaps as wise not to seek that message too energetically: "Isn't it better like that, moreover, isn't it better that parents refrain from reading their children's novels? What could they possibly find of benefit to themselves therein?" (80). What indeed could parents find to like in the writings of their child, that is, insofar as *they themselves* are concerned, and quite apart from any other story those writings might tell?

In other instances, however, we may have very little choice in the matter, and such is the narrator's case, I believe. Confronted again and again by women in green, she cannot turn her back on the message that they would seem to convey. For one thing, she senses early on that these encounters are not isolated events, but rather part of a pattern; at different stages in her life, the narrator is destined to meet women in green (27). She knows, too, that Katia Depetiteville takes her place in this series, as one among several: "I'll see her again, and we will almost be friends. I know that one day another green woman will replace her, one whom I have likewise not chosen" (28). Each woman in the series presents herself as a different one, to be sure, but there is an essential sameness about them that is as undeniable as it is uncanny, and it is that sameness, that *greenness*, which seizes the narrator's imagination. When she sees Katia Depetiteville for the last time, for instance, the narrator feels certain that something of Katia—if not "Katia" herself—will one day return: "Katia Depetiteville, forever a woman in green in my memory, opens in back of her the door upon which she had been leaning, and retreats backwards, a thin smile on her lips. I never saw her again. I never heard anything about her. Oh, she'll come back—but in what shape? She'll come back—but how?" (75). There is, of course, a ghostly quality to these women in green. They are *revenants* of a sort; they do come back, and they do haunt the narrator.

Yet I believe that something else is going on here as well, something more deeply embedded in the way this text functions as a fable of fiction, and in the way it dramatizes an extremely skeptical view of personal identity. As much as they trouble the narrator, put her to the question, and cause her to doubt the evidence of her own experience, the women in green nonetheless satisfy a deep desire on her part:

> Because I think of my mother, of Ivan's wife, of my stepmother, and I worry about losing my mind if all these women in green disappear one after the other, leaving me unable to prove their existence, and my own originality. I wonder, in my sisters' tidy kitchen, how I would bear a life bereft of women in green, projecting their equivocal silhouettes in the background. In order to get through these moments of torpor, deep boredom, and disabling languor, I have to remember that they adorn

> my thoughts, my subterranean life, that they're here, both real beings and literary figures, without whom the bitterness of experience seems to burn my skin and flesh right to the bone. (77)

Indeed, the role these women in green play for the narrator could hardly be clearer. They fire her imagination in crucial ways. They satisfy her need for the extraordinary, the exceptional, the *romanesque*. Their stories are the only ones that really interest the narrator. Those women, and the stories they tell, enable the narrator to dream, to invest her "subterranean life" with meaning all the more pungent by virtue of its alterity, and eventually to create. They are the embodied ideas of fiction in this text which, more than anything else, puts on offer a sustained reflection on the process of literary ideation.

As such, the narrator recognizes that her relationship with these women in green is impelled by something more powerful still than desire, something close to absolute exigency or requirement. It is not for nothing that the tune she hums to herself after her children fail to see Katia Depetiteville is "*You're the one I need*" (11). She knows that the women in green will come back, and finds that knowledge comforting. Moreover, each successive return, each incarnation of the woman in green, seems to come a little bit closer to the narrator, and seems thus to implicate her in that greenness a little more deeply, from Katia Depetiteville, to her former friend and current stepmother, to her own mother. As she thinks about what the future might hold, the narrator senses the ineluctability of such a process—and also, insofar as she herself is concerned, its profound necessity: "I dream that one morning perhaps, in fifteen or twenty years, I'll hear the doorbell ring, and I'll see before me a small girl with dark hair, saying 'I'm your half-sister, Bella,' in a shy, trembling voice in which something green can be heard—green like her eyes, her sweater, her pants, so that things will never be finished" (91). Each of those women projects her greenness upon the narrator, and despite her doubts, hesitations, and uncertainties, the narrator clearly basks in that greenness. And with each encounter, she is able to inhabit that greenness a little more closely. Such greening, if only by proxy and through ideation, is deeply satisfying to the narrator.

It is important to recognize, however, that the narrator's greening is not a matter of simple projection. To the contrary, it results from the recognition of a profound alterity in these women in green, and the perception of a strangeness in them which resists the narrator's interpretive efforts at every juncture. These women are fundamentally unfamiliar to the narrator, and indeed they must remain so if she wishes to be greened in her turn. Their otherness clearly puts the narrator's vision of her own identity painfully to the question; but at the same time it enables her to imagine a life beyond her familiar world, one that is far more ample, intriguing, and colorful.

One may wonder if the same is not true of Marie NDiaye herself. If the narrator is greened through the mediation of women whom she has very largely imagined, might NDiaye be greened by the narrator she has created? And just as the women in green announce for the narrator the possibility of living a creative life, might the narrator guarantee the same possibility to NDiaye? It is a commonplace to suggest that a writer invests herself in the characters she creates, and in a sense lives through them. In the case of Marie NDiaye, that commonplace may deserve more attention than we usually accord it, for from the beginning she has refused to engage in debates about identity politics, and has stoutly resisted narrow, reductive efforts to recuperate and classify her, whether as a "Francophone writer," a "woman writer," or a "black writer," claiming instead her right to be, well, a *writer*. The staking of such a claim is one of the principal goals of this *Autoportrait en vert*, I believe. Responding recently to an interviewer's question about whether her position with regard to the idea of "race" has changed over the course of her career,

Marie NDiaye replies, "well, me, no . . . I can't see myself, for my part, as a black woman" (Asibong and Jordan 199). Perhaps one may read, in the *greening* that colors this *Autoportrait* from first page to last, NDiaye's will to define herself in a rather different manner, as the person she wishes to be, quite apart from the expectations of others, and strictly on her own terms.

Jean Rolin's Explosion

Just as a matter of observation, it is a curious tale that hinges upon the rupture of a radiator hose. Yet that is precisely the case of Jean Rolin's *L'Explosion de la durite* [*The Explosion of the Radiator Hose*] (2007), the chronicle of a trip whose purpose is to convey an automobile from Paris, the capital of Darkest France, to Kinshasa, the capital of the Democratic Republic of the Congo. It is a pleasingly subtle text, a narrative as sly and canny as one is likely to find in contemporary French literature. One doesn't quite know what to call it, however, in view of how lustily it plays on the boundaries of genre. Prose fiction, autobiography, travel narrative, participatory journalism, and historiography all compete with each other here, sometimes loyally and equally, sometimes in ways far less balanced. One might as well call the text a "novel," invoking that word as a default term, and for lack of a better one. It is a much-contested term, to be sure; but it is also extremely resilient, because the novel, these days (at least the novel of the "serious" stripe), is almost always a hybrid form, one wherein hallowed generic convention has ruptured no less spectacularly than Rolin's radiator hose.[1]

Turning once again to that event (as one must necessarily do, time and again, in any attempt to come to grips with this text), it shortly becomes clear that its narrative profile is indeterminate, and that, like certain experiments in graphic art, it changes shape as the angle from which one beholds it shifts. In one perspective, it is the text's center of gravity, the place toward which other events strain, either through prolepsis or analepsis. In another perspective, it constitutes the narrative "now" of the text, the moment when a variety of discourses engaging a variety of pasts find reconciliation in a present, however ephemeral the latter may prove to be. In yet another light, granted the fact that it is inscribed in the title of the novel, that event clearly enjoys a rare authority in the general economy of the text, though the uses of that authority are not immediately obvious. Finally, it is possible to conceive the rupturing of the radiator hose as a kind of explosion of truth—insofar as one can imagine the appearance of truth on a narrative horizon that is otherwise so broadly furnished with hesitation, instability, and doubt.

Jean Rolin puts that event's preeminence on stage in the very first words of the text, making the first move in a game he will play with his reader throughout the novel:

> When the radiator hose [*durite*] exploded, the automobile, since its odometer had been reset to zero, had covered precisely ninety-nine thousand four hundred meters. It was traveling at more than 100 km/h, the needle of the temperature gauge lodged in the red zone. Before that, Patrice had stopped twice in order to open the hood and examine the motor, but he had deduced from his observations the conclusion that he could get back on the road and drive at that same speed. (*L'Explosion* 9)

A variety of things are going on in this passage. First and most obviously, the word *durite* (which the reader has already encountered in the title, of course) is a very arcane word in French, and functionally indecipherable to all but the most hardcore devotees of the internal combustion engine. It is an obstacle to understanding, placed at the very threshold of the text; and those assiduous readers whom this word sends scurrying to the dictionary may find that the definition they find therein does not bring significant illumination. The word is a very curious one, then, and it will shortly become the totemic word of this very curious novel. One might also notice the ironic manner in which Rolin introduces the notion of the journey in this incipit. The figure "ninety-nine thousand four hundred" may strike the reader as denoting a very great distance indeed; but when one realizes that meters are at issue, rather than kilometers, one is obliged to recalibrate. Granted that something just shy of a hundred kilometers is involved, one may be tempted to recalibrate one's expectations for this tale as well, because there is a suggestion here that its dimensions may be likewise short of epic.

Finally, Rolin takes pains in this passage to place the idea of reliable inference on trial, invoking Patrice's "conclusion" only to sabotage it, dramatically and irretrievably, in the very next sentence: "Erroneous conclusion, it was now easily understood, seeing the automobile immobilized at the side of the road" (9). This effect announces a narrative governed by uncertainty or, more precisely stated, by the principle of unpredictability. That principle is undoubtedly the most salient characteristic of *L'Explosion de la durite*, closely followed by others—instability, randomness, incongruity, for instance—clustering around it in loose affiliation. The fact of the matter is that very little is *given* in this text, very few things are axiomatic and beyond question. We know that a used Audi is to be transported from Paris to Kinshasa. We meet a narrator who remains anonymous until well into the text, when we learn that his first name is "Jean" (92); a bit further on, he seems struck by the fact that one of Joseph Conrad's fellow travelers up the Congo River in 1890 was named "Rollin" (106). The narrator has agreed to accompany the Audi, first by sea then by land, on behalf of a Congolese refugee named "Foudron" who resides in Paris, but has been obliged to leave his wife and children behind in Kinshasa. Put into service as a taxi upon its arrival, the Audi will provide a living for Foudron's family. Whereas Foudron's motivation is thus perfectly clear, that of the narrator is distinctly less so; yet he is careful to mention that, unlike Foudron, it was not money which prompted him to undertake this project (46).

There ends, practically speaking, that which we may know for certain about this narrative world. Indeed the deliberately constructed ambiguity of the narrator's motivation gives forth upon a whole tribe of cognate uncertainties that simultaneously vex and enrich this text. Chief among them is the unpredictability of narrative mode, as Rolin veers vertiginously, throughout *L'Explosion de la durite*, from one discursive register to another. One is at a loss to know where this novel is *going*, an effect all the more disconcerting in a narrative that wagers so heavily on the voyage tale, that most teleological of forms.

The diegetic path that Rolin takes is a wandering one, and he voices his story in a variety of ways. Upon occasion, his narrative verges upon fantasy, as when, in the Congolese night, the narrator hears spirits agitating a landscape that is otherwise utterly immobile (16). That tone contrasts sharply with a far more rationalist, flatly constative one that Rolin deploys frequently in the text in order to describe daily life aboard a merchant ship, for example, or the trials of getting a car through customs in a West African port of entry. Yet another tone is patently confessional and far more intimist in character. In that mode, Rolin postulates the strict identification of author and narrator, suggesting that the personal past which the narrator invokes is in fact his own. Sometimes the focus is upon small things, such as the plight of a bird that has lost its way and has become frightened and exhausted; sometimes the focus is far broader, for instance when Rolin discusses the political history of the Congo in the twentieth century.

Rolin himself is certainly aware of the equivocal nature of his narration, for the shifts in tone are so brutal as to make one conclude that they are deliberately staged, as part of a more general narrative strategy. From time to time, Rolin plays squarely upon the nebulous, dubious character of his enterprise, and in such cases it is legitimate to read his remarks doubly, both as commentary upon his trip and as commentary upon the writing of that trip: "Even before the incident that I am about to relate, it had not escaped me that the shadiness characterizing many of my maneuvers, whose real objectives are sometimes difficult to discern, or the dubious reputation of the countries, or even the people, that those maneuvers cause me to frequent, had awakened in certain people the suspicion that I entertained relations with the 'services'" (80). That he should be mistaken for a spy, in other terms, does not displease him. Moreover, that his account of his trip should display some of the more conventional features of the spy novel is perhaps not entirely coincidental.

In fact, if one reads *L'Explosion de la durite* against the backdrop of Rolin's work as a whole, one may begin to wonder if the former does not quite deliberately put into play the impressive diversity of technique and approach manifested in the latter. In other words (and having already invoked the notion of the hybrid in my liminary remarks), it is tempting to see in *L'Explosion de la durite* a hybridization of the various writerly gestures that Jean Rolin has practiced throughout his career.[2] There are passages of straightforward, traditional journalism here, reminiscent of some of the pieces that animate Rolin's 2006 collection, *L'Homme qui a vu l'ours* [The man who saw the bear]. There is "engaged" political journalism, too, of the kind that characterizes *Campagnes* [Campaigns] (2000), a series of texts focusing on events in former Yugoslavia in the 1990s; or like *Chrétiens* (2003), which deals with the fate of Palestinian Christians. *L'Explosion de la durite* incorporates a novelistic dimension of the sort one finds in *L'Organisation* (1996); yet here it is leavened by an even stronger current of autofiction. There is testimony based on participation, where the author injects himself into a given situation in order to report on it from the inside as it were. Many of Rolin's texts display that feature, but it is perhaps most obvious in *Terminal Frigo*

[Refrigerator dock] (2005). Finally, there is a close attention paid to the people and the phenomena of the margins, to the kind of stories rarely told in literature. That is a common thread in Rolin's work, one that is particularly apparent in texts such as *Zones* (1995) and *La Clôture* [Closure] (2002).

Granted the particular horizon that Rolin wishes to explore, the instability of narrative mode in *L'Explosion de la durite* is hardly surprising. Nor is it the only unstable site in the novel. Space, for instance, is constantly shifting in ways that are impossible to predict. One may jump without warning from a McDonald's in Paris to the bridge of a steamer in the Bay of Biscay; from a dock in Antwerp to an apartment in Kinshasa; from Gdansk to Berlin to Bordeaux to Abidjan to Brazzaville. It is difficult to navigate the narrative space in this novel with any degree of confidence—and indeed Rolin carnivalizes that kind of spatial uncertainty when he mentions that it is hard to find one's way around present-day Kinshasa, because the names of its streets are constantly changing: "These toponymical indications are of little real use, Kinshasa being the kind of city where nobody calls the streets by their current official names" (197).

Like space, time is a very problematic notion in this text, where temporal focus shifts without warning. Dramatically different moments rub elbows here, in astonishing propinquity, organized only tenuously by the rupture of the radiator hose and the comforting narrative present it defines. Thus, Rolin's account of his journey is constantly interrupted by evocations of other points in his personal history: the early 1980s in Poland, when he reported on Solidarity; May 1968 in Paris, when as a student radical he was wounded and had to be hospitalized; the mid-1960s, when as an adolescent he lived in the Congo; and so forth. Other, far less subjectivist junctures abound here, too: the final decade of the nineteenth century, when Joseph Conrad traveled into Africa; the Second World War; the heroic and less heroic moments of the Congo, from an oppressive colonial past to a fractured and uncertain present.

Thus, insofar as narrative mode, space, and time are concerned, Rolin plays fast and loose. Undoubtedly, his wish is that such narrative mobility may find its natural counterpart in a mobile reading, one that readily interprets the many apparent incongruities of this text as surface phenomena in a more subtle discourse that turns form into theme. For on the level of theme, incongruity is inscribed on practically every page of *L'Explosion de la durite*. In the rich intertextual fabric of the novel, for instance, two authors are preeminent. I have already mentioned Conrad; the other is Marcel Proust—and it would be difficult to imagine, I think, odder literary bedfellows. Nonetheless, they appear insistently in Rolin's text, and frequently together, as in this scene where the narrator's ship is stopped, far from shore: "Then, almost immediately, it began to list strongly toward the port side, just as though, in a sense, I were reading Proust (and being welcomed as a guest at La Raspelière) in circumstances recalling Conrad instead, and notably that episode of *Lord Jim* when the protagonist sins by irresolution, stamping his life with the fatal character which will determine everything that follows" (143).

Other effects play out a thematics of incongruity and unpredictability in different ways. Foudron, for instance, the Congolese refugee, has asked for political asylum in France; yet he is accorded the status of a "medical refugee" because he has a heart condition. When he does fall ill, however, it is not because of cardiac problems, but rather because of a lung infection (52–53). Under the influence of his readings of Proust, the narrator compares Marcel's introduction to the Duchess of Guermantes to his own introduction to the captain of the *San Rocco*, the vessel transporting him and the Audi to the Congo. All things considered, he finds his captain, a weathered Pole of few illusions and fewer words, a poor substitute for a duchess.

In similar manner, when he compares the three mates serving the *San Rocco* to the Three Musketeers, the narrator finds that fiction mocks life just as lustily as life mocks fiction.

Among all of these techniques and effects, what becomes clear is that *L'Explosion de la durite* is a text which—like a steamer with many years of service to its credit—takes its time, sets its own pace, and refuses to be rushed. As such, it is patently an example of what Ross Chambers has called "loiterature," that is, writing which wagers on the dilatory, which does not proceed directly to the points it wishes to make, but which instead proceeds indirectly, obliquely, by fits and starts, in a crab-like manner. Chambers points out that, despite its apparent innocence and naivety, loiterly writing is in fact subtly subversive with regard to both literary and social tradition:

> A reason I'm interested in loiterly literature, then, is that it has this characteristic of the trivial: It blurs categories, and in particular it blurs those of innocent pleasure taking and harmless relaxation and not-so-innocent "intent"—a certain recalcitrance to the laws that maintain "good order." In so doing, it carries an implied social criticism. It casts serious doubt on the values good citizens hold dear—values like discipline, method, organization, rationality, productivity, and, above all, work—but it does so in the guise of innocent and, more particularly, insignificant or frivolous entertainment: a mere passing of the time in idle observations or witty remarks, now this, now that, like the philosopher pursuing his ideas as he sits daydreaming on his bench. Or like the poet mooching along, his idleness a contrast to the busy street, going to the bank and the bookstore, doing this, then that. (*Loiterature* 8–9)

L'Explosion de la durite is "loiterly" from first page to last; yet the principle of the dilatory can be espied on far narrower textual horizons here, as well. Indeed, it is inscribed in each of Rolin's sentences. The latter take their time, too, stretching out over the page luxuriously, meandering, and—not coincidentally—putting the limits of readerly attention into question. This is, of course, a question of style, and Jean Rolin's style (both here and elsewhere in his work) wagers heavily on the lengthy, abundantly-furnished sentence, a bit like that of W. G. Sebald who, after Conrad and Proust, serves as one of the principal intertextual touchstones of Rolin's novel.[3] I should like to adduce a couple of those sentences, chosen practically at random among their fellows, in order to provide a sense of Rolin's loiterly style. The first one occurs early on in the text, after the radiator hose has ruptured, but before its repair:

> Each time that a truck appeared in the distance, before it began its descent, grinding its gears, I curled up on myself waiting for the collision, and it seems to me that I was able to make myself even smaller when the headlights lit up the ditch, then drew nearer very fast indeed, regaining my normal shape only after the truck had passed us, in a cloud of dust, the air that it displaced causing our automobile to shiver, from which one could conclude that a collision had been only narrowly avoided. (17–18)

At this point in the novel, the narrator is *waiting*. On the most obvious level, he is waiting for Patrice to return with a new radiator hose; yet also, quite simply, he is waiting for something—almost anything—to happen. That waiting is inscribed in somewhat different terms in the sentence I have just quoted ("waiting for the collision"), as the narrator waits for the road accident that seems to him inevitable. But, importantly, the sentence also projects a posture of waiting upon its reader, in the progressive accretion of clause upon clause, image upon image.

Such too is the case of a passage further along in the text that describes the *San Rocco* making its way—slowly, of course—up the Vridi Canal toward Abidjan, while the narrator gazes in loiterly fashion at the left bank:

> All of the latter, seen in deep shade from the wing on the port side of the bridge, is covered with a layer of mist that seems to become denser by the minute, casting thus more and more doubt upon the real nature of this left bank: does it belong to the bush, as the waves breaking noisily on its deserted shore lead one to suppose, or the low shrubbery, very dense, that one espies a short distance from that shore; or is it rather a well-organized plantation, as the tops of the coconut trees, perfectly aligned, might suggest, emerging as they do from the mist, and more and more numerous as the ship makes its way up the Vridi Canal? (136)

The dilatory effect of the utterance is accentuated by its interrogative character, in the first instance by the implicit question about the "real nature" of the left bank, in the second instance more obviously still by the explicit questions the narrator poses. In a sense, then, this sentence is very largely open on both of its ends, pointing toward a field of conjecture wherein narrator and narratee engage diegetic hypotheses in leisurely fashion. Within the general economy of *L'Explosion de la durite*, this moment stages itself as a respite of sorts, or as a diversion. Chambers points out, however, that such diversion can be highly motivated in character, rather than merely otiose, an effect of sleight of hand deployed in a textual shell game.[4]

Observing these dilatory effects in the aggregate, on a somewhat broader level, it becomes apparent that Rolin puts into play a strategy of digression in his novel. It is a canny move, I feel, and it deserves some consideration. Typically, we are conditioned in our culture to view digression in a negative light. It entertains a supplemental, even a parasitical relation to the real stuff of narrative. It distracts; it impedes the construction of meaning; it encourages sloth and a variety of other vices. As Christine Montalbetti and Nathalie Piégay-Gros put it, "Digression is a part of the text that should not figure in the text, a fragment that perturbs the economy—or transforms it. It's the divergence, the swerve away from the main point, it's a parasite sequence that delays, that muddies the waters" (5). Undeniably, though, there is also considerable pleasure to be had in digression, both for the narrator and for the reader, as they free themselves temporarily from constraint, and practice an agreeable "relaxation of vigilance" (Chambers, *Loiterature* 12).

What may be less immediately obvious is the idea of digression as a deeply purposeful narrative technique. However counterintuitive that notion may appear at first glance, upon further consideration it is perfectly reasonable—and especially when literary discourse is in question. We easily accept that an author and the narrator that he or she constructs may be quite different in voice, character, and purpose. Why should that difference not express itself in the attitude that each evinces with regard to digression? Or, as Montalbetti and Piégay-Gros suggest, "If the narrator goes astray, the author, undoubtedly, knows where he's going. In a literary text, digression is less a sign of going astray than the sham of going astray; it is not the sign of a lack of mastery of writing, but rather the fiction of a lack of mastery" (11). It is then possible to imagine digression, in a novel, as a fiction within a fiction, an embedded discourse that enjoys a performative status. Highly constructed, despite its appearances, it is also highly intentional. Like the stuttering of Père Grandet, it enables discursive traps to be set and, eventually, sprung. Yet in the same gesture it also provides a locus of discursive and creative freedom, a kind of speech relatively unfettered by rule and constraint.[5]

Moreover, if one is willing to accept those considerations, it is not then such a far stretch to imagine digression as possessing a critical dimension. Ross Chambers, for one, points out a clear instance of that: "Any digression enacts (although it may not intend) a criticism because, once one has digressed, the position from which one departed becomes available to a more dispassionate or ironic analysis: it must have been in some sense inadequate or one would not have moved away from it" (15). Christine Montalbetti and Nathalie Piégay-Gros are still more convinced of digression's critical vocation, characterizing it as "a technique of commentary which displays the complexity and the plurality of every text" (67), and enfranchising it fully in a catalogue of narrative devices: "A rhetorical instrument, a narrative process, it is also a critical tool which allows one to put into question the traditional working of the story" (69).

A close consideration of *L'Explosion de la durite* suggests that Jean Rolin uses dilatory effects and digressive techniques in highly purposeful ways. I think the same is true of certain other devices—unpredictability, incongruity, randomness, for instance—that seem, on a first level, to evince a lack of narrative purpose. On that first level, precisely, such effects suggest that the narrator is benighted, enmeshed in a story to which his narrative powers are not equal. His narration wanders, and we readers, perforce, wander right along with it. On another level however, one where a metaliterary voice makes itself heard, I am persuaded that those same devices enable *L'Explosion de la durite* to position itself as what I have termed elsewhere a *critical novel*, that is, one which comments pungently upon the limits and the possibilities of the novel itself as an evolving cultural form, through its own practice.[6]

One of the sites where such a dynamic is staged is the space where collective experience and personal experience compete with each other for the reader's attention. Quite deliberately, Rolin invokes both *history* and *his story*, as it were, vexing them against each other in order to see what kind of sparks may fly. On certain occasions, that effect may seem innocent enough, cast as it is in an apparently offhanded manner: "It was in Leopoldville that I learned to drive a car, a few years after Patrice Lumumba's death, and moreover to little purpose, since

I was to exercise that skill only very rarely thereafter, whenever chance happened to put me in the presence of a Renault 4L" (26). In a similar vein, he mentions that during a party, he had danced with the daughter of Joseph Kasavubu, the man who had stripped Lumumba of power, and that during that same period Che Guevara was fighting a guerilla war to the east of the Congo (30–31); that the first time he got drunk coincided roughly with the moment when Mobutu Sese Seko took power (36); that three years after singing *Allons, la mère Gaspard!* with the French ambassador's son in the Congo, he sang it again in the distant suburbs of Paris, in an attempt to recruit a family of workers to the "cause" (37–38).[7]

In this dimension of the text, of course, the suggestion is that the relation of author and narrator is one of absolute identity. Moreover, these moments are deeply intricated in the strategy that Rolin deploys in his efforts to claim narrative authority. As Ross Chambers points out, if the act of telling is unquestionably an exercise of power, that power is nonetheless not absolute, but rather "relational," since it must be authorized by the people for whom the narrative act is intended. "Consequently," he argues, "there is a sense in which the maintenance of narrative authority implies an act of seduction, and a certain transfer of interest (on the narratee's part) from the information content to the narrating instance itself (be it the person of the narrator, as in 'real-life' situations, or, as in the reading situation, the narrative discourse itself)" (*Story and Situation* 50–51). It is just that kind of "transfer of interest" that Rolin is trying to effect in *L'Explosion de la durite*, I think.

Or perhaps it would be more accurate to think of it rather as a *sharing* of interest, since Rolin clearly does not pretend to embody in his own person the entirety of narrative interest here. Quite to the contrary, he suggests that his story is in fact beggared by history; and in that sense his novel puts forth a compelling brief for a rehabilitation of historical sensibility in contemporary literature.[8] He returns time and again to the political history of the Congo in the twentieth century, a narrative quite as baroque and full of extraordinary—indeed, *explosive*—incident as any fictional work one might imagine. By contrast, his own story culminates in the rupture of the radiator hose. On the one hand, that event is the very incarnation of the banal, of the ordinary and uninteresting. On the other hand, it is the moment where the kind of sharing of narrative interest that I have described becomes apparent, where the subjectivity of narrative voice encounters the objectivity of the Congo, in precisely defined space (99.4 kilometers from Matadi) and time (September 9, 2005). Rolin presents that kind of encounter in various guises, but always as one that is unequal, exploiting that inequality in wryly humorous fashion:

> The circumstances that I'm referring to occurred in the year 1965. It was probably during the same year, the year of my first stay in the Congo, that I bought, in the Globe bookstore, a shop devoted to the diffusion of Russian literature and Soviet propaganda, a brochure entitled *Patrice Lumumba and African Freedom*. To what degree was I concerned about "African freedom" at that time? And to what degree was I concerned about anything at all? Today, it seems to me very difficult to understand why, at the age of sixteen, one adopts a given ideological posture rather than another. And how that posture, sometimes, eventually takes on the consistency of a conviction, even a fanatical conviction, such that what was once only a fancy, at least in part, can grow and strengthen until it has become more or less durably the tyrannical framework of a life. (28)

Clearly enough, however, something a bit more sober is going on in this passage, too. For Rolin is questioning the young man that he once was, in order better to understand the man that he has become. That process of interrogation is very largely sited on the ground of politics, whether in the Congo of the 1960s or the early twenty-first century; or in leftist activism in France in the aftermath of May 1968; or in Gdansk in the 1980s, as the Solidarity movement was just beginning to flex its muscles.

Such a perspective provides a useful lens through which to view Rolin's construction of the subject in *L'Explosion de la durite*. If it were merely an instance of autobiography, such considerations would be trivially conventional ones, for in that literary form everything (or nearly everything) is sacrificed to the subject, such that the latter may reign supreme in the text. That is not the case of *L'Explosion de la durite*, however. Instead, therein it is very much a question of reciprocity and complementarity. Pierre Bayard has advanced an intriguing hypothesis about the existence of an "intermediary" space where fiction and the real overlap, and which enables a productive conversation between illusion and reality.[9] For my part, I feel that Jean Rolin constructs just that sort of space with regard to collective experience and personal experience, a space wherein those two discursive (and phenomenal) orders engage in mutually illuminative articulation.

One of the other things that is illuminated thereby, not coincidentally, is literature itself—and here, once again, the "critical" dimension of *L'Explosion de la durite* becomes apparent. As he meditates upon what shapes the novel may assume in our vexed present, one of the techniques that Rolin uses is that of analogy, comparing *L'Explosion de la durite* to various other novels both obliquely and more explicitly. Those comparisons are both numerous and varied, as Rolin invokes figures from Sartre to Sebald, Hemingway to Alistair MacLean. I shall not catalogue them all here; instead, I'll focus on the pair that I have already mentioned, Conrad and Proust.

The former strides mightily through these pages, and constitutes therein a singularly imposing presence. Though Rolin mentions *Almayer's Folly* on a couple of occasions (27, 213) and

Lord Jim and *Victory* once apiece (143, 185), he is principally interested (for obvious reasons) in *Heart of Darkness*. He mentions that during one of his earlier trips up the Congo, in 1980, he felt like he was on a "Conradian pilgrimage" (81), and his current trip is full of uncanny reminders of *Heart of Darkness*: a shipping firm is named "Marlowe, whose Conradian denomination seemed to me to augur well" (165); a man toward whom Rolin turns for help in Matadi is named "Kurt," recalling thus "his Conradian quasi-homonym" (184). As much as Rolin is interested in the writer's work, so too is he intrigued by the *life*. For he senses that in the case of Conrad, there is a deep, causal connection between the two. Clearly, he is hoping that his own journey will "inspire" a work of literature, just as Conrad's did:

> When the *San Rocco* sets out to sea, in the afternoon of August 4, after having loosed itself from dry land by raising its gangway, then by casting off its mooring lines one after the other, it was precisely a hundred and fifteen years ago, day for day, that Joseph Conrad himself embarked from Kinshasa, aboard the steamer *Roi des Belges*, on that journey upriver which would inspire *Heart of Darkness*. (104)

Once again, however, just as in the case of history and his story, the analogy that Rolin invokes is unbalanced, in a way that inevitably ironizes his own project. For the moment at least, Jean Rolin cannot begin to claim the kind of writerly distinction that Joseph Conrad enjoys—but that is very much part of the game that Rolin is playing here, a game that puts the horizon of possibility of contemporary literature squarely on trial.

Neither is Jean Rolin a Marcel Proust, of course; yet Proust, like Conrad, is a constant presence in *L'Explosion de la durite*. Rolin rereads *A la recherche du temps perdu* [*Remembrance of Things Past*] during his trip, one of its virtues being the way that it transports him "to a universe diametrically opposed to the one in which I really was" (179). The implicit conversation between

Proust and Conrad that results is likewise starkly contrastive; but it is also a constantly suggestive one. Where Conrad enfigures the writer as a man of action, Proust may be taken to represent the writer as a man of thought—and, more particularly still, a man who reflects upon his past. Both of those stereotypes, and the writerly modes to which they correspond, are brought into play in *L'Explosion de la durite*. If on the one hand Rolin is trying to find a way to tell an adventure story in a cultural moment when such a gesture no longer seems possible in "serious" literature, so too on the other hand is he attempting to excavate a personal past in an effort to define a personal present. While those two projects animate *L'Explosion de la durite* in equal measure, their mutual relationship is constantly tensive in character, as each calls the other dramatically into question.

Clearly, that dynamic is bound up in a larger game of self-deprecation that Rolin plays throughout his novel. Some of the time, the moves he makes in that game are subtle ones, for instance when he wryly alludes to "the epic dimension with which I carefully adorned this enterprise" (42), or his admission that he may have invented one of the events from his past out of whole cloth: "But perhaps that too was a result of pure invention, like my claim of having once worked for the intelligence services" (213). Other moves, such as the insistent comparison of *L'Explosion de la durite* to *Heart of Darkness* and *Remembrance of Things Past*, are far less subtle. Still others are so explicit as to be absolutely unavoidable. Such is the case of a passage wherein Rolin tells a longshoreman named Jacques about his project, and recounts the latter's reaction: "Despite everything, Jacques thought that it was absurd to tell in written form the story of a car, and he suspected me of contributing to the underdevelopment of the region by importing a used vehicle" (151). What this passage constructs is an embedded image, a mise-en-abyme of narrative function, encompassing both production and reception. The reaction of Jacques, in that sense, provides a carnivalized image of the fate of *L'Explosion de la durite*, a funhouse mirror in which Rolin contemplates his text and its fate, inviting us to do the same.

A similar self-deprecative tone characterizes Rolin's reflections on the question of style, and especially insofar as his own style is concerned. He recalls for instance his adolescent habit of attempting to impress young women with his radical ideas, expressed in a studiously prolix language:

> For if the ideas that I professed, in an uninterrupted and undoubtedly exasperating spate of words, may have shocked them, the shining form in which I couched them, and in which they sometimes disappeared entirely, may have touched or impressed one or another of them, since it was obvious that I deployed those efforts only to please them, if only after the fact, and by no means to convince them. (29)

The victory of style over substance that Rolin sketches comments caustically upon his narrative strategy in *L'Explosion de la durite*. Patently, the game he is playing here is a version of the "loser wins" that Michel Beaujour has identified as a habitual gesture of certain avant-gardists.[10] In other terms, *L'Explosion de la durite* is doomed in advance if it pretends to compete with the modernist novel on any of the terms that modernist protocols set forth. The only manner in which *L'Explosion de la durite* (and other contemporary texts cast in a similar experimental mode) can hope to claim distinction is through a drastic reconfiguration of the rules of the game. It is useful, I think, to view that process of reconfiguration as a performance, one that is more than passingly ostentatious, and which is itself thematized in the novel. Thus, its author declares over and again his inadequacy with regard to the tradition of novels past. Thus, its narrative strategy relies not upon the unity and coherence of subject and event, but rather upon the multiplicity and fragmentation thereof. Thus, it does not seek to persuade us of fixed meaning, but seeks instead to enlist us in a collaborative search for a meaning far more mobile. Thus, it culminates not with a traditional explosion of truth—"The horror! The horror!"—but rather with the rupture of a radiator hose.

It is crucial, though, to see that moment for what it is. The title of the novel points straight at it, after all. Moreover, that locution—*l'explosion de la durite*—recurs again and again in the text.[11] Each time it does so, it can be imagined as a call to narrative order, that curiously reconfigured narrative order which Jean Rolin puts on offer here. While in one perspective the rupture of the radiator hose occupies the center of this story, in another perspective it frames the story. Just as that incident immobilizes the Audi in the first pages of *L'Explosion de la durite*, so too does it immobilize Rolin's telling, in a sense: in a narrative that wagers so heavily on travel through space, if the Audi cannot budge, then neither can the tale of the Audi. Seen from another angle, however, the rupture of the radiator hose is clearly the event that enables all the others, and makes this story possible. Furthermore, in all of its unadorned materiality, its obviousness and its banality, it performs the rejection of transcendence that lies at the very heart of *L'Explosion de la durite*. This is a novel that positions itself as a sketch of a novel, a set of prolegomena gesturing toward a new kind of novel.

That new novel hovers just over the horizon that Rolin adumbrates in *L'Explosion de la durite*, where we can anticipate it, perhaps, but not yet descry it. Indeed, Rolin may be pointing toward it, obliquely and ironically, as he brings his tale to a close. He mentions that his father was in the Congo in May 1968 when he received the news from Paris informing him that his son had been wounded, and taken to the hospital in critical condition. According to family legend, his father had decided that, should his son die, he would assassinate the French Minister of the Interior. "One may easily imagine," remarks Rolin in the final words of *L'Explosion de la durite*, "the course the 'events' might have taken if such a chain of circumstances had actually occurred. The July Revolution and the June Days would have been nothing in comparison. Someday, I will have to tell that story, the story of my heroic death and of the revolution that ensued" (221). There, finally, is the prospect of a novel worthy of the name; one that sits at the very antipodes of this one; one that takes place in a shiningly hypothetical, alternative world; one that deals in currency whose value can never decline; one that is uncorrupted by the real; and one that is truly, in a word, *explosive*.

Christine Montalbetti's Engaging Narrations

> BOVARISM: Illness named after Flaubert's heroine, Emma Bovary, and which consists in constructing one's vision of the world in function of the novels one reads. The incapacity of fictional universes to serve as models for the real world leads to a series of disillusions. By extension, the term designates a pathology of reading. *See Don Quixotism.*[1]

LIKE MUCH OF the most intriguing fiction produced in France in recent years, Christine Montalbetti's works defy easy description. Author of eight novels and a couple of collections of short stories, and a play adapted from Stevenson's *Strange Case of Dr. Jekyll and Mr. Hyde*, all published at the Editions P.O.L, Montalbetti writes books that put a keen consciousness of literary possibility on display, and that test a variety of narrative tactics from different angles of approach. One would be tempted to call her work avant-gardist, if that term were not so embattled these days, and apparently limping toward its dotage. Her writing has an experimental quality to it, yet the term "experimentalist fiction," which is often used to denote works produced in a radically formalist perspective, does not quite fit, either. Critics often invoke the notion of "serious" or "elite" literature in an effort to describe the kind of work that appeals to a learned readership; but those words are weasely ones, I think, and they beg far too many questions. John O'Brien has used the term "subversive" to characterize the kind of fiction that appeals to him as a publisher ("Interview"), and Montalbetti's works certainly do play out a dynamic of suave subversion with regard to literary tradition. For my part, I prefer to think of Montalbetti's writing as *critical fiction*, insofar as, whatever else she may be up to in a given text, the gaze that she casts upon fiction itself is critical in nature, one which insistently calls into question fundamental assumptions about literature and its uses. Moreover, through a finely-wrought and closely articulative narrative strategy, Montalbetti encourages her readers to approach her fictions in just the same manner, reading perhaps less for story than for discourse as we reflect upon what narrative can become, today. I am convinced that it is in just this sort of text that contemporary French fiction finds its deepest resources, and where it seeks to renew itself.

The key technique in that critical dynamic is the intrusive narration that colors each of Christine Montalbetti's novels and short stories. Allow me to be clear about what I mean (and to point out in passing that my own narration will itself be relatively intrusive). Gerald Prince defines the intrusive narrator succinctly as "A (distancing, engaging, ironic or earnest) narrator commenting in his or her own voice on the situations and events presented, their presentation, or its context; a narrator relying on and characterized by commentarial excursuses or intrusions" (*Dictionary* 46–47). Clearly enough, this is a matter of degree rather than one of absolute kind. Gérard Genette argues that any utterance bears some trace of the speaking subject, however minimal, and thus any narrative act testifies to the presence of a narrator (225). Elsewhere in *Figures III* he remarks, "It may seem strange at first glance to attribute to any narrator a role other than narration itself, that is, the act of telling the story; but we know that the narrator's discourse, whether in a novel or another kind of text, can take on other functions" (261). It is precisely those other functions that interest me in Montalbetti's case, for the narrators that she puts on stage in her fictions are unrepentant *talkers*,[2] extremely loquacious figures who condition our reception of the text in crucial ways. Even Wayne Booth, who normally takes a dim, proscriptive view of metadiscursive techniques, is forced to admit that intrusive narration can have important uses: “Though garrulity in narrators is as tedious as garrulity in acquaintances, though commenting narrators are, in fact, particularly tempted to be pompous and redundant, at their best they can yield a breadth of experience unlike that provided by any other artistic device” (199).

Robyn Warhol has distinguished usefully between two kinds of intrusive narrators, “distancing narrators” on the one hand, and “engaging narrators” on the other. The former tend to discourage the reader from identifying with the narratee, while the latter encourage it. The engaging narrator’s task, according to her, “is to evoke sympathy and identification from an actual reader who is unknown to the author and therefore infinitely variable and unpredictable” (812). That is just what Montalbetti’s narrators seek to do, it seems to me, proposing their stories to us in a highly discursive, dialogical game, one that plays cannily and spiritedly upon what we imagine narrative to be. In vertiginous and repeated gestures of romantic irony, her narrators lay bare the various illusions of their fictional worlds, summoning us to reflect upon process issues. In that sense, moments such as those function as shifters in the text, *engaging* us to pass from one level of reading to another.[3]

That phenomenon is difficult to theorize in a wholly satisfactory manner. One may certainly understand what a narrator is, and one may consequently envision the person whom he or she addresses as the narratee. Similarly, we may have little problem identifying the author and the reader, at least very locally, since both would seem to have a guaranteed status in the real world. More nuanced constructs such as “implied author” and “implied reader” may help us to mediate between one group and the other. Yet when those notional figures (who live in very different worlds, after all) are placed in an articulative, polylogical economy as mobile as that of Montalbetti's fiction, things quickly become more confusing. I should note right here that Christine Montalbetti herself is not prey to that sort of confusion. Or not, at least, when she is writing as a poetician, rather than as a novelist.[4] In an essay entitled "Narrataire et lecteur: Deux instances autonomes" [Narratee and reader: two separate cases], she takes an uncompromising position with regard to the reader's identification with the narratee:

> The narratee does not create a place for me in the story, any more than the characters do, or the narrator. I can identify with him or her, but only like I do with the others: not always, nor at any price, not inevitably, and without it being a case of substitution. [. . .] The narratee is neither my double, as many theoreticians would have it, nor merely an inversion of me [. . .]; he or she is an other, no more and no less than the narrator, no more and no less than a character. It is my responsibility, in each reading, to decide who resembles me—if indeed a resemblance is what I'm looking for in my reading. (8–9)

It is legitimate to read those assertions as correctives intended to counter the tyranny of a model that postulates the necessary and inevitable character of such identification. For surely enough, some kinds of texts encourage reader-narratee identifications more energetically than others; and some readers may be far more willing than others to succumb to the blandishments of engaging narrators. Nevertheless, it must be acknowledged that there exists an interesting friction between Montalbetti's theory of literature and her practice thereof, devolving precisely upon this point.[5] On the one hand, her fiction continually invokes the reader through the narratee, calling imperiously upon the former to engage in the process of creation through the mediation of the latter, and furthermore proposing that as the site where a productive engagement of author and reader may take place. On the other hand, she speaks in her theoretical work of the author-reader relationship as an "impossible communication," arguing that "communication between a real author and her readers, through the text of a novel, is a utopian concept" (*Images du lecteur dans les textes romanesques* 8).

For my part, I would like to propose a deliberately utopian reading of Montalbetti's fiction, fully cognizant of the fact that in doing so I am swimming against the current of contemporary critical fashion, and to proceed as if that sort of communication were possible in some shape or form, be it real or virtual. My reading will be a naive one, as one might speak about "naive mathematics," that is, an inquiry that is not axiomatic (in the first instance at least), and that relies more on induction than on deduction. If fiction typically calls upon us to suspend our disbelief willingly in order to *make sense*,[6] one can also practice that suspension at certain moments in certain kinds of interpretation. I am moved by the manner in which Montalbetti's books construct "the fiction of a desert island where people chat together" (*Nouvelles sur le sentiment amoureux* 27–28); I am persuaded that, as Philippe Lejeune said about Georges Perec, "there is in each of his texts a place for me, a place for me to do something" (*La Mémoire et l'oblique* 41); and if such a gesture seems excessively Bovarist (cf. "Quixotic"), then I can at the very least argue that I am in good company in identifying with a fictional construct.

In what follows, working by accretion, I shall attempt to catalogue the techniques Montalbetti uses in order to engage her reader, focusing principally on her first five books: *Sa fable achevée, Simon sort dans la bruine* [His story told, Simon goes out into the mist] (2001), *L'Origine de l'homme* [*The Origin of Man*] (2002), *Western* (2005), *Expérience de la campagne* [Experience of the countryside] (2005), and *Nouvelles sur le sentiment amoureux* [Tales of love] (2007). Some of those techniques may be attributed to her narrators; in other cases, we are encouraged quite explicitly to attribute them to the author. Sometimes a narratee is very clearly invoked; at other times, the reader is patently apostrophized in the very act of reading. My hypothesis is that Montalbetti deliberately casts the relations between those figures as fluid and mobile ones, for specific purposes. In commenting upon the narrative principles that subtend *The Name of the Rose*, Umberto Eco devotes several pages to a process he calls "constructing the reader" (*Postscript* 47–53). "What model reader did I want as I was writing?" he asks. "An accomplice, to be sure, one who would play my game" (50). The incipit of Montalbetti's first novel, *Sa fable achevée, Simon sort dans la bruine*, is conceived, I think, with just such a process in mind:

> First we have to specify things from a theoretical point of view, in the abstract, invoking our own experience, not in its singularity but precisely in what it has in common with mine, with Simon's, in short something that gently connects us and about which we likely agree—while admitting exceptions of course, and acknowledging that sometimes things are different, certainly not wishing to argue about it, certainly not condemning those differences, because we are broadminded folk, happy to occupy common ground, but also curious about landscapes with contradictory patterns, that's how I see things in any case. (7)

The insistence on first-person plural forms, the invocation of a commonality of experience, the suggestion that author, character, and reader are somehow linked and have something to share are intended to stage a reading dominated by the idea of complicity. These are seduction techniques, of course, as is the transparently diffident tone of the last part of the passage. The "I" appears only at the end, and as if by afterthought—yet it is clear, too, that it serves to call us to order, voicing as it does the notion of narrative authority. In retrospect, reading backwards as it were, the passage may be seen to announce a strategy that Montalbetti deploys and sustains throughout the novel (and indeed in each of her fictions), wherein she attempts to shape the reader to her purposes.

Sometimes those purposes are more specific and local; sometimes they are broader and less definite. In *Nouvelles sur le sentiment amoureux*, examples of both kinds may be found. One of the stories begins in the following way: "I don't know what you think, but for my part it's not the main subject that I consider in a painting, most of the time; rather, it's the little scenes in the background, the secondary subjects, painted with quicker brush strokes, perching precariously behind the central figure" (25). In that fashion, slyly and underhandedly, Montalbetti prepares her reader for the extremely discursive character of the narrative to follow, advancing the notion that discourse may in this case hold more interest for us than story, conditioning her reader to make that unusual leap of faith. Once again, she casts that proposition in attractive terms, calling upon us to follow her own authoritative example. In another of the stories, she describes a character happily lost in an amorous daydream: "He gives in to this sweet fiction, interpolating here and there a few personal snapshots of unidentified beaches, dunes, windblown grass" (91). Here, her purposes are far more general, it seems to me. Her character is a stalking-horse for the reader, and the latter is invited to identify with the former, confederates in the pleasures of fiction. An effect of mise en abyme lends force to this moment, for the character's reverie takes place within a collection of other reveries of the same order, that is, the short stories which compose the collection. If one is willing to imagine a set of reading instructions in this passage, they are clearly ones that embrace not only this moment in this story, but also the collection as a whole.

More than anything else, these effects are a matter of contract, a pact that Montalbetti seeks to seal with her reader. If the reader accepts the terms of that contract, the author will in turn set the table for a sumptuous feast. She will inform us; she will amuse us; she will intrigue us; she will please us—and all with the most extraordinary complaisance. She will never mislead us, and she will provide us with all the facts that we might wish to have. For that, after all, is a narrator's role, and it is legitimate that we should demand nothing less. In *L'Origine de l'homme*, Montalbetti offers a thumbnail version of that contract, invoking both the narrator's duty and the reader's right to *know*: "A story that you have the right to know, after all, and that I'm going to tell you" (86). As appealing as that promise may seem on the face of it however, it is prudent to consider it with a bit of healthy skepticism. Otherwise, one may very likely wander into these fables and never find one's way out.

All of Christine Montalbetti's fictions are characterized by a richly ludic pattern of pronominal interplay. Except when they are clearly marked as the voice of a character, first-person singular forms are always identified as feminine.[7] While most of the time we may be content to imagine that these utterances emanate from a narrator, sometimes the author speaks in her own voice, referring to herself by name. I shall return to that latter instance in a bit; for the moment, suffice it to say that the identification of narrating voice in Montalbetti's fiction as a feminine one, and the occasional, abrupt shift to an explicitly authorial voice, promote the identification of narrator and author in the reader's mind—or at the very least those effects prompt us to interrogate the relations that prevail between those two figures, serving as they do to put the idea of narrator and author as distinct figures belonging to distinct worlds dramatically into question.

As to the first-person plural and its various forms, Montalbetti often chooses to wager upon their performative potential as she inaugurates her texts. *L'Origine de l'homme*, for instance, begins thus: "Splash splash goes our man, delighted to see a half-dozen dragonflies flitting through the chilly air" (9); in similar manner, she launches *Western* with an imperative in the first-person plural: "Let us call him whatever we wish, this thirty-something man in a checked shirt rocking back and forth under the awning" (9). Once again, these techniques are designed to foster a sense of complicity in the reader, and to suggest that he or she is embarking upon an adventure along with the author, an adventure to be shared. In the first case, Montalbetti's wager hinges on the notion that author and reader are as it were co-proprietors of the character, and indeed her texts literally teem with effects of that sort.[8] In the second case, Montalbetti advances the idea that textual production can likewise be shared, and that the reader is free to imagine any name for the protagonist that he or she might wish. It is a sly gesture, of course, Montalbetti's apparent complaisance masking the fact that a crucial bit of information is being withheld from the reader, as Montalbetti plays on the latter's desire to know, setting in place in her first words an important element of the hermeneutic code in *Western*.[9] In such a manner, she seeks to enlist her reader in a textual dynamic based on the principle of collaboration, while at the same time whetting his or her semiotic desire.

Montalbetti exploits her reader's natural curiosity throughout the stories she tells, sometimes in rather unexpected ways. After putting forward a series of questions for the reader to consider in one of her short stories, she remarks, "Let's swallow our uneasiness and see what happens" (*Nouvelles* 56), suggesting in that manner that she shares our desire to know and sympathizes with it and, simultaneously, intimating that we shall not have to wait too long in order to satisfy it. At other times, she encourages us to put our plot-centered curiosity aside for a moment—graciously agreeing for her part to do likewise—in order to speak about other things, clearing the way for a narratorial excursus devoted to discourse, rather than to story. Typically, passages such as those are bound up in metadiscursive over-rationalizations[10] of various kinds:

> Let's stop our two heroes right there, in the middle of their reunion, and go back into the past a bit, if you wish, in order to make a few things clear. And I'm not thinking in terms of years here, a technique both offhanded and commonplace (those are not mutually exclusive) for manipulating chronology, upsetting sequences so much that all sense of the real is lost, dragging the reader along so inconsiderately that he or she becomes all mixed up, with a head spinning from so many bold leaps. No, all I'm asking for is a few minutes taken from the ordinary flow of time. (*Sa fable* 20)

Montalbetti's use of second-person pronominal forms poses problems that are thornier ones. To be sure, like most engaging narrators, hers often address their narratee as *vous*.[11] Upon occasion, those apostrophes sketch certain potential characteristics of the narratee in some detail; and in some instances they suggest that the communication between narrator and narratee is open to figures who would normally be excluded therefrom, such as fictional characters: "Well, you [*vous*] should be more sure of yourself, why would Jacques try to trick you, since you have accompanied him so kindly until now, and he's so grateful for your discreet, attentive presence, which warms his heart in his lonely bachelor life where nobody accompanies him in fact, and he hopes that you're single, too (I mean, you can have flings, but you're not attached, right?)" (*L'Origine* 205–06). Sometimes, however, the *vous* is not addressed to the narratee, but rather to a character, as in *Expérience de la campagne*, where the narrator addresses her protagonist, Simon, using that form (41–42).[12] Upon still other occasions, the author may apparently speak to herself in that manner, as for instance in Montalbetti's first novel, where the author ponders her own descriptive technique: "That's the operation you're asked to perform. An area, a number of rooms, sometimes a remark about orientation, or newness or disrepair, about furniture or absence of furniture, you have no more than five lines to paint your picture, before going on to the next one" (*Sa fable* 18).

Even those instances where the *vous* is not addressed to the narratee or the reader, however, participate intimately in the broad pattern of strategies that Montalbetti constructs in order to engage us. For the very indeterminacy of the pronoun, the fact that it is such a slippery deictic in these texts, functions to keep us very much on our toes, wondering in every case it appears if we might not be the object of the invocation it conveys. In "Narrataire et lecteur" [Narratee and reader], taking as example her own first novel, Montalbetti speaks about the uses of that sort of pronominal play:

> In the novel I published at P.O.L a little more than a year ago, if I may be allowed to speak about my own practice of fiction, the writing constantly played with the circulation of pronouns. The "you" could designate the narratee, but it could also designate the main character, Simon, whose experience was sometimes relayed in the second person (in a sort of staging of the identification of the narratee with the character). That second person could even designate the narrator, who could attribute to that "you" a memory of childhood which might serve to affiliate the narratee, but at the same time using it too precisely not to constitute, quite explicitly, a form of autobiographical speech. The very possibility of such circulation, its technical possibility I mean, testifies in my opinion to the fact that these instances of the narrator, the character, the narratee are all situated on the same level, not necessarily the same narrative level (the character being bound up in the

> diegesis, the narrator and narratee being extradiegetic), but on the same level when one thinks about the place the reader might occupy in the text, when one imagines an instance constructed, elaborated with a view toward that substitution; it's only the dynamic of identification that seems pertinent to me, once again, and it can apply to any of these instances. (9)

In short, the free circulation of the pronoun creates a discursive community that is polylogical, rather than dialogical, in nature. The boundaries of that community are deliberately loose and mobile ones, the better to foster an impression of hospitality. Clearly, too, that community straddles two very different worlds, the world of fiction and the phenomenal world; and consequently the voices animating it must have rather different status. Yet a key move of the game Montalbetti plays in her fiction is to intimate that those worlds are not mutually impermeable ones. Indeed, at certain moments in her books, she sketches dizzying, aporetic vistas wherein those two worlds happily collide. A passage in *L'Origine de l'homme* where the protagonist excuses himself to the reader for the tardiness of his arrival, saying that he had been taking his daily bath in the Somme, is a case in point (14).

Elsewhere in that same text, he addresses the author directly, and by name, using the familiar form of the second person, *tu*: "Listen, Christine, you [*tu*] can easily see that nobody believes in my silexes" (239). She responds to him, of course, and (interestingly enough) switches from the formal *vous* to the familiar *tu* in an effort to reassure him. Though such wormholes connecting fictional world to real world can be found fairly readily in Montalbetti's fiction, they are largely absent from her theoretical writings. And understandably so, for that way lies madness. Nevertheless, in a different perspective it might be argued that they are a source of considerable joy for the reader—and quite possibly for the author, as well.

Other techniques used by Montalbetti in her efforts to promote an engaged reading of her fiction are perhaps marginally less noble. A few examples will suffice to demonstrate the tenor of those devices. Chief among them is flattery, and it is also the most transparent. Montalbetti often casts her reader as the one individual who is equipped to understand the special kind of storytelling that she has chosen to put forward: "you are just the person I need, to imagine without fail the particular turmoil that the wretched hero of this story experiences" (*Nouvelles* 117). From time to time, she postulates certain characteristics of her interlocutor, traits that we are only too happy to claim for ourselves: "As a matter of fact, I'm calling on your common sense here" (*Nouvelles* 93). Elsewhere, she anticipates readerly reactions and inferences, complimenting us upon our perspicacity and assuring us that we are on precisely the right track: "You're right to suspect the evenness of his stride, to question it a bit. And I'll tell you why. This man has just returned from vacation" (*Nouvelles* 87). In that passage, the flattery is somewhat more developed and complex, for, just like the incipit of *Sa fable achevée, Simon sort dans la bruine*, it sets the stage for an affirmation of narrative authority. Cast in barefaced blarney, the message that it conveys is multifold: you are correct to be skeptical of this character's motivations; you are a canny and resourceful reader, indeed an ideal one; I have foreseen your readerly responses and have predicated my own narrative strategy upon them; I shall tell you everything you wish to know in this, *my* story.

Another technique, one closely akin to flattery, is cajolery. Montalbetti resorts to that tactic when she feels that the reader's attention might be flagging, or when she senses that the reader might be unwilling to make the kind of interpretive leap that a particular narrative situation demands.[13] In the middle of an especially garrulous passage describing a sunrise, Montalbetti enjoins her reader, "come along, leave it to me, relax, come on, there, gently, gently, let your body relax, passively, confidently, that's good, you should feel like you're on a little cloud, you're floating, you're swimming, come on, let yourself bask in the regressive quality of reading, that's right" (*Western* 20). In that mode, she constructs her reader as a passive recipient of textuality, one who readily responds to inveiglement of various sorts. She strokes her reader here as one might stroke a golden retriever, fondly and benignly. It is quite a different figure, then, from the one she habitually appeals to, a reader distinguished by intellectual acuity, by resourcefulness, and by active interpretive participation—in short, a seasoned hermeneut. Yet the manner in which she attributes shifting characteristics to her reader is very much a part of the game she plays in her discursive strategy, and its ludic quality is meant to be savored.

Every good dog deserves a bone, of course, and from time to time Montalbetti tosses us one, as for instance when the protagonist of *L'Origine de l'homme* remarks, "After all, I'm not in a twentieth-century novel" (26). Here, Montalbetti proposes a series of implicit jokes to her reader, with a wink. First and most obviously, her character, Jacques Boucher de Crèvecoeur de Perthes (1788–1868), is a historical figure who did not live to see the twentieth century. Moreover, he was a man whose attention was turned toward the past—and more particularly the Stone Age—rather than toward the future: an accomplished amateur archaeologist, he argued the existence of early humans in Europe, based on flint implements he had found in Picardy. The final joke is one that can be appreciated only from the vantage point shared by author and reader, for it is quite literally true that Jacques is not "in" a twentieth-century novel, but rather one of the twenty-first century, granted *L'Origine de l'homme* was published in 2002. All of this is intended to foster a sense of complicity, patently enough, as is the playful vexation of fictional and real worlds upon which this passage hinges.

In order that the reader should not become irretrievably lost in labyrinthine speculations of this sort, Montalbetti takes care to call us to order from time to time, and to attest that she, at least, is careful to keep her eyes on the prize. "Don't think for an instant," she assures us, "that the adventure has been forgotten" (*L'Origine* 212). That prize is plot and the manner in which it is developed; and as such it is the most traditional—and handiest—point of readerly interest in any narrative. Yet Montalbetti puts that notion forward with considerable duplicity here, since her fictions typically enact a massive displacement of story in favor of discourse, wagering as they do on a meandering, backing-and-forthing narrative style. A good portion of that dynamic is bound up in the way that Montalbetti adumbrates an ongoing implicit dialogue between author and reader. That gesture is particularly evident in the way the author anticipates questions the reader might raise. Sometimes she addresses those questions outright: "The shapes it assumes? Their rude invasion of dinners for instance, their interminable babblings around the dinner table" (*Sa fable* 22); sometimes she parries and defers them, as the situation requires: "Our man walks onto the bridge, not taking the time to notice a young woman (no, it's not Margot. Margot who? You'll see)" (*L'Origine* 21).[14]

Moments of narrative over-rationalization occur with some frequency in Montalbetti's fiction. Many of these are relatively laconic metadiscursive comments focusing very locally upon an element of the narrative that has just been presented: "I insist upon the personal nature of that custom" (*Western* 59). Brief as they may be, they function to draw our attention to narrative voice and enunciative situation, reminding us that the speaker is doing her utmost to provide a coherent account of things. Others insist more explicitly on the problems the speaker must negotiate in the difficult business of storytelling: "I haven't explained everything to you, but how can I, beginning a story is a tough thing to do, believe me" (*L'Origine* 32). They point toward process issues, of course, inviting us to consider the latter and the rigors they present, in a voice that is apparently guileless. They plead for our indulgence and our sympathy, as the speaker attempts to work her way through a series of unimaginable constraints: "I would like to make my thinking clear on that point, but I'm not in an easy position, I'm being nagged, I'm closely pressed, hindered, I don't have enough room" (*Sa fable* 42). With their implicit offer of franchise in the business of textual production, the conspicuous sincerity of their tone, and their blatant invocation of the idea of *difficulté vaincue*, passages such as these are intended to engage ever more deeply in our reading—and at the same time to redouble our sense of loyalty to the storyteller.[15]

Similar in the way that they play upon readerly susceptibilities, moments of narrative hesitation may occasionally be noted in Montalbetti's writing. They suggest that the speaker is uncertain about how to proceed, and consequently they, too, invite us, however momentarily, to reflect upon process issues. Typically, moments such as these are brief ones. It is moreover tempting to regard them as surface phenomena, transparently staged as such, for the hesitation they express is almost always belied by what follows. "Ted's voice is, how to describe it?" muses the narrator of *Western* (94), before launching into a lengthy and extremely detailed description of that voice. The game that moments such as these propose invites us to consider the rigors of narration, to speculate upon the alternatives that the narrator weighs in her efforts to solve her problem, and, eventually, to admire the elegance and the depth of resource to which that solution testifies so abundantly. In short, like many of the other devices that Montalbetti deploys, they serve to reaffirm the principle of narrative authority. Further, as we become more and more familiar with those devices, we come to understand the lesson that subtends them. As Montalbetti and Nathalie Piégay-Gros put it so pithily in *La Digression dans le récit* [Digression in stories], "If the narrator goes astray, the author, undoubtedly, knows where he's going" (11).

Narrative digression plays a crucial role in the textual economy of all of Christine Montalbetti's fictions. In *Western* most particularly, it is difficult to speak about narrative "action," since so little in the novel is devoted to event, the vast majority of the text being organized around narratorial dilations of various kinds. In most cases, digressions are clearly marked as such for the benefit of the reader; the narrator opens a parenthesis, as it were, and invites the reader to plunge into it. Speaking of a painting in *Expérience de la campagne*, for instance, the narrator remarks: "It was an original motif, and we should stop to consider it, if you're willing" (56). When at length the narrator draws her digression to a close, that point of closure is often likewise marked with some deliberation—and perhaps some reluctance, too: "But now it's time to go back to the scene" (*Western* 188).

In *La Digression dans le récit*, Montalbetti and Piégay-Gros speculate on the dilatory voice in narrative, in a theoretical perspective. They insist upon digression as a narrative feint: "In a literary text, digression is less a sign of going astray than the sham of going astray; it is not the sign of a lack of mastery of writing, but rather the fiction of a lack of mastery" (11).[16] It is a trick used in order to *divert* the reader,[17] in the fullest sense of that term. On the one hand, it is intended to deflect the reader's attention from other concerns such as plot and character. On the other hand, it is supposed to amuse the reader; indeed, Montalbetti and Piégay-Gros take care to underscore the ludic potential of that device (69). Speaking of what they call the "parodic" novel (and invoking by way of example works such as *Tom Jones*, *Tristram Shandy*, and *Jacques le Fataliste*), they argue that the digression that is so characteristic of the narrative strategy of works such as those is in fact a critical tool that destabilizes traditional narrative norms, enabling other, less conventional dynamics to come into play (45). They conclude, provocatively enough, by negating the idea of digression as it is habitually conceived, in order to dust it off and rehabilitate it on quite a different level: "Here at the end of this overview of digression, we come thus to a radical formulation that allows us to rethink the first question, that of coherence: 'Digression does not exist for the critic.' [. . .] A rhetorical instrument, a narrative technique, digression is also a critical tool enabling us to call into question the traditional workings of stories" (68–69).

Granted that it was published in 2000, and thus before Montalbetti's fictions, it is tempting to read in *La Digression dans le récit* a blueprint for the discursive principles that she puts to use in the latter. In such a light, digression is clearly a critical tool that is massively deployed in what I have called *critical fiction*. It is a device that displays by implication a skepticism with regard to traditional narrative norms on the part of the author, and one that exhorts the reader to think about process issues in the text at hand, appreciating the ways in which they adumbrate new narrative possibilities. It is interesting to note that, while Montalbetti bids us to exert our critical faculties in moments such as those, her invitations themselves are cast in a very dilatory mode. "Let's take a moment to look at the courtyard a bit" (*Western* 45), she proposes, as if we had all the time in the world. Elsewhere, that summons toward readerly idleness is still more explicit: "it's your leisure time, leave it to me, I'll take care of everything without rushing anything" (*Western* 21). Effects such as those are symptomatic of what Ross Chambers has called "loiterature," that is, a textuality that foregrounds the illusion of a leisurely, dilatory pace both in the process of production and in that of reception.[18] Like Montalbetti and Piégay-Gros, Chambers suggests that loiterly techniques serve to divert the reader, in a kind of textual shell game which the author plays out, and whose stakes involve the renovation of literature itself.[19] He also concurs that digression is critical in its vocation, interrogating as it does the very discourse that it apparently interrupts: "But if there's a *jouissance* of digression, the option in favor of digressiveness is also, as I've said, a critical act—the critical is, so to speak, the second side of digression's pleasurability. Any digression enacts (although it may not intend) a criticism because, once one has digressed, the position from which one departed becomes available to a more dispassionate or ironic analysis: it must have been in some sense inadequate or one would not have moved away from it" (15).

All of these arguments rely heavily, of course, on a construction of authorial intent; and when I take my Bovarist lenses off, I realize how very fragile such an edifice can be. If I wager upon it here nonetheless, it is largely because Montalbetti herself advances the notion of writerly intent so unrelentingly in her fiction. I would like to examine certain instances of what Genette calls "auctorial" discourse,[20] with a view to determining how they take their place in Montalbetti's arsenal of engaging tactics. The first and most obvious sort of auctorial discourse is when the speaker identifies herself as the author, by name: "Hear ye the sad fable that pits, in a seaside café situated on the main street leading down to the briny, Christine Montalbetti (me, that is, exposing myself thus to you in one of my familiar bunglings) and a tobacconist, the precise features of whose face I can no longer visualize" (*Western* 140). Montalbetti adorns this anecdote with a variety of engaging features. The mock-heroic style in which she couches it serves to distinguish it from that which surrounds it, and suggests that we should approach it in a different manner. She identifies it as a "very silly story" as she introduces it (140), framing it quite explicitly as a "sad fable." In so doing, she emphasizes its importance *as narrative* within the more general narrative economy, while at the same time she advances it as a trivial thing, at best. That patent discursive duplicity stands in stark contrast to the apparent candor of her address here, for she seems to cast aside the mediative figures of narrator and narratee in order to speak directly to her reader.

The inscription of her name is a powerful authoritative gesture, reinforced and guaranteed by the "me" that quickly follows it. It forces us to sit up and pay special attention—in short, it engages us. The notion that this passage constitutes a kind of narrative "bungling" (which is expressed parenthetically, but which is nonetheless crucial in her strategy), like the gently bantering, self-mocking tone of the passage as a whole, is intended to palliate the peremptory quality of the summons that Montalbetti issues here; and clearly those effects are also very engaging ones.

Instances such as that, where the author "exposes" herself to the readers, are privileged ones in Montalbetti's fictions. Stepping back from them a moment, it is undoubtedly wise to regard them as moments of false intimacy. As skeptical as we may choose to be, however, those instances are very striking—and very seductive as well. Sometimes authorial interventions are overt and unavoidable, like the passage I have just examined; sometimes they are more subtle and ambiguous. When the speaker in one of Montalbetti's short stories, for instance, proposes to tell the story of her great-great-grandfather (*Nouvelles* 62–66), we are tempted to believe that Montalbetti is speaking in her own voice. Yet is only toward the end of that passage that the name "Montalbetti" occurs (*Nouvelles* 65), serving thus to certify that voice as the author's, and confirming that our intuition was indeed correct. Similarly, when the speaker in another text says, "*e tutti quanti*, as my ancestors used to say" (*Western* 83), it makes sense to imagine that it's Montalbetti herself. Utterances that allude directly to the material conditions of writing work to the same purposes. "A bastard (my spell checker suggests bastion)" (*Western* 119), for example, suggests that we have caught a glimpse of the author in the very act of composing her text, in real time as it were. Briefly stated, the techniques that Montalbetti put in place are calculated to make us imagine that we are hearing the author's voice in each instance where that interpretation is even barely possible—and to make us feel, too, that that voice is addressing us readers directly and without mediation. Thus, for instance, when the speaker invokes a memory from a trip to Japan (*Nouvelles* 42) or an anecdote from a trip to London during her childhood (*Nouvelles* 136): whereas in another sort of textuality we might quite comfortably construe those utterances as emanating from a narrator quite distinct from the author, Montalbetti's fiction conditions us imperiously to ascribe them to the author herself, even in the absence of a clear signature.

That sort of readerly reaction is habit-forming, of course, and Christine Montalbetti wagers heavily on the idea that her readers are creatures of habit. One of the advantages that such strategies afford her is that they tend to render assertions of narrative authority more legitimate than they might otherwise be. The tone of such moments ranges from the relatively mild and benign—"I clear my throat a bit in order to extract you from your maritime reverie" (*L'Origine* 137)—to the baldly autocratic—"Here you mark a pause, you think about walking in general, and about your own way of walking" (*L'Origine* 263). Whether they be subtle or more obvious, however, each of those instances serves to remind us how deeply we rely on the storyteller. Other techniques reinforce that fundamental lesson. Foreshadowing, for example: when the storyteller in *Western* alludes to her protagonist's Smith & Wesson, she adds, "the time has perhaps come to alert the more timid souls that the odds of our thirty-something man putting that gun to use before the end of this book are very likely indeed" (121). In such a manner, she assures us that our ghoulish (but extremely readerly and, more to the point, highly *constructed*) anticipation of violence will be rewarded; yet she also implies that she will provide such reward in her own good time, and only when she sees fit. Montalbetti plays on her reader's semiotic desire mercilessly, intimating that the best is just around the next corner—"Just wait, there is better to come" (*Nouvelles* 134)—and providing us in the meanwhile with narrative satisfactions quite other than those we might have expected.

As she deploys this array of effects designed to grab and retain our attention, Montalbetti occasionally chooses to put that very process on display and asks us, with transparent sincerity, to consider it: "but what wouldn't one do to retain your attention, as you're well aware" (*L'Origine* 31). A cynic would interpret moments such as this as examples of narrative disingenuousness, for despite the manner in which they are couched, they are clearly control techniques, and the warning that they convey is in fact calculated on the contrary to disarm us. As such, in their intent and in the way that they manipulate the reader, they are not so very different from the injunctive, imperative discourse that recurs with such frequency in Montalbetti's fiction. "Look at them, our ancestors with their lost faces, having escaped from their daguerreotypes, howling at the moon!" the speaker exhorts us on one occasion (*Sa fable* 24–25), calling upon us to act in common with her. Other exhortations are more laconic, yet more compelling still. "Don't get me wrong," says the storyteller in *Sa fable achevée* (69)—and indeed, upon reflection, that's all she asks of us. It's little enough, I suppose.

Metadiscursive passages focusing on writing—most particularly the writing of fiction—and its protocols are likewise intended to draw us into the text in a broadly participatory manner. "You wonder fleetingly if to a certain extent writing a novel is not precisely that, arranging one's personal images without recognizing them, in order to construct a legible sequence," muses the storyteller in *Expérience de la campagne* (73–74). The lines of address are unclear in this instance: perhaps it is the narrator or the author speaking aloud to herself; perhaps she is addressing a character; perhaps she is addressing her reader. For my own part, I feel that Montalbetti leaves that question open quite deliberately in this instance, asking us to read that passage in all three modes simultaneously. In that fashion, she suggests that the question of what the novel *is* and may *become* is likewise an open one, a question that must be entertained and negotiated on a very local level, in a polylogue that enfranchises a diversity of figures both real and fictional. In other words, the future of fiction in the world will be decided both in fiction and in the world, in a debate that shuttles back and forth vertiginously between illusion and reality. It is in just such a spirit that Montalbetti invites us to speculate upon narrative hypotheses or alternatives that can just barely be glimpsed on the horizon of possibility: "That, you see, is what these pages might relate" (*Sa fable* 128).[21] These are dizzying perspectives, of course, granted the potential of narrative to ramify infinitely. Yet precisely by virtue of that, they underscore the kinds of choices a writer must make in constructing a fictional world—and the kinds of interpretive choices we make in our attempts to come to terms with that world.

In order to help us along in that latter activity, Montalbetti frequently enjoins her reader to call upon personal experience in order better to imagine events in her fictional worlds. "I'm sure that you don't have to search too far in order to find an episode like this one in your own memory," she says as she describes how her protagonist was slighted in the General Store (*Western* 139).[22] In that manner, she suggests that there are points of permeability between fictional worlds and the real, and that when one deliberately vexes the one against the other, useful sparks may fly. That invocation of the reader's own experience is especially marked when it is a question of sexuality. Describing—or rather, declining to describe—her protagonist's sexual initiation in *Western*, the storyteller remarks: "personally, as you have sensed, I don't necessarily wish to go into this scene in great—and intimate—detail, trusting you to project upon it, pardon me, the memory of your own loss of virginity"

(181). That scene, adumbrated as it is only by the most tenuous gesture, is clearly an example of what Gerald Prince terms the "nonnarrated."[23] Montalbetti treats questions of Simon's sexuality in much the same way, remarking parenthetically: "*nota bene*: Simon's coituses, I fear, given the way that things are going, will not be recounted. So much the better for prudish readers (and there are far more than you imagine); as to the others, they are inventive enough to supply the missing details" (*Sa fable* 23). In such a fashion, Montalbetti plays a double game. On the one hand, she voices her confidence in our readerly sophistication, for we are obviously *not* prudes, nor are we lacking in imagination (to say nothing of experience). On the other hand, she intimates once again that fictional worlds and the real can—and must—speak to each other, in a kind of infinite and mutually illuminative conversation.

Moreover, though moments such as these would seem to renege on the key term of the textual contract that she has proposed to us (the promise to tell everything, without exception), the fact that she frames these unnarrated scenes so candidly is very engaging in itself. "That there should remain in a story a few dark corners, you can accept," she argues. "That one should allow oneself, in passages where you might have welcomed more detail, a few ellipses, you can say yes, that's the way the game is played" (*Western* 147). She appeals, in short, to our common sense—and more importantly still, to our sense of something in common. That latter may be a category of experience we share with author or character: a sexual initiation, a visit to an aquarium, or a sunrise over a dusty village in the American West. Or it may be something else that we are invited to share, such as the invention of fiction. "You know the texture of a man's dreams," the storyteller whispers (*Western* 69), pointing simultaneously toward a cowboy's dreams and toward the far vaster and more amply shared dream that is fiction.

Optimally, each of those devices serves to foster a sense of complicity between writer and reader, based on the impression that, whatever may come to pass, we are and shall remain allied. "Let's remain calm," says the speaker in one of Montalbetti's short stories (*Nouvelles* 92), directing her advice to herself quite as much as to us, and postulating thus the fundamental harmony of our reactions.[24] If we in turn accept that notion of complicity, Montalbetti promises to reward us with a rare degree of franchise in the business of textual production. Toward the end of a description of a wall in that same dusty Western village, she adds, "and if a little zoological urge makes you want to have a few lizards climbing up it, go right ahead, it won't bother me a bit" (*Western* 46). Elsewhere, abridging her account of two characters in the kitchen, she remarks: "I'll let you fine-tune things" (*Western* 90), as if we were perfectly capable of assuming that task. Clearly, this is yet another game that Montalbetti plays with us. Yet she issues her invitation to that game with considerable delicacy, and in terms that are finely calculated to appeal to our imagination and our desire for shared experience: "Let's dream about that (shall we?)" (*Nouvelles* 17). Her fictions are welcoming ones in that perspective. They are texts governed by a refreshing code of hospitality wherein the author constantly assures the reader that he or she has a *place* in the fictional world, "for you're my guest, after all" (*Western* 140).

The notion that we might find just such a place for ourselves is a heady one, of course, and the hospitality that animates it is powerfully engaging. Montalbetti returns to that notion again and again, sometimes briefly (and as if by chance), sometimes in more extended narrative excurses. In the early pages of *L'Origine de l'homme*, for instance, when she stages a meeting between her reader and her protagonist, she puts on display a moment that is pungently emblematic of her narrative strategy. As the reader shakes Jacques Boucher de Crèvecoeur de Perthes's hand (16), a pact is sealed on a variety of levels. He or she accepts the protagonist's invitation to hear his story—and to place his confidence in the storyteller, moreover, whose competence the protagonist guarantees. He or she agrees willingly to play along, to make *as if*, to imagine a world where writer, character, and reader may for a moment get along together in the most harmonious and seamless articulation.

That gesture of hospitality is a transitive one, Montalbetti argues, one that may proliferate well beyond the boundaries that we normally impute to fiction. Walking us through the village's General Store in *Western*, Montalbetti remarks that we might like to buy a souvenir there. We could show it to dinner guests, she suggests, as an object of curiosity: "And that, where did that come from, where did you find it, where did you buy it, you would answer them, Oh, that came from *Western*, and, carefully putting the object back where they found it, they would reply, Oh (probably they would never have heard of it), and you could explain to them, sit them down facing you in an overstuffed armchair (they're your friends, an old pillow suits them fine), and undertake to tell them the adventures of our thirty-something man" (114–15). Just as a gesture of hospitality may ramify far beyond the instance in which it occurred, so too are stories passed from hand to hand, recast and reappropriated according to the specific demands of discursive context, in a potentially endless chain of narrative. Indeed, the situation that Montalbetti sketches in this passage is closely descriptive of my own, for in this essay one of the things I am doing is telling *you* a story about her fiction.

Clearly, my story is one in which the narrator suffers a number of pratfalls, stumbling as he has freely chosen to do through the overlapping, highly accidented terrain of real and fictional worlds. But such is the topography of the literary space that Montalbetti constructs. Any reader venturing into it may anticipate some missteps—and in fact they are not the least of its pleasures. That literary space is a broadly open one, and it provides considerable room for maneuver. It is designed to accommodate individuals of very different ontological status and to provide a site for the kind of conversations that would be nearly unthinkable in most of the spaces we inhabit. In the beginning of one of her short stories, Montalbetti invites us to gaze upon just such a space, and to dwell in it for a moment:

> You should imagine a place open to the public, any place you wish, according to your habits. In that place occurs an event, oh nothing very notorious, nothing interesting to anyone beyond a small circle of folk, a kind of occurrence whose nature doesn't matter, and which you can imagine as you wish, in function of your own interests and the events you usually encounter. What is important is that anyone can enter into this space (you and me, for example), and that there exists a federating event which justifies the fact that such diverse people should meet in the same place. (*Nouvelles* 129–30)

We should enter into narrative, she suggests, in a way that makes us available to the experience it offers, bringing with us all of the baggage that makes us ourselves. What we may become therein, however, is another matter, one that depends upon our inclinations, the suspension of some of our usual habits of skepticism, and our willingness to play a role in a collaborative dynamic that has been scripted for us. If those conditions are met, we exit from narrative refreshed and invigorated, seeing our quotidian reality in new ways, our readerly narcissism considerably chuffed by the experience we have just had, delighted to be accorded the final word:

> Floating between contrary emotions, as you finish reading about this very frequent experience, to which you can compare many personal examples, you return to your activities filled with Heraclitan ideas, knowing full well that, yes, everything must pass, everything must fall, same and other, and that the only fixed point in all of that, buffeted by so much diversity, sometimes

> savoring it lustily, sometimes feeling threatened by it, is you. (*Nouvelles* 125)

In such a manner, Christine Montalbetti engages us to wander through the ins and outs of fiction, turning now this way, now that, contemplating vistas that we might never have imagined in the company of people we otherwise would never meet, seeing our way, then losing it, perhaps seeing it again, in a world that we are finally entitled to call our own.

Antoine Volodine's Crossings

THE BODY OF work that Antoine Volodine has created over the last thirty years is striking by virtue of its ambitious scope, the originality of its vision, and the way that it resists conventional strategies of reading. Volodine imagines canny fictional worlds whose internal coherence is never in doubt, as strange as those worlds may seem when compared to our own. The men and women in his novels are peripatetic souls, constantly in motion and never in repose, as if mobility itself provided them with the surest guarantor of an otherwise dubious existence. More particularly, Volodine's characters are always crossing frontiers, changing from one state to another, or migrating into new territories. Sometimes the latter are sketched in highly figurative terms, sometimes in terms that are far more literal. These people cross over from waking into dream, from sanity into madness, from life into death—and back again, as often as not. Freedom and incarceration are two of the key territories that Volodine sketches, though the first one is typically far more hypothetical than the second. Other sites are more vague and unmappable still, yet Volodine invokes them no less insistently. The "here" and the "there," for example, are important constructs in Volodine's world, as are the notions of the inside and the outside. Those notions are slippery ones, however, and their mutual relations are subject to dizzying inversions. Some kinds of crossings are massive and collective, involving ideological shifts: thus, revolution gives way to reaction, and humanist thought is overmatched by the inhuman. No less important, I think, are the boundaries that loom on literature's horizon of possibility, boundaries that Volodine's writing puts dramatically into question. For there, too, it is largely a question of crossings: from the real to the fictional, from the name to the heteronym, from the exotic to the postexotic, from a passive mode of reading to one that is necessarily far more critical.

Reflecting on Volodine's *Dondog* (2002), Lionel Ruffel is struck by a passage wherein the eponymous hero perches vertiginously on the verge of a precipice, "on the edge of the void" (*Dondog* 26), wondering what might come next. Ruffel imagines that scene as an exemplary one, emblematizing the state of the novel at the end of the twentieth century and the beginning of the twenty-first, a "denouement [. . .] pointing simultaneously toward the past, which it transforms, and toward the future, which it authorizes" (*Le Dénouement* 11). More broadly, he sees therein a cultural moment where many different discourses collide and interrogate each other, enabling us eventually to stride from one era to another: "This articulation of discourse and figures tries to understand a century's end, that is, the *passage* from one century to another" (*Le Dénouement* 14). Other critics point to gestures in Volodine's work that are analogous to the one that intrigues Ruffel. Anne Roche, for example, speaks of "paradoxical spaces where one advances without advancing," and of interstitial sites such as "this no man's land between death and death" ("The Clarity of Secrets" 52 and 56). Marie-Pascale Huglo likewise recognizes a thematics of passage in Volodine, one that adumbrates a connection between the most disparate places: "In this universe fragmented in space and time, dreams and shamanic mediation are the privileged modes of 'transport' for post-exotic consciousness. The atemporality of dreams and rituals materializes the immaterial passage between places, consciousness, and fables" ("The Post-Exotic Connection" 99).

In all of these readings, and in others like them, it is centrally a matter of *crossings*, of shifts (or potential shifts) from one place to another. For my part, I would like to examine that topos locally, focusing on one of Antoine Volodine's most intriguing novels, *Songes de Mevlido* [Mevlido's dreams] (2007). Its landscape is classic Volodine: a postrevolutionary world in a time some three hundred years after our own, verging upon the end of history, when all but the most quixotic hopes for the future of humankind have revealed their emptiness, and where the future—such as it is—undoubtedly belongs to spiders. It is a place where institutional violence has been the norm for longer than anyone can remember. The world revolution had no sooner ended than the civil war began; the latter in turn was followed by the "black" war. In the pestilential present, a cynical nomenklatura persecutes those few folk who are misguided enough to resist it. "It is almost difficult to believe that we're in the real world," the narrator notes (135); and we readers undoubtedly share his difficulty.

Gigantic, mutant birds abound in this world: ravens, owls, seagulls, buzzards, guinea-hens, turkeys, chickens, and talking crows. Their cacklings assault the ear, and their droppings pollute the streets. The human fauna, by and large, is less attractive still. Comatose junkies line the curbs; former child-soldiers still kill for a nod or a wink; feral commissars and bent cops belabor a population of madmen and moral cripples. Mevlido himself is a policeman, charged with infiltrating Bolshevik cells in "Chicken Coop Four," the most notorious ghetto of Oulang-Oulane. He, too, is bent, but not in quite the same way as his colleagues, for he has been reborn in this world as a long-term deep-penetration agent, sent by the "Organs" in a final effort to save a foundering humanity. His wife, Verena Becker, had been martyred twenty years previously, and he lives now with Maleeya Bayarlag, a scarred woman who is often incapable of recognizing him. He is beset by dreams, nightmares, and reveries of various sorts, states that he cannot differentiate from his waking consciousness. They are his only means of communicating with the people who sent him to this foul place—and his only reality. It is perhaps fitting that his fate should be determined in "Chaos," a limitrophe sector of Oulang-Oulane that makes Chicken Coop Four look like the Club Med. It is "an intermediary site between the dream world and the real" (429), a place that beggars conventional ideas of right and wrong.

Like Dondog, Mevlido often finds himself perched on the edge of nothingness, either literally or metaphorically. When his superior, Berberoïan, frets that Mevlido might have a breakdown during a key mission, the police psychiatrist in charge of Mevlido's case reassures him: "That would surprise me, says Maggie Yeung. He's in control of himself. He's on the edge of the void, it's true, but he has no desire to throw himself into it" (83). Similarly, as he advances along "Memorial Avenue" in a city he might only have dreamed, Mevlido struggles to put one foot in front of the other: "His legs carried him with reticence. The palms of his hands supported him, like when one leans out over the edge of a precipice" (96). Each of these experiences anticipates a crossing of sorts, and each of those crossings is in its own way painful, involving as it does a leap into the unknown, and the trauma attendant upon it.

It is tempting to read in Mevlido's various crossings a scripting in caricature of the manner in which Volodine himself has traversed the literary horizon in France, since launching his career in the mid-1980s. He published his first four novels at the Editions Denoël, in a collection devoted to science fiction entitled "Présence du Futur." Those texts, including *Biographie comparée de Jorian Murgrave* (1985), *Un navire de nulle part* [A ship from nowhere] (1986), *Rituel du mépris* [Ritual of contempt] (1986), and *Des enfers fabuleux* [Fabulous hells] (1988), elicited very little interest, either among critics or among general readers. The indifference of the former can be explained, in part at least, by paratextual considerations. Appearing as they did in a low-status collection such as

"Présence du Futur," and marketed in cheap editions with impossibly lurid cover illustrations, these books were clearly beneath the dignity of the critical establishment. As to general readers, and more specifically the devotees of science fiction to whom Denoël's collection was notionally pitched, they may have found themselves nonplussed by a set of texts that quite obviously and deliberately overstepped the boundaries of mainstream science fiction. As Jean-Louis Hippolyte puts it, "Volodine's mystifying and uncharacteristic novels soon charted a terra incognita in the world of sci-fi, having little in common with the formulaic productions of other writers in *Présence du Futur*. His odd polyphonic novels challenged science fiction's orthodoxy, and the Volodine case soon degenerated into a new *querelle des anciens et des modernes*" (*Fuzzy Fiction* 168).

It was only with the publication of Volodine's fifth novel, *Lisbonne dernière marge* [Lisbon last margin] (1990), at the Editions de Minuit that specialist readers began to sit up and take notice of him. Minuit was an imprint that was difficult to dismiss at the beginning of the 1990s. Having launched the New Novel in the 1950s, its director, Jérôme Lindon, had confirmed his reputation for editorial prescience all over again in the 1980s by publishing a new generation of writers—people like Jean Echenoz, Jean-Philippe Toussaint, Marie Redonnet, Christian Gailly, Eric Chevillard, Marie NDiaye, and Christian Oster—who quickly established themselves as figures to contend with. The fact that Volodine's work should appear in Minuit's small but highly selective catalogue meant, quite simply, that he was worthy of critical attention. And indeed, as Jean-Didier Wagneur has pointed out, "It was only with the imprimatur of the Editions de Minuit that critics began to read him" ("Introduction" 3). Thus, it might be argued that Volodine changed camps early in his career, migrating from "popular" or "mass-market" fiction to "serious" or "elite" fiction. I myself would be tempted to argue just that, were it not for the fact that I can discern no substantial difference between his Denoël novels of the 1980s and his Minuit novels of the 1990s, either on the level of technique or of theme.[1] Consequently, I am inclined to think of this phenomenon as one of the instances of "paradoxical space" (to invoke Anne Roche's term once again), wherein "one advances without advancing."

There is another site where one may observe a more convincing crossing, however. Like the reception of Volodine's Denoël novels, it devolves upon concerns that are primarily extratextual, and more precisely on the manner in which Volodine came to imagine his own literary enterprise. Chary of readymade taxonomies, undoubtedly sobered by his experience at Denoël, and conscious of the real alterity of his writing, Volodine conceived the term "postexotic" for his project.[2] In an interview with Jean-Didier Wagneur, Volodine suggests that the fundamental coherence of his writings as an *oeuvre*—and their fundamental difference from other bodies of writing, as well—was something that dawned on him only gradually, becoming fully apparent only after his second novel for Minuit, *Alto solo* (1991), had appeared. "It was after that," he remarks, "after *Alto solo*, that I understood that I had in fact, quite simply and blindly, instinctively, written books that could take their place in a vast Anthology. It was then that an aesthetic and novelistic project that I named post-exoticism became clear to me" ("On recommence" 234).

Pascale Casanova invokes the idea of the foreign in order to characterize postexotic literature, suggesting that it is "a literature springing from elsewhere and going toward elsewhere—a foreign literature" ("A Fragmentary History" 49). Volodine himself has mentioned that the notion of foreignness colors his writing, and that he imagines his writings as originating in another language entirely:

> Putting it simply, one could say that my novels come from a place that is foreign to French literary reality.

> They constitute a literary object published in the French language, but conceived in another language, one whose nationality is unclear. A language that is not attached to a specific geographical region, and clearly "foreign," because it does not convey the culture and traditions of the French or Francophone world. ("Ecrire en français" 53)

He speaks moreover of his own status as a marginal figure with regard to the literary establishment, or rather as an outsider among outsiders, bearing the burden of a double alienation, as it were: "My problem was that I was a writer from the ghetto, but nonetheless an *alien* in the ghetto, where the perceptions of literature and literary culture were not mine" ("On recommence" 243). Marie-Pascale Huglo recognizes the alterity of Volodine's project, and she insists too upon its mobile nature: "Post-exoticism is a hybrid, migrant literature. It introduces migration at the heart of its writing about the end, in order to transform it into this infinite trance, from which one does not return" ("The Post-Exotic Connection" 106). That is a *crucial* idea in the fullest sense of the term, granted the manner in which Volodine's work foregrounds mutation, wandering, and the translation from one state to another.

In *Songes de Mevlido*, it is the writer Mingrelian who best embodies the postexotic aesthetic. "Mingrelian's art," says Volodine, "influenced by post-exoticism, plays with uncertainty, failure, confusion of opposites, and nothingness" (419).[3] Certainly it is just as well to be skeptical about the easy identification of Mingrelian with Volodine himself, especially in view of the multiple layers of irony in which Volodine wraps the figure of the writer. Nevertheless, Volodine takes the opportunity to have his writer voice certain principles of postexotic practice that he himself quite demonstrably puts to use. Faced with the constraint of closing his narrative—at the very moment when Volodine is faced with closing his own—

Mingrelian opts for a solution that puts the very idea of an ending into question:

> Mingrelian hesitates. Concluding so many trials in one single episode doesn't seem right. Neither *Attacks Against the Moon* nor *Chicken Coop Four* is an adventure novel. He thus chooses the post-exotic technique of narrative luffing, a technique that the Organs (who demand categorical answers) don't appreciate, a technique harshly criticized by adepts of official literature, who see in it yet another insult to their theory of fiction. As if the black wind of narration, at this key moment, were incapable of finding an appropriate direction, the story furls oddly back on itself, gathers itself, ready to proceed again, and suddenly it flutters against itself. Three versions will thus coexist, independently and inextricably, three sequences springing from the same narrative clay, with which Mingrelian deftly shapes an awkward ending for his story, and an unfulfilled eternity for his hero. (427)

It is perhaps not the idea of a triple conclusion, or even the notion of an "unfulfilled eternity," that strikes one as original here. After all, such gestures are common ones in postmodern practices. Rather, it is the image of *luffing*, of advancing in an uncertain wind with one's sail insufficiently filled. The itinerary of such an advance is necessarily interrupted and shifting, one that is guaranteed to shock the sensibilities of more conventional sailors. Volodine asks us implicitly to consider, however, that such a technique might be admirably suited to the kind of impossible conditions that he describes. Such is his wager, and such, too, is the leap of faith that he invites us to take here, both on the local level of *Songes de Mevlido* and on the broader level of his postexotic project as a whole.

One of the most particular traits of that project is the way that it turns its back upon literary tradition as we commonly think of it. Apart from autoreferential gestures, which are frequent, there are rather few conventional intertextual effects in Volodine's books. Instead of alluding to mainstream precursor figures in literature, Volodine generally prefers to point elsewhere, toward the foundational texts of Marxist-Leninist thought, for example, or those of Tibetan Buddhism. He seeks thus to underscore the otherness of his writing, insisting that it arises in a manner that is very largely independent. Moreover, he has noted that many of the texts which he most admires perform the same gesture with regard to the institution of literature; writers like Kafka, Borges, and Pessoa, he remarks, "are wary of literary references, and, most of the time, eschew them consciously. They try to take a stand outside of the system of official, normalized literature" ("On recommence" 240).

In opposition to an exhausted literary tradition, Volodine proposes to invent a new, mythological tradition,[4] and this, too, is properly viewed as a kind of crossing. For therein tired genres such as the novel, the short story, the romance, and the epic give way to imagined forms such as the *romånce*, the *shaggå*, the *narrat*, the *novelle*, and the *entrevoûte*, each of them offering itself as both new and old. New, because each iteration of the form is the first of its kind; old, because those forms are firmly anchored in a mythological literary history as venerable as any one might conceive. Volodine's renovated forms testify to his will to make things new, and to underscore the alterity of his postexotic project. Those forms enable Volodine to situate his project well apart from the literary mainstream, as he attempts to chart new territory for contemporary prose fiction. Jean-Didier Wagneur recognizes that cartographic impulse in Volodine's work, and the key role that the new forms play therein. "Volodine's universe is nothing less than a map of these fictions," he argues ("Introduction" 7), insisting on the notion of space, a territory that demands to be traversed and reconnoitered.

In *Songes de Mevlido*, those new forms play an important role; and we have seen that Volodine presents his character Mingrelian quite explicitly as a postexotic writer. Yet the manner in which Volodine casts those forms in his novel is curious, insofar as he describes them as belated and neglected in the world he constructs. They belong to a past that has lost its relevance, and they can no longer help humans to understand their impossibly vexed present. The interest they offer is anecdotal at best, and they are always damaged in one way or another. At one point in his mission, Mevlido happens across a motley collection of these relics: "Now he was examining the books—minutes of meetings that have taken place in clandestinity or indifference, in Ulan Bator, Iquitos, Zone Two, or here, right here in Chicken Coop Four. There was also a post-exotic romånce. The volumes were in shreds. The cover was missing" (89). He is one of the few remaining people whom such a text might conceivably interest—but this is undoubtedly because he himself is an impossibly belated figure. The interplay of the new and the old that Volodine constructs here teeters on the knife-edge of irony. In the fictional world, the *romånce*, the *narrat*, the *shaggå*, and so forth are exhausted forms, and whatever truth they may have conveyed in their time seems, now, quaintly dated. In the referential world—that is to say, the world which we inhabit—those forms function as the very signs of literary innovation, of a will to make things new. It is difficult, of course, to have things both ways, but the manner in which Volodine shuttles back and forth between those two perspectives is intended to guarantee a kind of ironic equilibrium. Furthermore, it is emblematic of the broader strategy of alternation that Volodine constructs in his work as a whole, as he leads us here, then there, then back again.

Another instance of that shuttling dynamic is the way that Volodine uses heteronyms. In the spring of 2008, Antoine Volodine went all Fernando Pessoa on us (as my students might put it), revealing that for many years he had been practicing literature under a variety of different names, in addition to his own. He is responsible, notably, for more than a dozen titles at the Ecole des Loisirs, a publishing house specializing in works for a young audience. "Elli Kronauer" made a name for himself there between 1999 and 2001, with five books for young adults; and "Manuela Draeger" launched the "Bobby Potemkine" series there in 2002. A few years thereafter, "Lutz Bassmann" penned two books for the Editions Verdier, *Haïkus de prison* and *Avec les moines-soldats* [With the monk-soldiers], both of which appeared in February 2008. Indeed, Bassmann has staked his claim to reality in a thoroughly modern manner, with an elegant, eponymous website (www.lutzbassmann.org) that leaves little room for argument. More recently still, Manuela Draeger has defected from the Ecole des Loisirs for the first time, authoring a book for a more mature audience, *Onze Rêves de suie* [Eleven dreams of soot] (2010), and publishing it at the Editions de l'Olivier. Putting that arduous and explicitly postexotic text on offer as she does, Draeger appears to be competing for attention with Volodine himself.

In the light of this tsunami of heteronyms, one may wonder what other contemporary writers Volodine has fathered. Michel Houellebecq? Christine Angot? Jean d'Ormesson? Is all of French literature merely a dream of Antoine Volodine—or indeed of Mevlido? For it should be remarked that this heteronymy colors not only the manner in which Volodine signs his books. It extends also to the characters in his fictional world, and most especially to those characters who are invested with the responsibility of telling his stories. Surveying Volodine's work from its beginnings through *Bardo or not Bardo* (2004), Jean-Louis Hippolyte finds no fewer than seventy-two heteronyms, in what he characterizes as "a Pessoan polyphony" (*Fuzzy Fiction* 161). In a brief consideration of "trashcan" literature (a term she invokes as a synonym for "postexotic"), Pascale Casanova sees Volodine's use of heteronymy as a resistance technique. "The systematic use of heteronymy is clearly conceived as a principle of subversion [. . .] by the authors of trashcan literature," she contends. "Against the principle of sincerity, against the stable and reassuring identity of the author, against connivance with the reader, against the academism of self-proclaimed avant-gardes, against the attempt to renew the novel, against bookshop manipulations" ("A Fragmentary History" 46).

It is useful to resituate Volodine's heteronymy in the broader context of his onomastic strategy. If his first four books share anything at all with mainstream science fiction, it is surely their anthroponyms, which underscore the alterity of the individuals they identify, in an attempt to convince us that the world which they inhabit is a very strange one indeed. Furthermore, those very bizarre names—and the slippage to which they are subject—serve to put the notion of personal identity on trial. Such a process is apparent in each of Volodine's fictional worlds, and it suddenly looms larger still, in the light of his recent revelations about his pseudonyms. For Volodine, a name is bound up in the task of speaking, and in the most crucial case, in the responsibility to testify. His narrators share the discursive stage with "metanarrators," second-degree figures speaking from beyond death, or from a carceral space, or from somewhere outside of the diegetic frame.[5] Narrators and metanarrators collaborate and compete with each other constantly; at times it is clear which sort of voice is speaking, at other times it is less clear. What is important—and importantly characteristic, moreover—is the manner in which voice shifts from one mode to another: clearly, this is yet another example of the sort of crossing that colors Volodine's writing so indelibly.

In *Songes de Mevlido*, the question of who speaks is a very difficult one. That question inevitably arises when a narrator speaks in the first person, intruding into a narrative pattern where the third person is the norm. Those moments can be jarring for the reader, as when, after having noted that Mevlido likes the atmosphere in a certain neighborhood, especially after dark, the narrator adds, "Me too" (45). That remark catches us unawares, and signals an abrupt shift from a dispassionate, objective narrative to one which is all of a sudden personalized. Other narratorial interventions are marked by an effort to claim a narrative authority that is by no means axiomatic: "Allow me to put a word in here. Nobody invited me to do so, and I don't even know if I'll be able to say what I'm thinking, but allow me nonetheless" (55). Still others testify to a need to put some order into the telling, to normalize and clarify: "I would like to return for a moment to Sonia Wolguelane, whose name was mentioned in Mevlido's dream" (55).

In none of these instances is the status of the narrator perfectly clear. We are unsure whether it is a man or a woman speaking; we don't have a good sense of what that individual's relation to the events he or she recounts might be; we don't even know whether that person can be thought of as a character in the fictional world. Indeed, the answers to those questions are themselves subject to shift, depending on the narrative instance—and that, too, is a very deliberate tactic in Volodine's general strategy.[6] Describing a scene in a crowded trolley car, the narrator notes, "All the shoes exhale an odor of wet shoes, especially Mevlido's, who is standing three feet away from me" (125), suggesting that the narrator is indeed a character in the fictional world, telling a story principally focused on someone other than himself, constituting thus what Gérard Genette calls an intradiegetic-heterodiegetic narrator (*Figures III* 254–56). Yet when, a brief moment thereafter, the narrator remarks, "Except for me, and I don't count, nobody accompanies him" (128), one may wonder why the narrator doesn't *count*. Is it because he is only a minor figure, and thus of no real importance in the story he tells? Or is it because he is not literally present in the scene that he sketches? The point may seem like a fine one, but I believe that it is crucial. All the more so in view of the context of this passage. For the scene takes place in a trolley car that is taking Mevlido toward Chicken Coop Four, and thus toward one of those crossings which test him so closely. At such a moment, the principle of narrative uncertainty—and stories are always uncertain in Volodine[7]—weighs very heavily indeed.

One may be tempted to identify Mingrelian, the writer, as the narrator of Mevlido's story. After all, it is he who is charged by the Organs with drafting the report on Mevlido's mission. We know, too, that Mingrelian and Mevlido had met during their special training. We learn that Mingrelian feels very close indeed to "his" character: "Mingrelian easily inhabits his character. No psychological barrier deters him or thwarts him" (418). Yet when the narrator (or rather *a* narrator) remarks, from afar as it were, that he likes Mingrelian's books, our efforts to locate a stable narrative voice in the figure of Mingrelian founder. Each gesture we make in that direction is likewise doomed to failure. When we encounter a narrative utterance such as "Thus did Mevlido's death—that is, mine—play out" (385), for instance, we are very much at a loss; and that situation is not remedied when, right afterward, the narrator remarks further, "We catch up with Mevlido on that day. Mevlido, or someone who looks enough like me to be me and to bear the same name that I do" (386). In short, what Volodine does in *Songes de Mevlido* is to traverse the spectrum of possibility offered by narrative voice, mapping that territory on his own terms, but taking care that we should never be able to situate ourselves precisely upon it.

He plays the same sort of game with the notions of the author and the reader. At one end of the spectrum of narrative voice, the territory of the metanarrator abuts that of the author, or more precisely the implied author. That latter figure is the one who interacts with the reader—or the implied reader—while both consider the text together. As Volodine casts them, the mutual relations of author and reader are significantly tensive in nature: on some occasions, the author seeks to draw the reader into an interpretive community; on others, the author seeks to distance the reader. Sometimes, Volodine underscores what

Lionel Ruffel calls "the participatory dimension of reading and analysis" ("Interrogation" 79), suggesting that the reader is an active, fully enfranchised partner in the production of literary meaning. At his most pressing, Volodine argues that the reader must project himself or herself into the fiction, that indeed there exists a strong commonality of purpose between author and reader—and between reader and character as well. There are moments in *Songes de Mevlido* when a narrative voice far more *authoritative* than that of any metanarrator may be heard. Typically, that voice directs our attention to literature itself,[8] and enjoins us to deepen our connection with the fictional world: "As Deeplane remarked about the relations between Mevlido and Mingrelian, we are linked to these books, to all of these books, by a total and painful complicity. Between us and Mingrelian, there is not even—alas! Yokog Gans would exclaim—the thickness of a cigarette paper" (420).

Elsewhere however, Volodine keeps us very much at bay, frustrating our interpretive efforts and suggesting that the text is fundamentally indecipherable. Throughout his work, there is a pattern of messages gone astray, and the very notion of communication is an embattled one in the fallen worlds that he creates. In her consideration of authorial and lectoral figures in Volodine, Mélanie Lamarre contends that "the work is haunted by the specter of bad reception" ("Ici Breughel" 150), and indeed that is often the case. Frédéric Briot goes further still when he argues, "The purpose of the story is to bewilder the reader, in the fullest sense of the term" ("Les Chimères" 206). For my own part, I view moments like these as part of a very mobile, shifting dynamic wherein Volodine shuttles between two visions of literature. The first vision is utopic, one where author, reader, narrator, and character collaborate harmoniously on a level that is very nearly isotopic, and each of those figures may claim the fictional world as his or her own. The second is dystopic, one where the figures I mentioned are mutually alienated, where meaning is continually deferred, and where the human subject is a stranger in the world he or she pretends to inhabit. Those two visions put each other into question in Volodine's fiction, and thereby enrich the metaliterary dimension of the latter. They serve moreover to make readers reflect about what we look for when we pick up a novel. Surely we cannot expect utopia each time we do so, but by the same token we anticipate that there will be some room for us in the novels we read. In other terms, what Volodine puts on stage here is readerly desire and its changing fates—and in this one instance at least, we may be forgiven for imagining that he is speaking directly to *us*.

The dream world that the title of Volodine's novel so clearly invokes is constantly at issue in the text; and indeed the characters in *Songes de Mevlido* are always migrating from the waking state to the oneiric, and back again. Mevlido himself is subject to nightmares, "nocturnal hallucinations" (170), and dreams of all sorts; yet he confesses to Maggie Yeung that he is unable to give an account of those dreams, as if they were fundamentally untellable—or as if his own narrative powers were unequal to the task. In another session, he tells her that he can never determine if a given memory arises from waking experience or from dream (74). His problem is undoubtedly complicated by the fact that he himself is a champion dreamer, and has been identified and recruited as such by the Organs. For once he sets off on his missions, the only contact Mevlido will have with his controllers will be through dreams. It is through dreams, too, that he comes into contact with Verena Becker, who has been dead for twenty years.[9] Explicitly forbidden to seek her out oneirically—"I remember Deeplane's instructions. It is forbidden to establish contact" (462)—Mevlido cannot determine whether she is a figure in his dream, or he in hers. It is a familiar paradox (one thinks of Zhuangzi's dream of the butterfly, or of Alice and the Red King), and yet it is no less pungent for its familiarity.

That very confusion is a central feature of the world that Antoine Volodine creates, one which is highly intersubjective and where boundaries are meant to be traversed. One can never be quite certain which consciousness contains the other, or which regime, dream or waking reality; and the limits of those states are always fluid and shifting. Any narrative at all resembles a dream in Volodine, precisely by virtue of its narrativity. Frequently in *Songes de Mevlido*, narratives (even the most banal ones) are explicitly cast as dreams. Such is the case when Mevlido's controller, Deeplane, asks him to read an account of a forensic dissection: "You see, Mevlido? said Deeplane. It seems like a chaos of weirdness in a dream" (203). In a pinch, that description might serve to describe the novel itself, of course, and in fact Volodine peppers his text with metaliterary moments very much like it. One of the resistance slogans that echoes through Chaos exhorts whoever hears it, "DREAM A THOUSAND YEARS, DREAM A THOUSAND YEARS WITHOUT BELIEVING THAT DREAMS EXIST!" (160), calling for the abolition of the distinction we habitually draw between dream and waking reality. That distinction serves dream very badly indeed, Volodine suggests, and tends to keep people in a state of subjugation.

To Volodine's way of thinking, dream is potentially liberating in its effect—and thus so is fiction. For dream is largely synonymous with fiction in his work, where each term, in parallel or in concert, sets out an alternative to an oppressive waking reality. On the simplest level, Volodine causes his characters (and his readers, along with them) to reconsider their perception of the phenomenal world. In Alban Glück's store, for example, Mevlido reflects, "It's almost difficult to realize that we're in the real world. The shop itself seems like it came straight out of a dream" (135). On a more complex level, Volodine emblazons dream within dream and fiction within fiction, such that any phenomenal reality they may invoke seems, at best, anecdotal. Thus, he takes a canonical work of fiction, Mikhail Bulgakov's *The Master and Margarita*, and inserts it into his fictional world, where it becomes part of the mythology of a revolutionary past. Borrowing a scene from Bulgakov, Volodine creates a reconfigured, second-order fiction in *Songes de Mevlido*, carefully calling our attention to what happens when fictional worlds collide:

> A few centuries ago, just after the beginning of the First Soviet Union, one of our favorite Russian novelists, Mikhail Bulgakov, described a man's decapitation by a streetcar. The conductor was a conductress. She belonged to the Communist Youth. Careening down Bronnaya, she gave herself the pleasure of neatly beheading a man who had fallen on the rails. The head of the victim rolled elegantly along the ground. So it goes in fiction, but here we were smack in the middle of reality, and the woman in green's head had not been neatly cut off, to the contrary. The iron wheels had crushed it disgustingly, after dragging and mutilating her body. As to the conductor, it was not, like in *The Master and Margarita*, a frisky young worker on her way to a radiant future. It was a fifty-something man who, even if he had been sympathetic to the Komsomols ages ago, no longer expressed that sympathy, not for a long, long, long time. (107–08)

In such a fashion, Volodine invites us to reflect upon a variety of concerns. For instance, he asks us to think about the context in which each of these fictions arises, about the different literary horizons on which Bulgakov and he himself stake their claims. He invites us to savor the way in which a fiction can be recast as reality—as a reality suspended within another fictional world, that is. And by extension, he demands that we exercise a readerly agility which is itself worthy of consideration. Most importantly however, Volodine wraps the easy distinction of fiction and reality in aporia, and suggests that we cannot know for certain where we stand in the world that he creates. And inevitably, there arises the question that Richard Saint-Gelais articulates with regard to Volodine's work: "what happens when the text becomes its own fiction?" ("Faction Antoine Volodine" 104).

In one sense, it is otiose to pursue that question much further, for that way lies madness. Yet that itself is one more boundary which Volodine urges us to cross, if only virtually. It is certain that his own characters migrate back and forth between sanity and madness with regularity. Mevlido tells his psychiatrist, Maggie Yeung, that he feels that he is slipping into insanity (139). Elsewhere, he imagines mental illness as a pervasive, contagious presence: "Mental illness lurks too close to me, he mused. It's everywhere" (169). His companion, Maleeya Bayarlag, recognizes early on that Mevlido's dreams are those of a madman[10]—but in view of the fact that she herself is as crazy as a jaybird, can we trust her assessment of Mevlido? Once again, it is a question of stance and, consequently, perspective: can one recognize a dream from within a dream, or fiction from inside of fiction, or madness from a state of madness?

That same sort of question may bedevil us when we consider other frontiers that Volodine causes his characters to cross. Freedom and incarceration, for example, are cast in Volodine's work as states that are mutually implicative. The carceral condition is dominant, and it is often from there, or from another place of constraint, that his protagonists speak.[11] They speak because they must, in the first instance, but also because speech affords them the only kind of autonomy they can hope to find in an oppressive world. Speech thus holds out the possibility of liberation—even if that possibility remains a very distant one. Yet one may be prompted to wonder if Volodine's protagonists can actually descry anything other than the condition they are doomed to inhabit. Their existence is inscribed in what Erving Goffman calls "total institutions,"[12] and Mevlido, controlled as he is by the Organs, is no exception to that rule. Throughout Volodine's work, there is a tension between the notions of the inside and the outside—but the outside remains very largely virtual most of the time, something that shimmers on the edge of the horizon of possibility. Charif Majdalani sees in that tension a fable of literature:

> In a metaphorical or analogical way, the schism between inside and outside proclaimed by post-exotic novelists can easily appear as the expression of an awareness, ever-clearer and more painful, of the schism between, on the one hand, the writer immured in a stubbornness to speak outside of all worlds, outside of all conventions, in his own language, and, on the other hand, a world that no longer pays attention to literature, a world distracted by the interminable chatter of the media, a world that turns away from authentic voices, and whose historic and social conditions (veritable or media totalitarianism, flabby democracy, conveyor of mediocrity and of a self-forgetting, according to Volodine) are the proximate or distant causes for literature's becoming "inaudible." ("Post-Exoticism, or Internal Literatures" 64–65)

The fictional world that Volodine imagines is a fallen, corrupted one, certainly. Literature—or indeed any other kind of interpersonal communication—is in an extremely embattled, parlous state in that world. We have seen that when Volodine invokes literary texts they come to us as cultural vestiges, as artifacts of a civilization that was, but no longer is. For the revolution has long since given way to reaction, and the shift from one to the other has occasioned disastrous consequences for humankind as a whole. The reality that Mevlido and his fellows must come to terms with is stamped by "abortive revolution" (56); they live in the ghetto of Chicken Coop Four, in a landscape furnished by catastrophe, genocide, apocalypse, heinous collaboration, and a resistance that is always foredoomed. Moreover, they are tragically and inescapably belated.[13] "We are after the global revolution," Deeplane explains to Mevlido. "Long after. It's not the same thing. Not really the same geological period, you know" (196). According to him, such belatedness has caused a significant change in humans, and in the behavior they display. As if to mock the early promises of progressive ideology, postrevolutionary humans have become, in Deeplane's view, nothing better than beasts.[14] As goes the species, so too goes the individual, and Mevlido can feel that very process at work within himself, he can sense the way that his better self is slowly coming apart.[15] It is undoubtedly the most exquisite torture to which he is subjected.

A ruined world like this one offers Antoine Volodine a privileged crucible in which to test his human subjects. Asked by Jean-Didier Wagneur whether he is drawn toward the ruins of epics, he responds:

> Toward epic, toward revolutionary epics, yes, and also toward ruins in general. But I feel even more drawn toward the extraordinary and seemingly inevitable mutation of revolution into its own parody or betrayal. It's a tragic thing, in human terms; but in a novelistic perspective it's riveting, because you don't know beforehand what the ruins will look like. Anything is possible, even the most awful things. I love the idea of an epic that swerves toward forms that are always original, unknown, nightmarish. My characters stand at different points in that process. They are armed with two certainties: on the one hand, the liberation of human beings through revolution is the only activity that justifies their existence on this earth; on the other hand, revolution will necessarily degenerate and crush them. That's why they are so much in their element in camps and prisons, where those two certainties are most in harmony. ("On

recommence" 236)

It is a very brutal world indeed, one that beggars individual will and moral sense. That Mevlido can continue to envision something better, and act in function of that vision, suggests that he is capable of crossing the frontier between the world as it is and the world as it ought to be, if only through ideation. His struggle is fundamentally quixotic in nature, but it is no less exemplary for all that. Like Volodine's other protagonists, Mevlido plays out a drama of loss that is all the more poignant since he is fully aware of the fate that awaits him. Pascale Casanova argues that Volodine's work is marked by "the heroism of those who are going to die anonymously" ("A Fragmentary History" 45), and such is undoubtedly Mevlido's lot. It is useful to recognize, however, that the frontier between life and death in Volodine's fictional worlds is an open one, and his protagonists cross it frequently—in both directions.

When Mevlido arrives at the office of the Organs for his interview with Deeplane, the narrator complaisantly tells us that his death is forty-nine years in the future (193). It is a statement that seems simple enough on the face of it, and it appears to function unproblematically in the pattern of narrative time that Volodine proposes. Things quickly become more complicated, however, when one interrogates the way Volodine uses the notion of "death." For when Deeplane eventually sends Mevlido on his mission to Chicken Coop Four, it will be as a reborn or reincarnated deep-penetration agent. In other terms, Mevlido's existence at that point will be beyond his death—or at least beyond *one* of his deaths.[16] During his training, which lasts for forty years and more,[17] Deeplane teaches Mevlido to anticipate that moment of metamorphosis. "In a half century a man named Mevlido will be as old as you are today," he tells him, adding moreover that Mevlido will be a "good guy" (220). He will be called upon to cross over from life to death, and from there to another kind of life, where another kind of death undoubtedly awaits him. Unless Deeplane can exfiltrate him before he dies once again, that is. "We'll try to exfiltrate you beforehand, Deeplane promised. You know we always try. But most likely we'll have to focus on the only moment that's a hundred percent sure: your death agony. We'll get you back during that" (205).

When the time comes, however, such an outcome might be still more difficult to achieve than Deeplane foresaw. Because he himself is considerably enfeebled, having wagered on humans rather than spiders in the struggle for power, and having lost that wager. At best, perhaps he can manage to exfiltrate Mevlido into dream, if not into phenomenal existence—and that will have to suffice. The lesson that Volodine sketches here once again devolves upon the analogy between the individual and the species. For just as Mevlido has mutated, so too has humankind. "Something had changed in them. It was as if they could no longer tell the difference between living, dreams, and death. [. . .] Yes, humanity was a detestable species which had systematically betrayed every hope that had been placed in it" (200). Once that boundary has been crossed, there is very little room for maneuver left to the human subject, in a posthumanist world where every new beginning takes place after things have ended, "today, at the end of history" (10).

In his efforts to characterize such a world, Antoine Volodine has often invoked the image of the *bardo*, the transitional state of being mentioned in the *Bardo Thodol*, the Tibetan book of the dead. "Bardo, as one finds it in many post-exotic texts," he remarks to Jean-Didier Wagneur, "is a black space where oppositions are abolished, that is, where life and death, present and past, imaginary and real are the same, etc. The boundaries between You and I, author and character, author and reader are erased. Obviously, it's a very rich site for a novelist" ("On recommence" 261–62). It is a stateless state, a negative image of what we imagine existence to be. It does not lack for danger, but it also presents very significant possibilities of liberation and understanding. Importantly for Volodine, it is a utopian world, because habitual communicative boundaries are abolished therein, and meaning circulates freely. Whoever wishes to attain such a state—whether it be a writer, a reader, or a character—must be prepared to exercise a conscious effort of will, and a mobility that might have been, until that moment, latent and largely unsuspected. The process of transformation is arduous, and its results are uncertain. But the first step is an easy one: "That's just what I thought, I muttered. One only needs to cross the wall to change places" (388). It is just that act which Volodine's characters are called upon to perform, no more and no less, over and over again; and it is that, too, which Volodine asks of his reader, should he or she be inclined to play along.

Marie Cosnay's Roman-Fleuve

MARIE COSNAY'S *Villa Chagrin* [Villa sorrow] (2006), the third title in a body of work that now includes twenty books, may not be a roman-fleuve in the strict sense of that term (indeed it may not even be a novel), but a river most certainly runs through it, from first page to last. That river is the Adour, as seen from its right bank, across from Bayonne, the capital of the French Basque Country, in a place called Saint-Esprit. At some seventy-five pages, this text is certainly no *Jean-Christophe*, no *Chronique des Pasquier*. Nonetheless, it flows in full spate, picking up and melding along its way an impressive variety of narrative currents: the story of the painter Bram van Velde and his companion, Marthe Arnaud-Kuntz; an examination of the nature of disaster, conceived both as a collective phenomenon and as a personal one; a love story wherein absence looms far larger than presence; a meditation on the image and the fate of the image in representation; a parable of writing and its uses; and more besides. Like the Adour, *Villa Chagrin* is very fluid, very dynamic. Its author, a classicist by profession, is well placed to understand why a river seemed so apt to Heraclitus as a figure of time; and just like a river, this novel (for that is what I shall call it) is mutable in astonishing ways.

Michel Charles has argued eloquently for a vision of the literary text as an artifact constantly in motion, one that is difficult to apprehend in any way other than on the run, as it were.[1] That way of looking at textuality is particularly productive in the case of a work such as Cosnay's, wherein a powerful continuity is achieved through a narrative technique that seems, on the face of it at least, constantly interrupted. The multiple diegetic threads that I mentioned contribute to that sense of interruption. More telling still is the fact that Cosnay structures her novel like a diary, with dated entries and a progressive intercalated narration. Maurice Blanchot reminded us long ago that any discourse at all relies in some measure on interruption for its coherence,[2] and in that perspective it is easier to understand how Cosnay enlists multiplicity in the service of singularity. The image of the river is also helpful in that regard, as is Michel Charles's characterization of literary textuality as "essentially a long discourse, where the story appears intermittently" (199). One important consideration that such a manner of conceiving a work of literature suggests is that any reading we bring to it must strive to be as mobile as the text itself—a tall order, certainly, and one that inevitably calls us to attention.

The incipit of *Villa Chagrin* invokes both time and space, and appears to situate the narrative instance precisely: "On the November 15 I stayed at home, avoiding the fog on the Adour and the cottony flow I saw last night around seven forty-five, when I went out into the invisible, driving toward the most familiar place in the city" (9). Yet that invocation relies significantly on imprecision for its effect, and the narrator insists upon phenomena ("the fog," "the cottony flow," "the invisible") that serve to thematize the notion of imprecision. It is a technique that Marie Cosnay will exploit throughout her novel, and one that is deeply imbricated in the fluvial images that teem therein.

Those images are extremely various, and they serve a variety of purposes. From time to time, Cosnay personifies the river, in order to underscore the narrator's state of mind, either by identification or by contrast: "The river was imperturbable" (10). It is a thing both alive and reactive, whose spirits and modes of being change continually: "Not far from the Villa

Chagrin, in Saint-Esprit, I gazed at the Adour. It was spewing a bit. Successive bridges crossed it. The fog came" (35). Like the narrator and every other human whom she puts on stage, the river has traversed a significant span of both time and space in order to arrive at the *here* and the *now*: "A city where a small river meets a bigger one, which up to that point has traversed two hundred kilometers of hills, red with heather" (10). Though one might have imagined that the prison which lends its name to the book would have served as the center of Cosnay's novelistic topography, it is in fact the river instead. Speaking of her own house, the narrator remarks, "No, it's not far from the prison. Nor from the Adour, which is in relation to the Mandrill corner the symmetrical place" (11).

That symmetry marks *Villa Chagrin* indelibly, and the point upon which it hinges is the river itself. In that perspective, it is the river which guarantees the rest of Cosnay's landscape, conceived both literally and figuratively. As the narrator tells the story of Bram van Velde, for example, the incidents and anecdotes she provides take their place in a chronology that the river certifies, through metaphor. Moreover, in contemplating the river, the narrator becomes convinced of a broader existential lesson, one that might have seemed obvious from the start, but whose truth is so trivially conspicuous that it demands confirmation at a deeper level: "Life goes by indeed" (62). The river perceives each of the narrator's gestures, and serves as a mute witness to her circumstances and her thoughts. It observes her both as she acts and as she refuses to act: "I come to the corner of the Boulevards Alsace-Lorraine and Jean-Jaurès, not far from the Adour, and not far from my house. I threw away the photos the man I love had taken, I laid down, perhaps suffering from malaria, from new chills, I laid down in the sun that gazed upon the Adour, here I am, now it's time. Not yet" (56).

Finally, and as if inevitably, the river serves as an image of the text itself. Both are phenomena whose nature is difficult to grasp upon first encounter, things that change and that change again, but which are nonetheless governed by a directional logic—that is to say, both of them *go somewhere*. Importantly, the manner in which the river resists representation limns a discourse on representational difficulty that flows unabated through *Villa Chagrin*. "The man I love," mentions the narrator, "whom I describe as going from bridge to bridge, took a picture on the Adour: the sky choked the river, the bridge brushed the edge of the photo, the liquid expanse, above, was cottony, supple, whitely reflective" (44). Framed by sky and bridge, the river is hard to seize. One can perceive only its surface; the rest must be imagined. That surface is imprecise, elastic, and reflective, furthermore, which surely does not simplify matters. Anyone looking into it too closely runs the risk of encountering nothing other than his or her gaze. Yet that problem is, of course, one which a critical reading of a critical text must often negotiate—and, for choice, sooner rather than later.

Let us then turn our own gaze toward disaster and the suffering that attends it, as indeed Marie Cosnay invites us to do. Like the image of the river, the theme of disaster takes many different shapes in *Villa Chagrin*. It can be political and broadly collective; it can be more personal; or it can be utterly singular and strictly intimate. Whatever form it assumes, however, disaster calls out to disaster, as Cosnay sketches points of affinity and resemblance between the various kinds of catastrophe that she puts on offer. If she finds an exemplary figure in Bram van Velde, it is undoubtedly for two reasons. On the one hand, he was an artist, and through him Cosnay can conveniently invoke the issues of representational difficulty that are clearly on her mind. On the other hand, disaster seemed to follow Bram van Velde like a dog, whether it be on a massive scale (the Spanish Civil War, the Second World War, the Algerian War of Independence) or on a far more intimate one (poverty, professional failure, madness). Through him, and more particularly through a painting entitled *Femme au poteau de torture* [Woman at the torture stake], Cosnay seeks to tell a fable about what she calls "the sufferings of humans" (26), shifting from the singular to the plural.

Abraham Gerardus van Velde was born in 1895, but *Villa Chagrin* picks him up in 1932, when he and his wife Lily, beset by poverty in Paris during the Great Depression, decided to go to Majorca to live. There, life was far less expensive, and the village they chose had already welcomed other artists, among them several Germans seeking to flee rising Nazism in their own country. Cosnay tells the life of Bram van Velde in fits and snatches, sampling his biography to suit her own narrative needs, offering us an event here and an anecdote there without regard to linear chronology. Early on, it becomes apparent that personal and political disaster collide in the painter's life. Lily dies shortly after the Spanish Civil War has broken out. As Bram van Velde mourns her, he recognizes that the disaster in Spain announces others to come: "Spain struggled. The world would struggle" (44). Moreover, as Marie Cosnay tells it, Lily's death is explicitly inscribed under the threat of Nazism:

> On October 30, 1936, Lily has just died. Wijnand, the son of Edouard H. Kramers, a patron, writes to Bram: "[. . .] Only my fierce struggle against the murderous Nazi enterprise gives me the strength to continue. Even though we might avoid this catastrophe, I suppose, I feel that it is getting dangerously closer. It seems to me that the whole spirit of Europe is crushed by this depravity, which is always on the increase [. . .]." (17, ellipses in original)

Fleeing wartime Spain, Bram van Velde will find no real refuge in France. Quite to the contrary, in fact, and that is what interests Cosnay so intensely. For in 1938, he runs afoul of the law: "Arrested in Bayonne, Bram is arraigned in criminal court. A Dutch citizen returning from Spain, or almost, with no identity papers, he is condemned to four weeks in prison" (63). That law is a patently egregious and shameful one, enacted in a reactionary, isolationist spirit and directed against those people least equipped to defend themselves: refugees, unpapered foreigners, people with neither title nor standing.

In the present time of her narrative, Cosnay tells of her own inquiry into that law and its historical circumstances:

> February 21, 2005. Archives of the Bayonne Public Library. On the microfilm records of newspapers from the month of June 1938, I read, dated June 1: "A legislative decree, enacted on May 2, 1938, establishes a new and very strict set of rules for foreigners residing in France. According to the said decree, any foreigner residing for more than two months in our country must possess an identity card, or a residence permit replacing the latter, which he or she must obtain at the police headquarters, or town hall, of his place of residence." (41–42)

Once again in present time, Cosnay remarks upon her inquiry: "March 20, 2005. I got this story from June 1938, I got the place where on the Adour homes are reflected, near the prison called Villa Chagrin" (43). She uses the word "story" (*histoire* in the original French) in the fullest sense, I think, meaning both *story* and *history*, that is, both the dilemma that Bram van Velde finds himself in and the far vaster political situation that necessarily inflects the former. Those two regimes find their point of correspondence in the notion of disaster, Cosnay suggests; and in the first instance, disaster involves a failure to respect the fundamental laws of hospitality.

Those laws are typically put to the test most dramatically when it is a question of the stranger, and for Cosnay the painter Bram van Velde offers an especially exemplary figure of the stranger. That he should have been arrested, tried, and imprisoned for no good reason, in her own city, strikes her, even at a remove of some seven decades, as scandalous and utterly intolerable. Her outrage is one of the forces that impel *Villa Chagrin*—as is her conviction that, insofar as our view of the other is concerned, not much has changed between 1938 and 2005. In that sense, Cosnay's tale of Bram van Velde ramifies very clearly in the present, as does her meditation on the theme of disaster.

More than any other character in *Villa Chagrin*, it is Marthe Arnaud-Kuntz (whom Bram van Velde met after Lily's death, and who became his companion) who bears the weight of that meditation. She is marked by disaster from the moment she enters the story—and indeed before that moment, too, for Cosnay mentions that she had been a missionary in the Zambezi, and that there, "Marthe had known disaster, several kinds of disasters" (14). Cosnay insists upon the word "disaster," grafting it onto the figure of Marthe and according it totemic status in *Villa Chagrin*. "Marthe had already survived a disaster," Cosnay remarks of her early on (17); "Marthe had already been touched by disaster" (20); "You might think, insofar as Marthe is concerned, that she was gifted for life, including disaster" (27).

Especially "gifted" for disaster, Marthe suffers because of what she had witnessed in Africa. It is a truth that she finds hard to bear, and one that will eventually lead her into outlandish behavior and madness. "Marthe sometimes cried out strangely, haunted by memories of Africa," says Cosnay. "There, right by the promenade and the bridge, she squatted down, and caused a scandal" (14). Marthe's notorious *squattings* will become her signature, in effect, the sign of her particularity and of the particular illness that afflicts her. Cosnay exploits those squattings again and again in *Villa Chagrin*,[3] in part because she possesses very little other information about Marthe's life. "Until now, I have been unable to find any reliable information about Marthe Arnaud, about her work, the love she gave, her revolt, her squattings," Cosnay confesses early on (27), and thus she offers Marthe's squattings as the very posture of suffering, of *chagrin*, and of disaster.

If Cosnay chooses to deploy such a tactic, it is perhaps because disaster is difficult to represent in more conventional, direct ways. It beggars the imagination for one thing, escaping from our capacity to conceive it rationally because its dimensions are never stable, and they tend toward the infinite. "Disaster is not our business," argues Blanchot, "it is indefinitely infinite, it cannot be measured in terms of failure, nor as loss pure and simple. [. . .] Nothing suffices for disaster, which means that, just like destruction in the pureness of its ruin does not suit it, neither can the notion of totality define its boundaries" (*L'Ecriture du désastre* 9). Another reason that disaster resists traditional representational strategies, according to Blanchot, is that it is bound up in forgetting. That is, just as disaster itself challenges our capacity to understand, so does it put into question our ability to remember.[4] Potentially at least, in Blanchot's view, each catastrophe (whatever its scale may be) is thus double, first misunderstood, and then forgotten. One of the things that Marie Cosnay seeks to accomplish in *Villa Chagrin* is to reverse that process, by first remembering, then understanding a set of events in the past that most people would regard as obscure.

The *chagrin* that Cosnay invokes in her examination of the past is abundantly echoed in the present, and notably in a figure identified only as "Pierre M." The narrator claims him as a friend, and describes him as a man whose distress proved, ultimately, unbearable. The first time he is mentioned in the text, Cosnay wagers on understatement and economy of expression in order to express the dimensions of his suffering: "On August 27, 2003, Pierre M. killed himself in his apartment in the Rue Saint-Maur. After a stay in a psychiatric hospital he tried to find blood" (18). The disaster is his, of course; but it is not his alone. For it afflicts the narrator as well. She imagines that she sees him, a year and a half after his death, strolling on the far bank of the Adour (18). She remembers gazing at her friend's dead body, a body suddenly rendered "transparent" by death (50). She mentions that Pierre M. had been a writer, and that during the night before he committed suicide he wrote about the very difficulty of writing (42). Pondering his death, there is at least one thing that the narrator perceives very clearly indeed: "I saw, materially, my death" (18). In short, the narrator finds herself reflected in Pierre M., and his suffering is in some sense a mirror of her own.

Like other mirrors in *Villa Chagrin*, it is perhaps not entirely faithful to the subject it reflects. Or maybe the fault lies in the subject herself. For when the narrator is first confronted by her image in a real mirror, she fails utterly to recognize herself: "I was going out. Suddenly, someone was there in front of me, all teeth, I hesitated about its gender, it was a *she*: she was ready to leap, to bite, she was coming at me, there she was" (22). The topos that Marie Cosnay presents here—happening upon a mirror and seeing therein not oneself but another—is a familiar one in contemporary literature and film, so familiar that it has become a commonplace.[5] Typically, it testifies to another kind of disaster, a more intimate one this time, the moment when we realize that the human subject is not only alienated from the world but also from herself or himself. A scene such as this one may be taken as a dramatization of Rimbaud's pithy "I is another," and it wagers upon the same sort of uncanniness. Something additional is going on in this case, however, for this scene takes its place in a broader discourse on perception and interpretation that Cosnay elaborates in *Villa Chagrin*, one that centers upon the act of reading. In the first instance at least, the narrator's mistake stems from a failure to read the image correctly. That failure is all the more ironic insofar as we actual readers have no trouble understanding that the narrator is gazing at her own image.

"Would writing, in the book, be something like becoming legible for everyone, but for oneself, remaining indecipherable?" asks Blanchot (*L'Ecriture du désastre* 8), encouraging us by the same occasion to think about the uses of writing. Certainly, in the early pages of *Villa Chagrin* the narrator's writing seems to lead her away from herself rather than toward herself, into self-doubt instead of understanding and acceptance. Yet the narrator does ultimately recognize her error in that first mirror scene, even if that recognition remains a caustic one, fraught with fear and outright loathing: "Then I recognized myself in the mirror, which, at the far end of the huge room, seemed to lead to the exit. I had seen someone, almost a woman, ugly and perhaps dead and grimacing" (23).

The parable that this first mirror scene adumbrates is played out more amply in the novel as a whole, for as the latter develops the narrator learns to recognize herself more and more easily—she learns, in other terms, to read more and more fluently the images of herself that she encounters. Thus, for example, when she considers a photograph taken of her at age eleven, disguised as a clown, she understands that it is indeed herself, though a powerful feeling of self-loathing colors that understanding: "how ugly I am, how profoundly ugly" (24). Thus, too, when she gazes at a series of photographic portraits of herself taken by her lover, the narrator makes the leap from other to self, from third person to first: "I recognize her right away, she's visible in the frame, her eyes are wide open, she sees, she is seen. It's me, in the man's frame" (49). That very leap is an essential part of self-recognition for the narrator, as if the lesson Cosnay wished to convey were that one can only recognize oneself through the eyes of another. Upon occasion, the text outlines such a lesson quite literally: "Sometimes my face has been reflected in the eyes of the man I love," remarks the narrator. "That happened to me" (61).

The phrase *the man I love* echoes throughout *Villa Chagrin*, designating a figure who remains an elusive one, but who nonetheless plays a significant role in the economy of the novel. His elusiveness results largely from the fact that Cosnay never brings him into close focus, relying instead upon the aesthetic of imprecision which colors the novel as a whole: "The man I love goes from city to city. He erects freedoms on the kernel of sentences, their grammar, on the time between one word and another, on the happening where dying is not" (15). If one were inclined to doubt the intentional character of that effect, one might look toward certain passages in the text where Cosnay suggests, to the contrary, that it is quite deliberate and studied. Upon occasion, she conveys that message in a straightforward manner; at other times, she proceeds through irony. The latter mode is clearly at work when she promises to particularize that man, yet her particularization leaves him as approximate as ever: "The one I love has this particularity: he says that words strike down death and all the dying" (44).

In reflecting upon this character and his role in the novel, three considerations deserve to be noted. First, Cosnay invites her reader to compare the couple that the narrator and this man form to the couple composed by Bram van Velde and Marthe Arnaud-Kuntz. Despite the fact that the former couple evolves in the present, while the latter is confined to the past, Bram and Marthe have a great deal more narrative flesh on their bones than do the narrator and the man she loves. It is a question of focus of course, and of the choices attendant upon diegetic prominencing; but it is also bound up in the difficulty that the narrator experiences in seeing herself and her situation, a difficulty that becomes particularly conspicuous in the mirror scenes. Secondly, the narrator's lover is deeply affiliated with the river: "Behind the door stands the man I love. I haven't said anything about him, except that he goes from city to city along the watery ribbon, between narrow streets or instead bypassing the vast incursions of huge blue surfaces spanned by unexpected bridges, red, ugly or old, forming arches under which barges float" (29). Constantly in motion, never static, the man is as hard to seize as the Adour itself. Yet just like that river, he occupies a privileged, central place, both in the narrator's real world and in the one she imagines. Finally, this man serves the narrator as a point of reference, allowing her to put her own subjectivity to the test: "That he (the loved one, the other) should be the object, or that I should be: the same temptation of uncertainty, of floating identity" (61). That activity accounts for a great deal of what goes on in this book, and the narrator's struggles are patently one of the lenses through which Marie Cosnay invites us to reflect upon *chagrin* and the various shapes it adopts.

The word *chagrin* defines one of the principal currents that flow through Cosnay's novel, and that current melds a variety of emotional states, from grief, to distress, to suffering, to regret, to sadness, to affliction. It is constantly apparent in the way that the narrator tries to come to terms with events in her world, whether it be Pierre M.'s suicide or the way that the image resists representation. Bram van Velde is also continually beset by *chagrin* in its different forms. His rootlessness is certainly one of the causes of that existential condition, and so is the fact that he is by nature a struggling man, one who always searches, often without finding. As he deals with Marthe's eccentricities and outright madness, his distress mirrors hers. When at last she dies, Bram takes care to hide his grief, he "doesn't show his sorrow [*chagrin*]" (56). The eponymous prison in Bayonne is a site where several different kinds of *chagrin* coalesce and interrogate each other. On the one hand, it stands for the arbitrary and ultimately absurd abuses of political power, and the oppression that results from those processes: "In 1938, they imprisoned in the Villa Chagrin everyone who tried to get into Spain, and everyone who tried to leave it" (63). As such, it is an inevitable and enduring civic monument to scandal. On the other hand, it is a place where an innumerable diversity of individual sufferings—and the narratives that they potentially sketch—are archived. In that perspective, Bram van Velde's story exemplifies all of the stories to which the walls of the prison might testify. Despite the fact that it is so far removed in time, the narrator views his incarceration as a very local event: "Prisoner in the Villa Chagrin, in that place almost exactly between the Adour and the house where I live, Bram the sorrowful sketches in ink on the letters that Marthe sends him" (65).

Finally, the fact that the term *chagrin* figures also in the title of Cosnay's book signifies eloquently, as well. It is clearly an overdetermined word, one that is disproportionately invested with meaning. Each time one encounters it (or indeed one of its cognates) in the text, one is necessarily reminded of the title, and one quickly begins to suspect that it serves to announce a current of reflection in the novel that engages art and its uses. I do not mean to suggest that it is the only effect to do so, only that it is the most obvious one. That function is apparent, for instance, in the passage I just quoted, where, confined in the Villa Chagrin, Bram draws on Marthe's letters, quite literally imposing the visual image on the verbal. But it is equally apparent in the novel's epigraph, a brief passage that Cosnay borrows from Samuel Beckett. The text that she cites, entitled "Peintres de l'empêchement,"[6] is one essay among several that Beckett devoted, in part or entirely, to Bram van Velde.[7] In that piece, Beckett invokes the difficulties of writing on painting. He finds himself ill-equipped to speak about the painting of the van Velde brothers, Bram and Geer, and pungently remarks, "That's what happens when you let yourself be conned into writing about painting. Unless you're an art critic" (*Disjecta* 137). This is the reaction that interests Marie Cosnay, and this is the passage that she uses in her epigraph.

Beckett reappears at strategic moments in *Villa Chagrin*, and it might be argued that he constitutes a kind of *éminence grise*, a crucial point of reference in a text wherein the technique of intertextual allusion is very largely eschewed. For just like Beckett, Marie Cosnay has set herself the task of coming to terms with the image through words, and she finds that to be no simple thing. In the first instance, any object resists representation, and the more focused one's glance, the greater that resistance may seem. Thus, Beckett imagines Bram grappling with the object; and, over Beckett's shoulder, Cosnay imagines Beckett imagining Bram: "About Bram, in Bram's place, Beckett writes: 'I cannot see the object in order to represent it, because I am what I am'" (61).[8] The fundamental truth about representation that Bram van Velde recognizes, according to Beckett, is one that doubly vexes any attempt to "see" the artistic image clearly (as both Beckett and Cosnay attempt to see it), because the difficulties inherent in the first, creative situation necessarily inflect and constrain the second, interpretive situation. Moreover, in *Villa Chagrin* Cosnay takes care to register Beckett's recognition of that latter consideration, and carefully stages it as one of the major questions of her own writerly project: "'What remains representable if the essence of the object escapes representation?' wrote Beckett about Bram van Velde" (74).[9] Calling upon Beckett's struggles with the image and the word in such an overt, even theatrical manner, Cosnay's own struggles can be relativized. More importantly still, they can be situated in a recognizable tradition of speculation and aesthetic endeavor.

Cosnay underscores again and again the problem of the relations of the image and the word, and that problem subtends much of what *Villa Chagrin* has to say about art and its uses. "I'm coming to it, I'm coming," she assures us, "to my subject, to the point of impact" (51), and surely one of the things that term designates is a site where the verbal and the visual meet and meld, as do the currents in a river. It is a site that remains just over the horizon, continually deferred and never quite attained. For the passage from image to word—or from word to image, for that matter—can never be achieved in an entirely satisfactory manner, according to Cosnay, try as one might.

The example of Marthe is interesting in that regard, since it presents an ironic fable of writing and its fate. Cosnay tells us frequently that Marthe is haunted by the images she had seen in Africa, and she notes moreover that Marthe is animated by the need to write (47). She mentions that Marthe published an anticolonialist text entitled *Manières de Blancs* [White people's ways] at the Editions Sociales Internationales in 1938 (64),[10] and she remarks, too, that when Marthe died she had been working on a manuscript. "Under her arm, she had a manuscript. It was in 1959, twenty years after their first meeting, twenty-one years after the Amelia and Bayonne. It was August 11, 1959" (53).[11] That manuscript, Cosnay suggests, is in fact a lifework. Yet it palls in comparison to the life, or rather lives, that it chronicles, and like those lives it is deeply afflicted by a process of loss and forgetting:

> Concerning Marthe's love for Bram, I know very little. In the forties, Marthe writes down everything the huge man by her side says. When she dies, on August 11, 1959, run over by a car, he's in Tardais, in Normandy.
>
> Forty-seven pages, the carbon copy of a typescript, belonging to the Jacques Putman Archives. Of these pages, written by Marthe and tracing their life from Bayonne, in 1938, to 1947, only thirteen remain. (32–33)

The implicit question that Cosnay puts forward hinges upon the analogy of Marthe's writing and her own. Will her writerly efforts meet the same outcome as Marthe's? Are her own efforts to seize the image and come to successful terms with it through words equally doomed? Cosnay buttresses that analogy with the suggestion that the narrator's lover is absent, having merely left behind him some images:

> The man I love left behind him a shadow that I marry,

> every evening, at eight o'clock. I stay with the shadow for a few sweet hours. I have thrown the images away, each trace of him possessed. I only kept the bridge over the Adour that brushes the photo's edge. I wrote in ink on the clouds in the photo. I didn't have enough room. I kept on writing everywhere I could, on pages ripped from a notebook, on printed pages, on the covers of the books that surrounded me. (66)

The narrator's gesture may be compared to Bram van Velde's, but in the negative as it were. He draws images on Marthe's letters while imprisoned in the Villa Chagrin; she writes words on her lover's photograph of the Adour and the bridge that spans it. Her writing is necessarily fragmentary and interrupted, bearing the trace of disaster and testifying materially thereto.[12] In that light, it is Marthe's example rather than Bram's that comments most powerfully upon Cosnay's own position. Moreover, just as it does for Marthe, the image comes first for Marie Cosnay, demanding that one address it as a matter of absolute priority. "That's what I've been wanting to get at, since the beginning," she remarks, "through images and everything we don't see" (64).

There is the crux of the matter, I think: the image and the unseen. For in a sense the perception of the image, and even the first, graphic rendering of that perception are small matters compared to the rest. Indeed, Cosnay suggests just that as she speaks about the genesis of *Villa Chagrin*:

> At first it was easy to draft an outline, that wasn't the problem. The real difficulty was to identify the thing itself. After that, I couldn't imagine identifying that thing without there being a love story involved. In fact, something had begun there, between the Villa Chagrin and the Adour, where chance caused me to live. Caused me to live. The question involved Bram and Marthe. It concerned me, too. (44–45)

It is precisely that *something* which is at issue here, and that *something* is intimately bound up in the other currents that flow through this novel: catastrophe and its human consequences, the way the past inflects the present, the shifting affiliations of subject and object, the fragility of human relations, and so forth. Yet it is clearly the image itself that serves as the common denominator of those various discourses, the one invariable integer in Marie Cosnay's literary algorithm. Wordless and properly mute, the image nonetheless questions us, Cosnay argues, demanding that we come to terms with it in a manner that is fundamentally critical. For her, it is a matter of seeing, and more particularly of seeing in an especially penetrating way, so that one perceives what is normally unseen. When she mentions that her way of proceeding in *Villa Chagrin* necessarily involves a meditation on images "and everything we don't see" (64), Cosnay is thinking not so much of sight, but rather of *insight*. She invokes that notion—seeing what is usually unseen—on several occasions in *Villa Chagrin*,[13] and it is reasonable to assume that it is a key feature of her aesthetic.

At certain moments in the novel, the narrator's capacity to see insightfully is put dramatically to the test. One of those moments occurs in the opening pages, in a part of *Villa Chagrin* entitled "Image I." Searching through her bedroom, the narrator discovers a photograph of a naked woman, perhaps something that her lover has misplaced. At first glance, she fails to recognize that woman, yet as she continues to look at the photo, recognition dawns: "On January 18, I didn't know what I was looking at. The sex was gaping, in the photo's foreground. The woman's face, unrecognized until then, suddenly became familiar to me" (12). It is the objectivity of that image, and its very undeniability, that strike the narrator and challenge her. One of the particularities of the photographic image, as Roland Barthes has noted, is that it testifies to presence, it guarantees a kind of *being-there* in space and time.[14] It is chiefly that aspect of this image that troubles the narrator. She senses moreover that mere seeing and recognition will not suffice in this case. "I would like to see with eyes wide open, it could be autopsied," she remarks, "I want to see the gaze he directs upon the woman" (34)—as if the only satisfactory way of seeing this image were to understand the gaze of the photographer who framed it.

The parable that Cosnay sketches here has a lot to say about the techniques that she deploys in her novel, for those techniques are deeply bound up in the idea of the gaze. In the part of *Villa Chagrin* entitled "Image 2," Cosnay offers yet another parable centered upon the photographic image, explicitly and overtly casting it this time in the framework of a story, as narrative. "There was this story of another image," says the narrator, "or of *a* possible image, seen by the other, once, superbly. [. . .] The perfect photo of a precise woman, beautiful, white, recognizable, of sex and hair, proved at last that something had been visible" (48). Immediately thereafter, the narrator comes upon another photo, one that is already familiar to the reader because it has already been introduced: the photo that her lover took of the bridge over the Adour. That image is a foundational one for *Villa Chagrin* insofar as it captures the principal site of the novel's topography. It is innocent enough, as images go, and yet it is subtended—quite literally in this case—by other images that are far more troubling:

> March 2, 2005. In one of the man's bedrooms. The black-and-white photograph of the bridge over the Adour that brushes the edge. The clouds in the image, above the water, are so white, they look like they've been washed. I'm attached to it, I'm attached to that image, to the sky and the river, captures, and I know what it will cost me. I pick the image up gently. Bridges, skies, cities. The next fifteen photos are portraits of a woman. I recognize her immediately, it's me all right, she's calling, with her mouth, the man who's looking. (48–49).

Those images are all the more troubling when the narrator

realizes, quite simply, that they *cannot be*, recalling all of a sudden that "*He never took a portrait photo of me, fifteen times*" (49). What she sees before her, in other terms, is "the image, repeated fifteen times, of me who am not" (50).

The impossibility that the narrator confronts, dumbfounded, comments eloquently, I believe, on *Villa Chagrin* as a whole. For what Marie Cosnay puts on offer here is a fable of ideation, and more precisely a fable of how the image enables ideation, bringing it into being and then structuring it. Once again, the moral that this fable conveys is that the image is absolutely primary with regard to textuality. Certainly that is the case of *this* textuality, if we are to believe what Cosnay says about its genesis, on the penultimate page of *Villa Chagrin*:

> It was in the Bayonne Public Library. Opening the ledgers of 1938, on the little table near the window, I had photographed an old map in black and white. Unfolded, it sagged a bit, it was frayed on the creases. I had chosen a closeup of the Boulevard Alsace-Lorraine, by the Villa Chagrin, the Adour, and the railway trestle. On the photo of the 1938 map, the Adour's wide artery crosses and cuts the image, flatly. And again: the 1938 ink on Marthe's letter, from far away I see the center, flat, luminous, broad like a river, the center a bit yellowed, and around the maze, the slopes, even the arches of the bridge. (74)

Here, in superposition or juxtaposition, images inform each other and call each other into question through the ideational process that they engender. That business is a critical one, and it is organized in narrative terms. Each of the different tales that Cosnay tells in *Villa Chagrin* springs from an image, she argues, whether it be the tale of Bram van Velde's incarceration, the one of Pierre M.'s suicide, that of the narrator's difficult relations with the man she loves, a broader fable about how society views outsiders, or the story of how a story comes to be. Just as each image inflects every other one it encounters, so too do these tales comment upon and illuminate each other. In the course of that process, they take their place in a dynamic that serves to channel their mobility while at the same time impelling them, together, toward a newly-identified place. Such a dynamic can be imagined, I think, as something much like a river—or something much like a novel.

Patrick Deville's Novelty

SPECULATING ABOUT THE present state of things is always difficult, because the present is so hard to seize. It escapes from us just as we try to grasp it; it is mutable, elusive, and fundamentally ephemeral; its dynamic nature puts our own intellectual mobility to the test in crucial ways. Nevertheless, most of us feel the need to come to terms with the present, with the *new* and the *now*, and we devise different strategies in order to do so. Writers are no exception. Like the rest of us, they too try to account for the present in various ways, and traces of that process can be observed in literature. The contemporary French writer Patrick Deville is a case in point. Right *now*, he is producing some of the most intriguing writing one might hope to find. His is an agile and ever-changing body of work that insistently asks the question of what the novel is in our embattled cultural present, and what it may become in a future we can only dimly descry.

Deville's oeuvre is all the more astonishing granted that he seems to have reinvented himself in mid-career. From the mid-1980s until the end of the century, he published a series of five novels at the Editions de Minuit: *Cordon-bleu* (1987), *Longue Vue* (1988), *Le Feu d'artifice* [Fireworks] (1992), *La Femme parfaite* [The perfect woman] (1995), and *Ces deux-là* [Those two] (2000). Based on that body of work, many critics described him surely and definitively as a minimalist, an impassive fictionalist, and a paragon of the Minuit School.[1] In the new century however, Deville migrated to the Editions du Seuil, and the six texts that he has published there to date—*Pura Vida: Vie & mort de William Walker* (2004), *La Tentation des armes à feu* [The temptation of firearms] (2006), *Equatoria* (2009), *Kampuchéa* (2011), *Peste & choléra* [Plague and cholera] (2012), and *Viva* (2014)—are very unlike his Minuit books, suggesting a writerly retooling of a very rare sort. Among those more recent works, I am most particularly interested in *Pura Vida*, *Equatoria*, and *Kampuchéa*, because they appear to constitute (for the moment at least, that is to say, *presently*) a trilogy of sorts, one that circles the globe at the equator, and whose heroes seem in each case to be places, rather than people.[2] Or perhaps, in another perspective, one might argue that the protagonist of these texts is the novel itself, because each of them—and whatever else may be at issue—puts forward a vision of the novel searching for a *new* shape, right *now*. That process is a compelling one, inasmuch as it testifies to the way that culture itself shifts, right before our eyes. In what follows, I would like to focus closely upon *Kampuchéa*, because I believe that it builds upon the texts that precede it, and responds to them in key manners. Moreover it is in *Kampuchéa* that Deville puts his new writerly skill set to work most adroitly.[3]

Like *Pura Vida* and *Equatoria*, *Kampuchéa* presents itself as a novel, complete with the term *roman* emblazoned on its cover. Yet there is very little fiction here—if indeed there is any at all. Focusing upon Cambodia, roughly from Henri Mouhot's "discovery" of the temples of Angkor Wat in 1860 to the present time, *Kampuchéa* (the title is the Khmer word for "Cambodia") puts on offer a meditation on history, on geography, on politics, on culture, and on the way those categories necessarily overlap in a place that has always found itself precariously situated "between the anvil and the hammer" (187). The event that draws Deville[4] there is the Khmer Rouge Tribunal, and especially the trial of Kang Kek Iew, or "Duch," the first of the five former Khmer Rouge leaders to be indicted, and who would be convicted of crimes against humanity and sentenced to thirty-five years in prison in July 2010. That trial provides the text with its principal narrative thread, around which Deville weaves an impressive variety of other stories. That of the French Mekong Expedition in 1866–1868, lead by Ernest Doudart de Lagrée and Francis Garnier, for instance. Or that of Marie-Charles David de Mayrena, who declared himself King of Sedang in 1888. Or that of Vann Nath, who survived the Khmer Rouge camps by painting portraits of Pol Pot. Or that of Pol Pot himself, a man who returned to Phnom Penh after his studies in Paris in order to teach Vigny, Verlaine, and Rimbaud, and whose clandestine activity eventually resulted in his being named Prime Minister of Democratic Kampuchea. The regime that he presided over was a short-lived one, lasting only three years, eight months, and twenty days, yet it left a very bloody legacy. In Patrick Deville's view, the task of sketching a panorama of such dimensions demands a new kind of narrative form. If he calls this book a novel, he does so at a time when the horizon of possibility of that genre is constantly in question (one thinks of the recent work of Jean Echenoz, Pierre Michon, Marie NDiaye, Jean Rolin, Lydie Salvayre, Olivier Rolin, Marie Cosnay, Iegor Gran, and Emmanuel Carrère, to name just a few). That questioning is intended to restructure and reinvigorate our manners of writing and reading, to be sure; but what is also at stake, clearly, is the way we understand our world.

One of the most common ways of coming to terms with the world is through history, and Deville gives us plenty of that. But it is a special kind of history, one that is carefully honed and teleological. "The trial of the Khmers Rouges is the end point of a story that began a century and a half ago," remarks Deville (128), and it is legitimate to see in that remark one of the theses of *Kampuchéa*. History always seems to point toward the present of course, or toward *us*, in other terms; and it seems inevitable, for we organize it in a narrative fashion, and narrative is necessarily teleological. Yet Deville provides another kind of logic to the particular chunk of history that interests him here. As I mentioned, it begins with Henri Mouhot, the French naturalist and explorer. His presence may be felt throughout *Kampuchéa*, for example when Deville mentions, "We are in 41 post-HM" (118), that is, 41 years after Mouhot's "discovery" of Angkor Wat, or 1901. Mouhot is a *conqueror*, and Deville stages that notion very deliberately in his text, according it a place of privilege. Mouhot will be followed by other conquerors: Doudart de Lagrée and Garnier, for instance, and Mayrena, and Auguste Pavie, and André Malraux, and, in a sense, Charles de Gaulle. Thus, in one of its dimensions at least, what Deville gives us in *Kampuchéa* is the history of French colonialism in Indochina. Yet the end point of that narrative comes well before the present, at the battle of Dien Bien Phu in 1954: "It's the end of the delirious European dream, the one of the French and the English. Their empires are melting like icebergs in the ocean" (210).

Other dimensions of this project quickly become apparent: an account of how colonial subjects take their history in hand; a reflection upon political idealism and its fate; an evocation of the manner in which the collective beggars the individual and history obscures the story of any single life. In conversation with a longtime French expatriate in Phnom Penh, Deville remarks, "I sketch for him the principal lines of my little Braudelian project. I would like to put the Khmer Rouge trials in perspective, with regard to the last century and a half, since Mouhot, running after a butterfly, bumped his head, raised his eyes, and discovered the temples of Angkor" (143). That "perspective" is mainly a question of context and causality, in Deville's view, but it is something that must be carefully constructed. Thus, he evokes a moment in the early 1940s when the future Khmer Rouge leaders were in high school together, and then how they went to study in Paris, and how that Parisian past rejoins the Cambodian present in unexpected ways: "They are members of the French Communist Party. There, Khieu

Samphân meets Jacques Vergès, who is now his lawyer" (46). Deville examines Norodom Sihanouk as well, a figure fully as fabulous, as *novelistic* as any character in a novel: "The Prince is a magician, a master of illusion on the stage of the music-hall of History" (49).

History itself is often examined in close focus. Deville is especially intrigued by the way that people experience what we commonly call "history." During a visit to Hanoi, he notes, "In the street I cross the gaze of Vietnamese just as old as me, who have lived through the American bombings of Haiphong and the Red River delta. The gaze of old folks, like the tobacconist, who witnessed the arrival of victorious troops on the Paul Doumer Bridge, and the French retreat. Those people had seen the eyes of their grandparents, who had witnessed Garnier's crazy campaign" (215). History is mostly about wars and conquest and inhumanity, and it has a great deal of narrative punch when compared to any given human life. Yet by the same token, we necessarily measure history with the tools that are closest to hand: "An average human life is a good instrument to measure History" (239), for in a sense, we have no other way to gauge it, other than to project a life—*our* life—upon it. When we do so, however, we are likely to find that history belittles our story, and that a panoramic view tends to trivialize the details of which it is composed. What meaning can one claim for a life, or even a million lives, when they are set in "historical" context? "One could forget them, the Khmers Rouges," argues Deville in the final chapter of *Kampuchéa*. "Let them die in their air-conditioned cells. One or two million deaths in four years. Not even the record of the century. Six million in the Nazi camps. Twenty in the Goulag. Fifty perhaps in Mao's China" (252). What is it about history that wreaks such havoc on "lives," that is to say, stories of lives? How can one attenuate that effect when putting history into play in a novel? Is a humanistic history possible? Those are some of the questions that Deville seeks to address in *Kampuchéa*.

One of his avenues of inquiry involves the disparity between ideal and practice, more particularly, a meditation on the way that revolutionary ideals go awry. To Deville's way of thinking, Cambodia offers an excellent test case in that regard, because among all of the revolutions one might name, the one that transformed Cambodia was the most ideologically pure. It was at the outset, Deville suggests, "A revolution as perfect as a laboratory experiment" (32). Nevertheless, in something less than four years, Cambodia became "an immense concentration camp" (36). What went wrong, so quickly and so dramatically, allowing utopia to become dystopia? What is there about the revolutionary ideal that becomes perverted in the world? Is there something about that ideal that breaks down in practice, or when it is called upon to assume human dimensions? Does the fault lie in political philosophy or in the very nature of people? Like many humanists before him, Deville tends toward the former explanation of things: "Terror is the armed branch of Virtue," he argues. "Political utopia, like religious utopia, detests humanity in its monstrous incompletion" (41).

Yet that consideration does not resolve the most pernicious questions that Deville asks about revolution. He wonders, for example, whether culture—and especially literary culture—can have any effect upon revolution, either for the better or for the worse. How can Duch, the former head of the Khmer Rouge internal security apparatus and commandant of the Tuol Sleng prison camp, a man accused of having tortured and murdered thousands upon thousands of people, how can Duch recite Vigny at his trial? It is not the first time that the question of culture and terror has been asked, of course. There are many other instances where that question arises, most notably in examinations of the European Holocaust. Yet Deville's interrogation is no less important because it is not absolutely original: it, too, takes its place in history, after all. If Deville focuses so closely upon literature, it is because, as a writer, he is quite naturally concerned about the uses and abuses of literature. I shall have more to say about that in a moment; for now, let us note Deville's recognition that Romantic poetry is not in itself a sufficient prophylactic against mass murder.

In other instances where Deville sees degraded revolutionary ideals, more obvious forces are at work. Human greed, for instance, and the allure of new capitalism can account for some of those examples. Strolling through Saigon, he notes, "it is curious to see the blood-red meteorite of a Ferrari Testarossa parked in front of the Louis Vuitton store, located on the Street of the General Insurrection" (93). That scene is an ironist's dream, but it is clear that Deville himself takes things far more seriously, and that the corruption of revolutionary ideal offends him deeply.[5] Sharing a meal with a survivor of the killing fields, he admits, "in the middle of the 1970s, I dreamed of tabula rasas. Call a halt to everything, and begin anew. The slogan echoed from Europe to Latin America" (38). In a sense, then, Deville's inquiry is very personal indeed, and very deeply bound up, by his own account, with his personal history.

Clearly, he hopes that the trial of the Khmers Rouges will provide answers to some of the questions he is asking. A trial is a forensic dynamic, first and foremost, one that is intended to discover the truth. As Duch's trial begins in 2009 (he was the first of the five former leaders to be tried), Deville still hopes that it will afford some resolution to a history that remains scandalously unresolved. Though he had imagined a process that would be absolutely riveting, he quickly finds that it does not interest him as much as he might wish: "They quickly become boring, these never-ending accounts, these procedures, these repetitive testimonies. It's also admirable. This dilation of time. One or two million dead people in Cambodia in less than four years. All of these years to judge five people" (105). In other words, the trial is lacking in *narrative* interest, and that is an important concern for Deville. Moreover, far from being a high-minded process of discovery, the trial seems to him to be a kind of grossly commercial theater: "The trial is a huge, corrupt industry, which commands substantial sums of money" (144). By the time Duch is convicted and sentenced, a year and a half after his trial began, Deville is thoroughly disillusioned. Like the revolution, the trial has gone badly awry. It has been put to uses for which it was never intended, and it tells a story that is very different from the one that a forensic fundamentalist might have anticipated.

When he himself is not in Phnom Penh, Deville follows the trial in newspaper accounts. Newspapers are yet another way of coming to terms with the world, but unlike history they focus upon the immediate, upon very recent (and indeed ongoing) events. In the first pages of *Kampuchéa*, Deville makes it clear that newspapers are very much a part of the narrative fabric that he intends to weave. Reading an issue of the *Bangkok Post*, he remarks: "I fly over daily events at the controls of my twin engine plane, a cigarette in my mouth and my feet on the rudder pedals, a bottle between my knees" (12). That kind of *overview* allows him quickly to invoke, one after the other, the Khmer Rouge trials in Phnom Penh, the arrest of the head of a drug cartel in Mexico, the trial of ex-President Alberto Fujimori in Peru, the International Criminal Tribunal for Rwanda in Tanzania, and the trail of former Croatian generals in The Hague. This moment is an important one in terms of the way he chooses to stage things in *Kampuchéa*. First, it allows a brief contextualization of the Khmer Rouge trials in terms of contemporary events. Second, it serves to remind us that crimes against humanity are not lacking in the world, and that what happened in Cambodia was not absolutely exceptional. Third, it suggests the narrative perspective that Deville will adopt in *Kampuchéa*, that is, an overview of a century and a half of Cambodian history. It might be argued, moreover, that this kind of approach has characterized all of Deville's work since he left the Editions de Minuit; and he himself has pointed out the fundamental role that newspapers played in the conception and execution of his first book for the Editions du Seuil, *Pura Vida*.[6]

Even more so than history, when Deville puts newspapers into the mix of this new kind of novel that he is attempting to write, the question of the relations of reality and fiction necessarily arise. His Minuit novels clearly privileged the latter over the former. The world that they sketch is not a particularly referential one, and little regard is given either to history or to the phenomenal present. As Pierre Hyppolite puts it in his discussion of *La Femme parfaite*, "Capturing the moments of hesitation where image and reality intermingle, where the character moves from one mode to another, the text not only questions the relation of the real and the fictional, it inverts those relations in a hyperrealist reversal" (69). In *Kampuchéa* however, Deville very deliberately and strategically promotes the real as a central element of the novel. Thus, when he invokes the visit of Charles de Gaulle to Cambodia in 1966, and the famous speech he delivered praising that country—"a history laden with glory and pain, an exemplary culture and art, a fertile land with vulnerable borders, surrounded by foreign ambitions, and above which danger always hovers" (49)—the Charles de Gaulle that he gives us is less the fictionalization of a real person than a figure who is supposed to come to us with his political, historical, and ideological heft very much intact. Yet the passage has still more to say about the dynamic of reality and fiction, I think, because de Gaulle's speech was written by André Malraux, his Minister of Cultural Affairs, and Malraux is in turn the author of one of the novels that inform *Kampuchéa* most deeply, *La Voie royale* [*The Royal Way*] (1930). In this affiliation, what we see is the suggestion of a process in which fiction and reality cannot be usefully—that is to say, *productively*—disintricated.

Such reflection raises still another question for Deville, that of literature and its uses. It is an especially burning question for him, regardless of the shape it assumes. What can literature achieve in the world? What are its possibilities and limitations? What is its proper role, and what is its responsibility? What can one expect of it? *Kampuchéa* asks questions like those on virtually every page. Again and again Deville returns to the early apprenticeship in literature—and notably French literature—of many of the Khmer Rouge leaders. That astonishes him, patently, and it scandalizes him, too. It is not only Duch reciting Vigny that shocks him, it is also the fact that Pol Pot himself studied literature as a young man, went to France to pursue those studies, and returned to Cambodia to become a teacher of literature. No less a figure than Soth Polin, the Khmer writer and newspaper editor who was forced into exile by the Khmer Rouge regime, can testify personally to the excellence of Pol Pot's pedagogy:

> In junior high school, Soth Polin had the future Pol Pot, freshly returned from Paris, as his literature teacher. "I remember his elocution: his French was soft and musical. He was obviously attracted by French literature, and especially by poetry: Rimbaud, Verlaine, Vigny. . . . He spoke without notes, hesitating sometimes but never at a loss, eyes half-shut, carried away by his own lyricism. . . . The students were under the spell of this affable teacher, always dressed in dark blue trousers and a white shirt." (247)

It would be difficult to find two contemporary Cambodian destinies more different than those of Pol Pot and Soth Polin. Yet both were deeply informed by literature. Does literature then have absolutely no effect upon human beings and how they behave? Or is it more a matter of what one *does* with literature? Deville tends toward that latter conclusion. And if his efforts to renovate the French novel have a political dimension to them, those politics are in the first instance communitarian; that is, they embrace the idea of literature as a kind of community. Speaking at a colloquium on contemporary literature at the Centre Culturel International in Cerisy in the summer of 2003, Deville explains why he chose to attend that event: "For me, there's a kind of complicity in what we do whenever we write, or read, or if we're book dealers, or academics, etc., all that is part of the same activity, an activity that is sorely endangered. I feel that we belong to a very small resistance network, and that, consequently, it's the least I can do to support this kind of event" ("Plus formaliste" 311). The notion of *resistance* is a crucial one. It is a central term in his theory of literature, and it is a key figure of all of his recent writings. In Deville's view, literature must be promoted *as literature*, but also as a way of coming to terms with a world and a reality that can be very oppressive indeed. Literature is, and must be, both artifact and tactic.

In *Kampuchéa* a broad metaliterary discourse animates the text from first page to last, and it deserves close attention. Intertextual allusions abound, invoking figures from Herodotus to Jean Rolin, and mentioning along the way Pliny, Pascal, Descartes, Boileau, Montesquieu, Vigny, Hugo, Verlaine, Rimbaud, Michelet, Kipling, Conrad, Loti, Gide, Paulhan, Cendrars, Breton, Aragon, Farrère, Mauriac, Malraux, Greene, Simenon, Orwell, Lowry, Robbe-Grillet, and Soth Polin. A couple of things could be noted about that referential field. For one, it is very heavily skewed toward Western writers, and more particularly still toward French writers. For another, Deville wagers heavily upon fairly recent literary history, mainly that of the nineteenth and twentieth centuries, because that is the historical period he chooses to examine in *Kampuchéa*.

Among the many writers who stride through this novel, two are preeminent on Deville's horizon. The first is Joseph Conrad. He appears in *Kampuchéa* as a precursor figure, a traveler and a writer who found a way to turn the rich experience of his travels into novels. Two of his texts figure heavily in the intertextual weft of *Kampuchéa*. First, *Heart of Darkness*, both as a tale of the Congo and as a tale of Southeast Asia. Let me explain. On the one hand (and most obviously), Marlow's story of his travels on the Congo exercises a strong pull on Deville's imagination—all the more so granted that he himself has spent a lot of time traveling in the Congo, thinking about that region's vexed history, and writing about it. All of that activity resulted materially in *Equatoria*, the book that immediately precedes *Kampuchéa*. But another version of *Heart of Darkness* is just as important for Deville, Francis Ford Coppola's adaptation of the novel in *Apocalypse Now*. In that film, the Marlow-figure, Benjamin Willard, follows the fictional Nung River all the way into Cambodia to find his "Kurtz." That Deville is indeed thinking of the film, as well as the novel, is confirmed by explicit references to Coppola in the text.[7]

The second Conrad text is *Lord Jim*, and its role in the intertextual economy of *Kampuchéa* is still more important than that of *Heart of Darkness*. Jim is a very uncertain hero, of course, and it is perhaps the dubious nature of his heroism that appeals to Deville. Yet Jim is also patently associated with the idea of fiction itself, more so than Marlow, more so even than Kurtz, and when Deville puts him on stage he quite deliberately underscores that trait: "And with every Malay cigarette, the smoker remembered Lord Jim's heroic end, 'the man with a romantic conscience,' the one who makes his way up the Patusan River in the jungle in order to atone for his sin" (52). It is precisely that "romantic conscience" that seizes Deville's imagination. It is moreover the crux of the analysis of Jim's character that Stein offers to Marlow in Conrad's novel:

> "I understand very well. He is romantic."
>
> He had diagnosed the case for me, and at first I was quite startled to find how simple it was; and indeed our

> conference resembled so much a medical consultation—Stein, of learned aspect, sitting in an arm-chair before his desk; I, anxious, in another, facing him, but a little to one side—that it seemed natural to ask—
>
> "What's good for it?"
>
> "There is only one remedy! One thing alone can us from being ourselves cure!" The finger came down on the desk with a smart rap. The case which he had made to look so simple before became if possible still simpler—and altogether hopeless. There was a pause. "Yes," said I, "strictly speaking, the question is not how to get cured, but how to live." (*Lord Jim* 136–37)

That question is a sobering, powerful, crucial one for any hero—or indeed for any writer. And much of what Patrick Deville puts on offer in *Kampuchéa* is intended to address it.

The second preeminent writer in the novel's intertextual economy is André Malraux. The epigraph that Deville chooses for his text is borrowed from *La Voie royale*, and indeed that novel serves as the principal intertext in *Kampuchéa*. The passage that Deville quotes comes from the early pages of Malraux's text, which present a discussion between Claude and Perken focusing on the idea of sexual perversion. Provocatively enough, Perken argues: "There is only one 'sexual perversion,' as the imbeciles say: it's the development of the imagination, the tendency toward dissatisfaction" (*La Voie royale* 10). That is a curious note with which to introduce a novel, to say the least; yet it puts on stage two terms, imagination and dissatisfaction, that will be extremely important ones throughout *Kampuchéa*.

Just as in the case of Conrad, it is both the author and the character that interest Deville. Malraux is clearly a strong precursor figure for him. Like Conrad, he is a writer who has traveled broadly and who has brought that experience to bear in his art. Yet Perken appeals to Deville too, for he embodies the ideal of the adventurer. That idea is a powerful one for Deville, and he puts it into play explicitly on several occasions. Two of those instances deserve attention. In the first one, Deville speaks of Malraux in the 1920s and 1930s, and the circumstances of publication of *La Voie royale*: "In 1930 he publishes his autobiographical novel and invents his double, Perken. Literary fame is his, but it's not enough. He still wants to act, to weigh upon History, to leave the library" (71). The epithet "autobiographical novel" is intriguing, insofar as it suggests a very transparent reading of Malraux's novel. The vision of Perken as Malraux's "double" is likewise interesting, most especially because of what it suggests about Deville's own writerly strategies. Moreover, it is legitimate to see both of the terms that I mentioned a moment ago, *imagination* and *dissatisfaction*, at work in this passage. Were "invention" and "imagination" and "literature" not enough to satisfy Malraux? Will they not suffice to satisfy Deville, either? In the other instance, Deville quotes Malraux's own use of the word *adventurer* in *La Voie royale*, in a remark that has since attained the status of aphorism: "Any adventurer is first a mythomaniac."[8] Thus does a boat captain describe Perken to Claude; but for Deville, the same might be said of Malraux. Adventure, after all, is a kind of heightened, sharpened experience, experience viewed through a narrative lens and organized according to principles of narrativity. A mythomaniac is someone who exaggerates the truth, who embellishes the truth, who imagines things because the truth alone is not satisfactory. In other terms, Malraux's remark points to the very essence of what a novelist does, and when Deville adduces that remark in *Kampuchéa* its specular function could not be more obvious.

Deville finds Malraux exemplary by virtue of his energy, his will to play a variety of different roles—traveler, novelist, publisher, journalist, soldier, politician, intellectual—and to leave his signature upon his time. More than anything else, it is a question of *reach*. Yet in Deville's view, Malraux's reach was not only horizontal, but vertical as well. That is, as much as he figured prominently in his own time, so too did he take his place in history. That is quite clear insofar as literary history is concerned. Deville mentions that Malraux had read Pierre Loti, and that Loti's influence in *La Voie royale* is fundamental. He remarks further that the young Loti had been inspired by Henri Mouhot. Thereby, Deville traces an affiliation in which he, too, takes his place—all the while recognizing that Malraux is an exceptionally hard act to follow. Literary influence, both as burden and as opportunity, is very much on Deville's mind in *Kampuchéa*. When he remarks, "Often, it's the fear of not equaling their fathers that drives adventurers" (74), he is speaking about Marie-Charles David de Mayrena's relationship with his father, but he might just as well be speaking about his own relationship with the writers whom he puts forward as his precursors.

Yet another dimension of Deville's intertextual strategy is played out in a series of allusions to his own writings. Those allusions engage *Pura Vida* and *Equatoria* almost exclusively; there is only one allusion to *La Tentation des armes à feu*,[9] and none at all (none that I could identify, at least) to the five novels from Deville's Minuit period. A few examples of Deville's tactics will suffice. When he mentions William Walker (61, 239) anyone even passingly familiar with his work will inevitably think of *Pura Vida*, whose subtitle is *Vie & mort de William Walker*. Likewise, when he invokes Nicaragua or the Sandinistas (22, 65, 85) one thinks of *Pura Vida*. When Deville remarks that he had traveled up the Ogooué River "following Brazza's tracks" (83) however, he is clearly alluding to *Equatoria*. More interesting still are passages where both of those prior texts come into play. In one of those, Deville mentions Pierre Brazza and then quickly thereafter William Wilson (167), sketching in the lightest of strokes two of the central figures in the broad historical panoramas that he paints in *Equatoria* and *Pura Vida*. And when he remarks, "In the year 1979, the Sandinista revolutionaries took power in Nicaragua, and the CIA organized the Contras in Honduras. The Soviets invaded Afghanistan, and aided the Cubans and the MPLA in Angola" (229), the effect is similar, except that this time what is at issue is the very recent history that he describes in *Pura Vida* and *Equatoria*. Those moments in *Kampuchéa* serve to affiliate that text with *Pura Vida* and *Equatoria*. In other words, the autoallusive tactics in *Kampuchéa* appear to be driven by the desire to suggest the mutual intrication of *Pura Vida*, *Equatoria*, and *Kampuchéa*, and to postulate their coherence as an oeuvre.

One consideration that is beyond dispute is that those three texts are very, very different from the five Minuit novels that precede them. That difference is everywhere apparent: in the conception of the texts, in their execution, in the concerns they display, in the way that they attempt to engage the world, in the inflections of their narrative voice, in the stance they adopt toward the reader, and so forth. Together, they testify to an extraordinarily bold decision on Deville's part to cast off his former writerly habits and to innovate, to experiment with new and untested models of prose narrative. Deville has not said a great deal about that process, but the few things he has said leave little doubt that he went about it in a conscious and programmatic way. In the conversation at Cerisy in the summer of 2003 that I mentioned earlier, he speaks in veiled and hesitant terms about his work-in-progress, *Pura Vida* (which would appear a few months later):

> And my next project . . . I don't like to talk about it, but . . . it's really something like an encyclopedia, that is, exhausting . . . well, it's impossible to exhaust, but . . . an effort to exhaust a subject completely, to master it absolutely, to read everything, to translate . . . because most of the information was not available . . . and to write from a mass of knowledge, to

construct a novel with that. ("Plus formaliste" 326)

What is intriguing about Deville's remarks is that while he seems to be uncertain about the process, he is very sure indeed about the product: there is no doubt in his mind that the result of his experiment will be a *novel.*

A year after those remarks (and thus after the publication of *Pura Vida*), in an interview that appeared in *Le Matricule des Anges*, when Thierry Guichard remarks to Deville that *Pura Vida* displays a radical departure from his usual style, Deville responds with more assurance. "It's because I tried to do something I didn't know how to do," he says. "And to reinvent ways of writing. I was up against a wall for a long time, I tried different things. It was just like changing instruments, in music" ("La Fabrique du héros" 21–22). The notion of reinvention is a compelling one, and it is absolutely fundamental to Deville's project. As he imagines it, the problem is to get from something that he does know how to do as a writer to something that he doesn't yet know how to do. In both cases however, that "something" is a novel, and clearly the task that Deville sets for himself is in the first instance a formal quest. In that perspective at any rate, he remains faithful to the principles that have always animated his writing. Speaking of his first novel, *Cordon-bleu*, he remarks: "I'm always a bit of a formalist. I had to find a form" ("La Fabrique du héros" 18). And a bit further on in that same interview, he makes it clear that for him the quest for form is essential to the aesthetic gesture, whatever guise that gesture may eventually assume: "Writing a novel, composing a symphony, or painting a picture, it's always creating forms; simple at first, they become more and more complex" (20).

The dynamic of formal creation, of innovation, of *invention* is thus both crucial and indispensable for Deville. He suggests that a great part of the satisfaction he derives from his craft is bound up in that process. "Moreover, what pleases me the most, I think, is inventing forms," he says. "It's a great pleasure to invent or use forms" ("Plus formaliste" 319). The will to make things new is of course central in art; and in the twentieth century it became the signature imperative of the avant-garde. Indeed, it became such a tyrannical diktat that one might argue it was the key factor leading to the avant-garde's exhaustion. The way the principle of innovation plays out in Deville's work is a bit different, however. More than anything else, it is a question of the search for new possibilities of expression in a literary genre that is—and indeed has always been—a significantly protean one.[10]

For the *new* is the lifeblood of the *novel.* Indeed the very name of the form—at least in English usage—suggests just that. We have been hearing reports of the novel's demise for a good half-century now. In fact, many people of my generation cut their readerly teeth on novels that had somehow escaped from that very death sentence. And thankfully, writers continue to produce novels, despite proclamations that the novel as a cultural form is doomed. In point of fact however, the history of the novel suggests that the novel has *always* been in crisis, such crisis being more or less dire in any given period. What does seem to be true is that certain traditional models of narrative are no longer as viable and performative as they once were, and Jean-François Lyotard was undoubtedly correct when he argued, in *La Condition postmoderne,* that we are far more skeptical with regard to "grand narratives" than we used to be (7). What is also demonstrably true is that contemporary novelists, since the New Novel in the 1950s, have steadily elaborated new models for the genre, and have proposed them to the reading public, with varying degrees of success. Patrick Deville takes his place in that experimental tradition consciously and deliberately. Moreover, he inscribes that gesture in the books he writes, putting his quest for a new kind of novel broadly on display, in the very middle of that quest.

Looking closely, one can see in Deville's career an evolution that plays out the recent history of the novel itself. His five Minuit books are relatively conventional with regard to the norms prevailing at that time (roughly, the last decade of the twentieth century) and that place (France, more specifically Paris, more specifically still the Editions de Minuit). They are traditional, even *classic* novels, as Deville himself is quick to point out: "To my way of thinking, the first five books are indisputably novels. They couldn't be more novelistic . . . They read like Madame de Lafayette in fact!" ("Plus formaliste" 324). Then, to all appearances, Deville decides that that kind of novel is no longer valid, and he undertakes a dramatic renovation of his own writerly practice, looking for new and more invigorating possibilities for prose narrative. Those early texts are nevertheless marked by a strong specular dimension, one that insistently asks the question of what a novel *is* and *can be*.[11] And when Deville turns away from those models, he is clearly still grappling with that very question. "The goal is always to make a novel," he remarks about *Pura Vida*. "I used several genres in that book: epistolary, novelistic, poetry, journalism, the personal diary, and historiography" ("La Fabrique du héros" 22).

That hybridity may seem extreme when viewed in the strict focus of any given text; but in a broader perspective one recognizes that the novel has *always* borrowed from other genres. Indeed, the generic specificity of the novel is notoriously difficult to define, undoubtedly in part because the novel has always spoken in a variety of accents. Patrick Deville's novelty wagers precisely upon that aspect of the genre, upon the way it changes shape while still remaining a novel. He wagers also that some point of connection will be made between his desire to write new kinds of novels and our desire to read them. Throughout, he is guided by an idea that he articulates in each of his texts. Sometimes he expresses that idea subtly, sometimes more overtly, but whatever form it may take it is clearly for him a confession of faith: "I persist in thinking that the novel is the major literary genre" ("Plus formaliste" 323). Think what one may of that notion, it would be difficult to find a writer in France (or anywhere else for that matter) who has defended it more vigorously and more boldly than Deville, in what we think of as our very own literary and cultural *present*.

Gérard Gavarry's Ceremony

There are very few writers who reinvent themselves with each book, who bring to each of the projects they undertake a willingness to see things differently and to account for that new vision in fresh ways. Gérard Gavarry is one of those writers. Mutability is undoubtedly the most striking feature of his work when one regards the latter in long focus, from the late 1960s to the present;[1] and it is one of its most appealing qualities, too. Yet it also makes Gavarry an elusive writer, one who is difficult to situate with regard to his contemporaries, and in terms of the taxonomies to which we usually appeal in an effort to understand culture in the present tense. That elusiveness helps to explain why he has not yet attracted the measure of critical attention that his work deserves.[2] For my own part, I would like to address Gavarry's elusiveness quite directly, in an examination of one of his most slippery texts.

Allada (1993) is a puzzling, challenging, and consistently rewarding novel, one that wagers firmly upon the principle of literary innovation. The title itself is sufficient to alert us that something uncommon awaits the reader. It is a sonorous, richly assonant word, yet its signification is not immediately apparent. It is certain to pique the reader's curiosity, and by virtue of that one can imagine it as the first element in what Roland Barthes called the hermeneutic code of the text.[3] People who know world geography better than most will recognize that Allada is a small city in Benin some twenty miles inland from the Gulf of Guinea. People with ready access to atlases, encyclopedias, and other kinds of reference works—that is to say, many people, *now*—will easily learn that "Allada was the capital of the most powerful kingdom in Ajaland before it fell to the armies of Dahomey"; that Toussaint Louverture was a scion of Allada's royal house; and that consequently Allada is regarded by Haitians as a sacred city. The quotation and the information that follows it comes from the entries on "Allada" on *Wikipedia*, in the English and the French versions of that site, respectively. But let us not forget that when *Allada* was published in 1993, people did not have such data at their fingertips, and access thereto required a great deal more energy and readerly activism than it does now.

It should probably be noted, too, that those few individuals who, like me, read Gavarry's *Façon d'un roman* [*Making a Novel*] (2003) before reading *Allada* may recall a chapter entitled "Retour d'Allada" toward the end of the former (171–72). Yet that chapter is so brief and elliptical that it sheds very little light on the current problem. What I mean to suggest is that the title Gavarry chose for his novel is deliberately obscure for the reading public he is addressing, if one imagines the latter to be primarily Metropolitan French, as seems likely. Moreover, that very group will recognize a dimension of exoticism in this title, a tributary to a current that has flowed broadly in French literature, particularly since Baudelaire. It may be the case, however, that this appeal to the tradition of literary exoticism is a surface phenomenon—or, in other terms, a distractive gesture in the writerly sleight of hand that Gérard Gavarry practices in *Allada*. For the impact that he seeks to achieve, in the first instance at least, may be one of radical obscurity rather than one of simple (and easily reducible) exoticism, something calculated to suggest that the fictional world we are about to enter will be strange and difficult to map.

The novel's incipit does little to dissipate that obscurity: "In that period, he is Mr. Director. He lives in an official residence next to the lagoon, near the place where every year, during the

Tabaski Feast, the Muslim shepherds from the North camp out, among the odors of greasy wool and the bleating of sheep" (9). The man whom Gavarry puts on stage thus is a shadowy figure; and he will not be particularized by name beyond the honorific that figures in the first sentence. The word "Tabaski" is a powerful element of the hermeneutic code, like "Allada." Furthermore, in a curious, almost subterranean manner, it points toward that latter word and underscores it. For "Tabaski" in West and Central Africa designates Eid al-Adha, one of the two most important holidays in the Muslim calendar. On the formal level, the homonymic relation of "Allada" and "al-Adha" is immediately striking. On the thematic level, Gavarry exploits that correspondence to put a number of things in place. In the first instance, it serves to put the notion of *sacrifice* squarely before the reader, because "Eid al-Adha" in Arabic means "The Feast of the Sacrifice," which commemorates Abraham's willingness to sacrifice his son Ishmael. Typically, the celebration of that holiday involves sacrifice of one sort or another, whether actual or metaphorical; and one may imagine that certain of the sheep mentioned in the first sentence of *Allada* are destined for sacrifice—and for the feasting that the holiday authorizes.

In a broader perspective, Gavarry uses this semiotic network in order to introduce the notion of *ceremony*, and to prepare the reader for the hieratic, ceremonial aura that will characterize his novel from beginning to end. The epithet that designates his main character, "Mr. Director [*Monsieur l'Ordonnateur*]," likewise figures in that topos, for to a French ear the word *ordonnateur* inevitably invokes the expression *ordonnateur de pompes funèbres*, or "funeral director." And indeed the events of the novel take place in an atmosphere of solemnity and ritual resembling that of a funeral. If one can speak of "events" in a text where the principle of action is as flattened as *Allada*, that is. For nothing much occurs here, if by occurrence one means something that clearly distinguishes itself as significant by force of contrast with the fabric of daily life. To the contrary, most of *Allada* is devoted to an event that seems very ordinary indeed: a simple haircut. The actors in that little drama are very few: Mr. Director; the custodian or security guard who looks after his house; a barber; and the barber's young apprentice. The stage is the Director's home, and more precisely a site in front of his house, in the middle of his walled-in property, where the barber sets up a chair for his client.

As banal as it may seem, Gavarry takes exceptional care to present that drama as a ceremony. Even before the Director arrives for his haircut, Gavarry offers the custodian to us as a kind of officiant: "Standing at the threshold of his hut, the custodian hums softly in a nasal tone. One might think it were a prayer, some ritual chant to appease fate" (17). When the Director arrives, he descends the stairway leading from his house to his yard, slowly, processionally, stopping occasionally in order to gaze about him, and in order to confirm through that gaze that everything he sees belongs to him. As the three other individuals assembled in waiting gaze in turn upon him, the impression that he makes is a very powerful one indeed: "the first glimpse one had of him: a man measured not by a piece of land or by a single city, but by the five continents and all the oceans of the globe" (19–20). When he takes his place with great dignity in the barber's chair, the barber himself is struck by the physical presence of a man who has occupied so much space in his imagination as a virtual presence.

Once Gavarry has put all the elements in place, the scene is stark and symmetrical: "In the center of the yard sat the Director, very straight, his back against the chair" (26). What movement there may be is largely figural rather than literal, and the image that Gavarry sketches resembles a still life. "He is seated," he remarks of the Director, "his head offered up to the instruments of the man in the white boubou" (54). He is immobile, awaiting the razor, much like the sheep just outside his walls. In other words, and in terms of the outward trappings of the situation, the Director is the central figure in a ceremony that resembles a ritual of sacrifice. Moreover, Gavarry describes the barber explicitly as "the man of art" (72–73) and "the artisan of tradition" (76), describing his manner of working as "this spectacle" (74), despite the fact that there is very little going on that might strike us as spectacular in the conventional sense of the term. Nevertheless, each of the participants in the drama is conscious of the solemnity of the occasion. And even the neighborhood children are transfixed by the event, gazing on it from outside of the property, as if spying upon "some forbidden scene" (103).

It is legitimate to imagine that their gaze stands in for ours, and that our readerly gaze is likewise heightened by the idea that we are looking in from the outside, in mild violation of taboo. That the object of our fascination is a ceremony in which we have not been invited to participate. Or is such in fact the case, strictly speaking? For there is another ceremony being performed here in parallel with the one in which the barber officiates. Just like that latter ceremony it involves an artist or an artisan, and a spectacle. In a text entitled *Façon d'un roman, ou Comment d'après le Livre de Judith j'ai inventé une histoire de banlieue, et à l'aide du cocotier, du cargo, du Centaure, écrit trois fois* Hop là! [*Making a Novel, Or How, Following the Book of Judith, I Devised a Story of the Suburbs, and with the Help of the Coconut Palm, Cargo Ship, and Centaur, Thrice Wrote* Hoppla!] (2003), in which he discusses the structural principles of his novel *Hop là! un deux trois* [*Hoppla! 1 2 3*] (2001), Gérard Gavarry characterizes the novel as a construction site, and he speaks about the making of a novel as a kind of ceremony: "It's one of these construction sites that we're going to visit in the pages that follow. We'll learn what materials were assembled there. We'll also learn what sort of machine was built there, what motor powered it, and how its parts worked. In short, through what work or what play—or what ceremony—it sometimes happens that a novel is constructed" (*Façon d'un roman* 11). My own sense is that the ceremonial aspect of *Allada* is consistently double, playing out simultaneously on the level of narrative event and on the metaliterary level, that is to say, as the novel itself comes into being and as it proposes that very process as spectacle.

Despite the fact that all four of the individuals who participate in it are apparently alive and reasonably well, a funerary mood pervades that ceremony. Allusions to death, some more overt, some more literal, abound in the text. Before the Director arrives on the scene, for instance, the barber chides the custodian for having welcomed him too casually, and threatens jokingly to cut his throat, "like the shepherds do with the sheep, over there" (14). The custodian's reaction is curious: "One senses that he is disoriented, probably vexed by contrary desires, incapable of satisfying any of them, struck by the same stupidity into which our awkwardness turns—should we flee, howling? should we get closer, to see better?—when we are confronted by the spectacle of Death dancing in the forest, at night, by the light of the flames, when the palms or the mallets of the fetish musicians beat on the tight skin of the drums" (14–15). The effect is clear, however, for the custodian's reflections upon a ceremony of death and sacrifice in the forest serve to set the tone for the ceremony that will be performed in the Director's yard.

When the Director takes his place on the barber's chair, he is swathed from neck to foot in a white sheet, like a shroud. His body is indistinct beneath that sheet, Gavarry tells us (98), and the other participants in the scene might well have imagined that he was naked underneath (69). The custodian remarks to the barber's apprentice that the Director is old and feeble, speaking aloud and apparently without regard for his employer, "as if the Director were not there, or as if he didn't count" (62). From the moment when the Director first appears, his presence is dubious and contingent: "one soon got the impression that the Director was there without being there, as if he had invisibly retired from the present in order to slip wholly into an unfathomable past" (28). That ontological thinness clashes with the social status that his honorific suggests; moreover, it is precisely *here*, surrounded by his possessions and by people devoted to his service, that the Director ought to be most fully present. "Here in Mr. Director's home," remarks Gavarry, "one might assume that the master of the house might behave like a king in his palace. The master of the house is quiet" (88). His silence is eloquent. It suggests an absence of sorts, a phenomenon that Gavarry limns subtly but surely. Even kings are sometimes hard to locate, he mentions. "No photo has ever been taken of a king's remains, because kings do not die. They leave for Allada, the cradle of the three kingdoms of the South" (87); and when someone remarks, "The King has left for Allada," everyone understands what that means (88).

Can we imagine that Allada is simultaneously an actual place in the real world *and* a mythological graveyard of kings? Can we also imagine that the Director is simultaneously alive *and* dead, like Schrödinger's cat? Can we contemplate those states together—or rather, in rapid and continual alternation, like a lenticular image, such that each comments upon the other, and enriches it thereby? Gavarry himself, it should be noted, is intrigued by the notion of images arranged in superposition, in overlay, such that they may be perceived together in a complementary manner, as mutually refractory as they might otherwise seem. According to him, that is the effect he sought to achieve with the three distinctive parts of his novel *Hop là! un deux trois*, through a tensive dynamic of similarity and difference.[4] Alternatively, we might imagine that we are in the presence of parallel universes in *Allada*. In a recent book entitled *Il existe d'autres mondes* [Other worlds exist],

Pierre Bayard has speculated productively on the possibility of multiple worlds, arguing that literature most particularly affords us the possibility of shifting from one world into another and back again, without incident (55).[5] Or indeed of existing simultaneously in several different worlds—Bayard himself claims to be not only a writer, but also a British detective, the conductor of the Korean National Orchestra, and Scarlett Johansson's lover (13–17). He has very interesting, provocative things to say about the principle of simultaneity, and about the way that such a principle can enrich our manner of reading: "The model of simultaneity, however, gives us the right to think of both something and its contrary at the same time, with equal sincerity; to contradict ourselves in successive sentences without that fact causing reproach; and most especially to live several simultaneous lives, being attentive to the plurality of universes and to the complexity of our own" (150).

In my opinion, it is in just such a spirit that Gavarry offers *Allada* to us. One that allows us—indeed *encourages* us—to consider things both as they are and as they seem; to imagine the Director as both quick and dead; to see the events in the novel as both ordinary and utterly exceptional; to view the text as both rehearsal and requiem. All of this in simultaneity, at once, privileging neither one regime nor the other, allowing them a mutually enriching interplay. Without a doubt, such an approach to *Allada* demands a great deal of readerly agility, and I furthermore believe that that is one of the sites wherein Gavarry invests the principle of mobility that I alluded to a moment ago. For to all other appearances, *Allada* is a very static text indeed. Its vibrancy resides in ideation—more precisely in the ideational gestures of the writer and the reader, and in the productive articulation they describe, together, as both of them test out new protocols of writing and reading.

It should be pointed out that such mobility is difficult to achieve, and that certain states are more readily imaginable than others. As a practical matter (and in very simple terms), in *Allada* it is far easier to imagine the Director as alive than as dead. It offers the course of least resistance, it puts less strain on our interpretive faculties. Yet demonstrably enough, Gavarry exerts considerable energy in an effort to coax us into a double reading of his novel, because everywhere we turn we are confronted with images of death. One of the most salient examples of that effect involves an issue of the *Journal Littéraire* that the barber's apprentice finds in a pile of magazines in the custodian's hut while everyone is waiting for the Director to arrive. Among pictures of Hemingway and Joyce, there is a series of nine photos entitled "Portraits doux à la morgue" [Tender portraits in the morgue] by Rudolf Schäfer, a German photographer known for taking pictures of cadavers in such a way that the figures seem not to be dead, but rather asleep.[6] The pages devoted to those images seize the apprentice's attention powerfully and immediately. But the Director's reaction when he catches a glimpse of those photos over the apprentice's shoulder is more intriguing still. He tries to avert his gaze, but he cannot. He is fascinated, galvanized by the images he sees—and at the same time scandalized. He leaps out of his seat, howling in protest, calling upon the others present to confirm the despicable, abject character of the images. "How can people tolerate that sight?" he asks (42), perhaps not entirely rhetorically. And yet he cannot tear his eyes away from the images. Nor, in his emotion, can he account for them in coherent language. "Unable to speak coherently, the Director merely cries out, in a raw voice," remarks Gavarry (51), suggesting that the Director is in fact struck wordless by these images.

Throughout all of this drama, Gavarry insistently solicits our readerly gaze, asking us to consider Schäfer's images—virtually, that is to say through *ideation*—right alongside the apprentice, then the Director. Moreover, he invokes three kinds of gaze, putting them into articulation here: the gaze of the photographer, the Director's gaze, and our readerly gaze. "On photographic paper," he writes, "everything is fixed, just like the gaze of the lens, with which our own gaze inevitably mingles" (66). That immobility is a striking feature of these photographs, an effect that more than any other confirms the deadness of the subjects they portray. Is it not fair to wonder, however, whether immobility is a surface phenomenon, either in "still" photography or in a literary text like *Allada* that seems to wager so heavily on the static? "Thus, in the portrait," remarks Gavarry, "movement is sometimes invoked by the image of its interruption, sometimes by that of its retention, depending on whether the person is photographed spontaneously or while posing" (66–67). One may legitimately read a moment of metacommentary in that remark, I believe, because what Gavarry offers in *Allada* is indeed a portrait, posed for the most part, where the principle of immobility is used to suggest death, or at least death's imminence. What the Director sees in Schäfer's photographs is nothing other than death, and more particularly his own death. For their part, the other people present muse upon the analogy between Schäfer's shrouded cadavers and the Director, draped in the barber's sheet: "Did they imagine that the Director too was naked, under the sheet fixed at his neck and which stretches to the ground, covering both chair and body?" (69). But the Director sees more than mere analogy here. His reaction to the photos is crucially literalist, and indeed Gavarry calls our attention to it explicitly again and again,[7] because what the Director perceives therein is a specular image of his own condition.

Many other effects in *Allada* contribute to this network of signs. Whiteness recurs throughout the novel, for instance. The barber is dressed in a white robe; the Director is wrapped in a white sheet, and his head is wrapped in a steaming white towel; white vapor escapes from the pot where water is put to boil for the Director's shave. Indeed whiteness colors the sky itself, as the Director assumes his hieratic pose on the barber's chair: "unmoving, with his face turned toward the white sky" (32). In many cultures, of course, white is the color of death and mourning; and granted Gavarry's insistence upon that color we can safely imagine that white plays that very role in the semiotic economy of *Allada*, too. But *blankness* is also at issue here, I think, as is the notion of emptiness. The Director's yard is empty before the ceremony of the haircut, Gavarry tells us (12). And after the ceremony is performed, emptiness will reign there once again: "No sign that humans exist or that one day they existed; nothing even out of which to make a sign" (128). In both cases, that emptiness, that void is clearly described as being lifeless. Yet if it is deprived of life, it is also deprived of meaning—and perhaps that latter deprivation is still more catastrophic than the former, granted the system of equivalences that Gavarry adumbrates. For it is not merely the case that no signs are inscribed in that void, there exists no *possibility* of such inscription there. That is an effect which testifies to something approaching absolute death, both on the level of the told and on the level of the telling.

Immobility is yet another important principle that Gavarry exploits in order to achieve his purposes in *Allada*. Whether it be the static quality of the landscape in the Director's yard, or the unmoving pose that the Director strikes in the barber's chair, or the stillness of the subjects in Rudolf Schäfer's "Portraits doux à la morgue," or indeed the unblinking gaze of writer or reader, immobility particularizes *Allada* in key ways. It is reflected in the paucity of narrative event, in the lack of descriptive prominencing, and in Gavarry's reluctance to equip his novel with a clear and unequivocal set of directions for use. If immobility is affiliated with death in the novel's fabric (and I am convinced that it is), it is also associated with the commemoration of death. Just as we sometimes observe a moment of immobility and silence in order to memorialize someone's passing, so too does *Allada* adopt such a pose—even if the object of that gesture is not immediately and obviously apparent.

Silence complements whiteness, emptiness, and immobility in *Allada*; and in a sense it trumps them, for it is both more insistent and more troubling than those effects. Gavarry carefully postulates silence as one of the fundamental conditions of *Allada* in the very first pages of the novel, when the barber arrives at the gates of the Director's house and attempts to rouse the custodian:

> —Anyone home? the barber calls out.
>
> Silence sets in immediately.
>
> Surely the custodian is home. He has family visiting, and friends from villages visiting the city, and colleagues from the neighborhood. But everyone stopped talking when the barber called out. It seems that the yard itself has become silent, so that in a few moments it might be all the more empty and immobile, a space no longer traversed by anything human, neither bodies nor voices, nothing living—so much so that a lizard, skittering under the rain gutter or climbing the papaya tree, seem incongruous. A space from now on similar to those evil places near which passersby stop talking and hasten their pace, tense in spite of themselves, frightened, shrunken, their insides shivering and their consciousness saturated by too many simultaneous alarms. (12–13)

Clearly, Gavarry suggests that the silence which reigns in the Director's yard is uncanny in quality, and significantly threatening to anyone who might dare violate it. There is also little doubt concerning its jurisdiction and its warrant: it is the house and the yard that are silent, and it is the Director who makes it so. From time to time, the silence of the Director's domain stands in contrast to the distant, filtered noise of the city outside the Director's walls, and of the festivities of Tabaski that currently animate the city. Yet on one occasion at least, right after the Director erupts in righteous anger against Rudolf Schäfer's photographs, Gavarry tells us that the city itself falls silent. "The Director's authority can be measured thereby," he adds, "the suspension of all noise, and the curious inactivity that it suggests" (35).

During the ceremony that the barber performs, the participants are careful to observe the rule of silence. Consequently, the soundscape of *Allada* is for the most part very muted indeed, and largely *objective* in character: "Nobody speaks in the yard, and the ambient noises, absent human voices, are those of the combs, brushes, scissors, and razor jostling together under the hands of the people readying them for use" (54). The two exceptions to that rule distinguish themselves in interesting ways. On the one hand, when the Director, faced with the scandal of the photographs, shouts his indignation, his utterance is nonverbal. It is primal, reactive, and powerfully performative, to be sure, but it is wordless. And the silence that follows his outburst seems deeper and more definitive still than the one that preceded it. On the other hand, when the barber upon rare occasion speaks to his client in order to perform his duties more efficiently, his quiet words inscribe themselves indelibly on the surface of that silence, as it were: "In the silence of the yard, the man of art's words resound clearly" (98). His speech is that of a priest officiating at a funeral; it is itself ceremonial and liturgical; it is dirgelike and hushed. It points toward death, in other terms, and it articulates mourning.

Gavarry's own language in *Allada* resembles that of the barber in significant ways. It, too, is sober and hieratic in tone. Gavarry eschews the "noise" that sometimes characterizes fiction, whether that "noise" be construed as emphatic discursive effect, or tritely conventional suggestions of exoticism, or gestures toward facile and bathetic emotionalism. To the contrary, his writerly tone is muted, measured, and workmanlike. That latter quality is an important one, I think. As I mentioned a moment ago, Gavarry himself refers to the barber not only as an "man of art," but also as an "artisan of tradition." For that man has *work* to do here, and the ceremony that he performs pivots around that work. One may recall that Sigmund Freud wagered heavily upon the idea of work in his celebrated analysis of mourning, emphasizing "the work which mourning performs" ("Mourning and Melancholia" 244). One of his key insights is that mourning is a gradual process, one that is carried out "piecemeal" (245) as the subject comes to terms with the loss of a loved one little by little. In the first stages, Freud argues, "a turning away from reality takes place and a clinging to the object through the medium of a hallucinatory wishful psychosis" (244); and thus during that time "the existence of the lost object is psychically prolonged" (245). For a while at least, the loved one is in a sense both alive and dead in terms of the subject's psychic experience.

Gérard Gavarry has seized a moment very much like that in *Allada*, I believe. The precise *object* of mourning is not transparently and explicitly manifest in the novel, and nor is the *subject* immediately apparent; but anyone who is familiar with the gestures of mourning will recognize its presence in *Allada*. Furthermore, I wonder if mourning does not play a role more fundamental still in the novel, something a bit deeper than thematics and prior to that, too. For it is generally acknowledged that mourning, as painful as it can be, can also fuel creativity. As Julia Kristeva puts it in *Black Sun*, "loss, bereavement, and absence trigger the work of the imagination and nourish it permanently as much as they threaten it and spoil it" (9). Allow me to be clear about this. I do not wish to argue that *Allada* is merely an account of mourning, prompted by the author's actual experience of mourning, for it is a great deal more than that. I do feel however that mourning is profoundly imbricated in the novel, both on the level of story and on the level of discourse. It provides an advantageous lens through which we may consider *Allada*, one that is particularly useful when it is a question of making provisional sense of certain features of the novel that may otherwise escape us by virtue of their uncanniness.

I say "provisional sense" because meaning is extremely mobile and multiple in a novel as rich as this one, ill-suited to reductive and definitive interpretation. Gavarry is abundantly aware of that, moreover. Indeed from an author's point of view it is important to him that meaning should have room for maneuver in his books. Speaking about *Hop là! un deux trois*, he remarks: "In other terms, I didn't write an apologue, but rather a novel, that is, a work of fiction whose form I intended to personalize and master, but whose meaning I by no means claim to monopolize or control. In this, taking risk. In that, exercising freedom. In the constant promise to oneself to lose sight of neither one, elementary moral of the writer" (*Façon d'un roman* 89–90). In that very perspective, it *makes sense* provisionally—that is, tentatively, situationally, heuristically, strategically—to identify a meditation on mourning in *Allada*. For beyond the other opportunities it offers, mourning serves efficiently and meaningfully to structure many of the ceremonies that we perform, be they as simple as a haircut or as complex as writing and reading.

Lydie Salvayre's Voices

READING LYDIE SALVAYRE is principally a matter of listening. A clamor of voices resounds in her writings: voices of rage, of loathing, of indignation, of sorrow, of fear, of desperation. They shout, they whisper, they castigate, they wheedle, they condemn. Some voices are maddeningly prolix, others are painfully laconic; some offer carefully reasoned insight, others speak to say nothing; some emanate from the lower reaches of society, others from points of rare privilege. Often they are monological, either by choice or by force of circumstance; and frequently those voices are anonymous ones. Some speak in bleakly literalist terms, while others layer irony upon irony in a discourse that is hopelessly contorted. Sometimes, people speak constantly, but soundlessly, in a silence more deafening than the most strident voice imaginable. As often as not, nobody listens—except for us, if we are willing.

The notion of "voice" in literature is of course an exceedingly slippery one. Eric Prieto recently pointed out that the semantic field of that construct has been considerably expanded in our time: "No longer exclusively associated with the spoken word and performance, voice takes on the more general meaning of 'personal style,' that is, those elements of written elocution that give us access to the specific personality and 'thought patterns' of a writer" (285). Susan Lanser, for her part, argues that the construct means different things in different critical registers. When feminists invoke the idea of voice, for instance, they typically use it as a general, mimetic, and political term; when narratologists deploy it, they do so in ways that are specific, semiotic, and technical (4). Maurice Blanchot famously described narrative voice as something always emanating from an "elsewhere" with regard to the putative "where" of narrative. Conceiving stories as bounded, or "encircled," Blanchot suggests that narrative voice speaks from outside of those limits: "one gets the impression that someone is speaking from behind, prompting the characters, or the events, telling them what to say" (556–57). If our reading necessarily encourages us to suspect the existence of such a point, however, its very eccentricity makes it all the more difficult to locate with any degree of precision. And the more closely we pursue it, the more quickly it flees into indeterminacy and aporia, "as if the circle had its center outside of the circle, behind and infinitely behind, as if the outside were precisely that center which can only be the absence of any center" (Blanchot 557).[1]

The notion of a vocal "elsewhere" is thus a very thorny one, as appealing and full of promise as it may seem. In Lydie Salvayre's case, it is still more problematic by virtue of the fact that the wings of the stage upon which her fictions are played out are, with very few exceptions, extremely exiguous ones. Most of her texts provide us with pure discourse, a character speaking to an audience—or indeed into the wind. In either case, that "other" is very largely voiceless; and it is very rare that an authorial (or authoritative) narrative voice intervenes to mediate what is said.

Clearly, if voice is a difficult notion to theorize, so too is the idea of hearing. "How can one make a voice heard using only the tools of written language?" asks Jean Rousset (140). Rousset himself proceeds metaphorically and analogically, suggesting that voice is like song, and relying upon the lexicon of music. Obviously, it is also very much a question of the ear, which Jacques Derrida describes as the most uncanny of organs since, while we can listen carefully or not at all, the ear is nonetheless always in a sense "open," always "offered" (*Otobiographies* 103). Rousset argues that Proust's ear is exceptionally fine-tuned: "Proust is not only a linguist (though untutored), he is a subtle acoustician, gifted with an ultrasensitive ear when his characters speak; he senses their phonic nuances, giving each a voice, which reveals those characters as much and better than the words the character speaks" (136). It is legitimate, I think, to make the same sort of claim for Salvayre's ear. As a practicing psychiatrist,[2] she is a trained, professional listener, attentive not only to what is said, but also—and perhaps principally—to how it is said. Furthermore, I believe there is abundant evidence in her writings to suggest that Salvayre is deeply intrigued by the performative aspect of voice, its effect upon the speaker himself or herself, upon the listener, upon the reader.

In examining Salvayre's poetics of voice, I shall focus upon the "vocal symptoms," as Rousset puts it (136), that her works display. I am persuaded by Derrida's contention in *La Voix et le phénomène* that consciousness is not possible without voice, and that indeed in a real sense, "voice *is* consciousness" (89). In the first instance, I shall use the construct like Lanser does when she speaks of "personal voice,"[3] in my efforts to come to terms with Salvayre's speakers. The characters in her works speak in a dizzying variety of voices, and their discursive strategies vary widely, ranging from the barely articulate to the extremely sophisticated and wily. In that polyphony, however, there are certain shared traits that become apparent, as if all of these different characters were speaking dialectical variations of a tongue common to all. Moreover, all of Salvayre's characters are very largely constructed *through* voice, in ways that are original and compelling. Once having examined some of those characters in detail, I hope to be in a position to offer a few remarks about Lydie Salvayre's own voice, one which is as distinctive, I feel, as any in contemporary literature.

The incipit of Salvayre's first novel, *La Déclaration*, puts in place many of the discursive techniques that she will rely upon throughout her career: "You are good. You have a soul. It is huge. But your smell bothers me, particularly the one which rises up from your stomach in the morning, undoubtedly linked to the corrosive action of tobacco on the gastric wall, and when you turn toward me for your little wake-up kiss, I feel an insurmountable disgust" (7). The speaker will hold the floor alone during the entire course of the novel. This monological principle is an extremely important one in Salvayre's writing, and it is one that characterizes the vast majority of her published works.[4] Moreover, the speaker is anonymous here, and will remain so; this is, once again, a familiar feature of Salvayre's writing. In those instances when Salvayre's monologists are named—"Suzanne" in *La Vie commune* [*Everyday Life*], "Louisiane" in *La Compagnie des spectres* [*The Company of Ghosts*], and "Maître Echinard" in *Quelques Conseils utiles aux élèves huissiers* [*Some Useful Advice for Apprentice Process-Servers*]—the name is offered offhandedly, by default as it were, and it does not guarantee the kind of stable personal identity that our semiotic desire prompts us to locate in narrators.

In the first pages of *La Déclaration*, the lines of address seem to be clear and unproblematic, as the narrator speaks to his wife in the second person. Yet it becomes clear that his speech is not literally directed to his wife, but is rather an interior monologue cast as an apostrophe. Moreover, as Brigitte Louichon has pointed out (312), the second-person narration gives way quickly to the first person and the "tu" becomes an "elle," as the narrator realizes the futility of addressing his wife, and gradually takes the measure of his own solitude. In short, this man is speaking to himself. That, too, would seem to be the rule in Lydie Salvayre's fictional worlds. The narrator of *La Puissance des mouches* [*The Power of Flies*], for example, speaks to a variety of people during his incarceration, a judge, a lawyer, a psychiatrist, a nurse (Louichon 310); yet the key here is in the preposition. He speaks indeed *to* them, rather than *with* them; and he is careful to preserve his discursive monopoly, allowing only a very bare ration of their voices to be heard, that ration substantially mediated and transformed through his own voice. Maître Echinard, in *Quelques Conseils utiles aux élèves huissiers*, and the lecturer in *La Conférence de Cintegabelle* [*The Lecture*] speak notionally at least to public audiences. Yet they both take care that their audience should have no real voice in the matter, no voice that might compete in any sense, that is, with their own.

Brigitte Louichon has argued that Salvayre uses the technique of "double enunciation" in her novels, a term borrowed from theater studies designating the way in which a character on the stage, speaking to another character, in fact speaks to the audience (310). For my part, I think it is fair to say that enunciation in Salvayre is always double, and that her characters speak in some sense through local situation to the reader; but I am struck by the fragility of pretense in the first term of that enunciative structure, as Salvayre presents it. For I am convinced that her speakers take very little account of their interlocutors; and it is easy to imagine that such dialogue as they engage in, like that of Clamence in Camus's *La Chute* [*The Fall*], might very well be illusory.

Speaking alone throughout the text, and anonymously, the narrator of *La Déclaration* resembles thus many of Salvayre's other protagonists. He is a man stripped of status, bereft of belief, and despairing of consolation. He is left with nothing other than his story—and his voice. On the one hand, he is, as Rousset remarked of Proust's Charlus, a "powerful speaker, lone master of words" (139). Yet on the other hand, to the degree that his words have rather little performative value, he speaks very largely in vain. As he tells his story, his voice becomes more and more insistent and obsessive; that kind of accelerative rhythm is also a common feature of Salvayre's writing. Like several other characters in her work, the narrator of *La Déclaration* will end up in a psychiatric clinic, his voice echoing plaintively through hollow corridors.

It is useful to view Salvayre's monological technique as an experiment in *suasoria*, that ancient rhetorical exercise which consisted in speaking in the voice of another, generally illustrious, figure, and often devoted to a question of conscience. Admittedly, most of Salvayre's characters are something less than illustrious; but they are nonetheless exemplary figures, insofar as they grapple with problems that are broadly distributed in society: alienation, injustice, oppression, personal and collective violence, and so forth. Moreover, the manner in which they voice those problems is clearly moral in tone, whether the moral outrage they display engages individual relations or social ones. Practically disincarnate (Salvayre allows us to "see" very little of her protagonists), they are in effect *embodied* by their voices, standing alone upon these otherwise barren discursive horizons.

They are, in other terms, soliloquists. Upon occasion, they recognize that function, and embrace it as a vocation. The narrator of *La Puissance des mouches*, for instance, mentions that he occasionally goes for walks in the countryside. He is not fond of exercise, nor does nature inspire him particularly. He loathes birds, and he fears countryfolk and the guard dogs that they keep. "Nevertheless," he says, "the countryside provides me with an inestimable advantage: I can soliloquize there in peace. I soliloquize then. I speak to myself for days on end. About everything. About nothing" (153). Yet the consolation which that activity affords him is fragile and precarious at best, for he comes to realize two very sobering considerations. First, the difference between speaking alone and speaking with others is a trivial one in the final analysis, granted that in neither case do his words have any power to change his situation. Second, what he has to say is of interest to nobody, not even to himself: "I have stopped soliloquizing. I don't find myself interesting anymore" (165).

In *La Conférence de Cintegabelle*, Salvayre constructs a

thoughtful—and infinitely ironic—meditation upon voice and its uses. The lecturer's subject is conversation, an art that was once, according to him, a preeminent feature of French culture, but that has now fallen into a deplorable state of corruption and decay. He is a man who does not quail at harsh truths—nor does he hesitate to belabor the obvious: "Given that most people speak to themselves, it would seem to us salutary to specify, ladies and gentlemen, that a conversation takes place between at least two people" (28). To his mind (a very idiosyncratic one, admittedly), nothing concerning conversation can be taken for granted. Inaugurating his remarks, he asks his audience to imagine a dinner party, and to adopt for the moment an anthropological perspective on the behavior there occurring: "Observe the guests. Scientifically. They turn toward their right and toward their left. Nod their heads. Execute with their right arms repeated gestures of pronation. Engage in mastication—mouths closed, I hasten to add. And between two mouthfuls, of very small volume of course, agitate their lips without cease. Like this" (9). All of the gestural apparatus of conversation is in place, he argues; but in reality there is no real conversation to be heard. Indeed, he may be the last person on earth who recognizes conversation for the art that it is; and he would be free to practice it, if only he could find an interlocutor worthy of his salt.

His conversations with his wife were less than wholly fulfilling during her lifetime, he mentions. Yet, since her death, they have become far more rewarding; in fact, they have become, by his own description, "ideal" (121). Perhaps he has not entirely despaired of finding a conversation partner somewhere in his audience, but whenever another voice appears to raise itself, he is quick to silence it. He praises the many virtues of dialogue in a voice that is unremittingly monological. Let us bear in mind too, that *La Conférence de Cintegabelle* is a monological novel. On a first level at least, we hear only one voice, that of the lecturer, arguing as it were against itself, disproving by force of example the very theses which it adumbrates. If there is a conversation here, it is one that is staged well above the head of the lecturer, and at his expense—a conversation, furthermore, that is very largely unvoiced.

Salvayre's lecturer speaks in moderate, complaisant, and measured tones. But there are far louder voices in her work too, voices that howl, roar, and shout. The father and the son in "Famille I," for example, know no other communicative mode—if in fact any communication is taking place between them. Their verbal violence, furthermore, presages the deadly act of physical violence upon which the text concludes. Suzanne, in *La Vie commune*, has often to suffer the shouted reproaches of her daughter, who becomes unhinged by her mother's constant complaining: "Ah no! cries my daughter in a strident voice, you're not going to plague us your whole life long with your ridiculous, simpleminded women's tales!" (50). In one sense, Suzanne is indeed simpleminded, for she lacks the thoughtfulness and the perspective that would enable her to relativize the small vexations of "everyday life." Moreover, *La Vie commune* is certainly a woman's tale, and clearly coded—albeit ironically, playing cannily upon hoary gender stereotypes—as such. Part of Suzanne's dilemma resides in the fact that she cannot bring herself to shout, much as she might long to. The eleventh chapter of the novel is devoted to one single utterance: "NO! I wish I could yell a no which would have the power of a punch, and which would take the place, if it were written, of all the words in a book" (63). Clearly, Suzanne can no more write a book than she can make herself shout. She is condemned to voice her discontent in whispers, and largely to herself, and that very lack of articulative possibility will be her undoing. Yet, stepping out of the fictional world for a moment, we may realize that this "no" is indeed written. Not by Suzanne of course, but by Salvayre, who voices in bold letters what her character cannot, and constructs in that manner a kind of economy of creative naysaying that one finds in her work from

La Déclaration through *Contre* [Against].

The loudest shouter in Salvayre's novels is undoubtedly Rose Mélie, the mother in *La Compagnie des spectres*. Her vituperations, screamed at the top of her lungs, become the most notable features of that novel's aural texture. There, too, a daughter finds her mother's voice unbearable. "I didn't want to hear her howl," says Louisiane. "Hearing her howl had made me ill. [. . .] For my mother does nothing other than sleep. Or howl" (23–24). The mother's howls are directed against Maître Echinard, the bailiff who has come to evict them from their apartment in a poor suburb of Paris. Though the action of the novel takes place in the 1990s, the mother's imagination confuses the present with the years of the Occupation, when her brother was coldly murdered by the collaborationist French Militia. She is certain that the bailiff has been sent by the Militia, and she curses him with every imprecation she can muster. When Salvayre finally gives Maître Echinard an opportunity to speak in his own voice, in *Quelques Conseils utiles aux élèves huissiers*, he tells his students that being verbally assaulted in this way is something that they can expect, granted the profession they have chosen: "This slatternly female, for I forgot to mention that this individual named Rose was disgustingly dirty, this slattern, I was saying, became a veritable Fury when she invoked the Collaboration, yelling, gesticulating, and apostrophizing me in the most brutal of manners" (28). In providing his students with this exemplary tale, he relies also on one of the first principles that he instilled in their minds: "poor people, you will learn, are often excessively emotive" (12).

Clearly, Rose Mélie is crazy. Louisiane says as much to the bailiff, in an effort to excuse her mother; and she herself undoubtedly suffers from the way that her mother lives constantly in two worlds. But perhaps Rose Mélie is not quite crazy enough for comfort. Perhaps there is some logic in the way she sees the bailiff, and though that logic certainly escapes Maître Echinard (for he is a man who is superbly and irremediably unaware), it may not escape us. When Rose Mélie howls at the bailiff, she is decrying scandalous injustices both past and present, in the only way she can. The manner in which she conflates the past and the present serves, for well-adjusted folk like the bailiff, as the very proof of her madness. Yet in the wings of this fiction, we may possibly hear another, more muted voice suggesting that social and political justice in France has not made quite as much progress in the last fifty years as the voices of power would have us believe.

Shouting, then, does not guarantee that one will be heard in Lydie Salvayre's universe—if one means "hearing" as "understanding." Even when construed more simply, the act of hearing, as commonplace as it may seem, becomes a very thorny issue in her work, deeply intricated with the problem of voice. In the best of cases, her characters find it difficult to make themselves heard by others. And upon occasion, they cannot even perceive their own voice: "No word suffices. And everything I say adds to my agony. And that agony is endless, for it awakens another, still more fearful one, deeper and more deadly, that of being unable to say anything about anything, because my mind is so weak that as soon as I concentrate, it's the sound of passing cars that I hear, rather than my own voice" (*La Déclaration* 69). At the other end of the spectrum, some of Salvayre's characters hear too much. In *Les Belles Ames* [Beautiful souls], for example, Olympe's loud laugh disturbs the bourgeois tourists, "Who have developed a hypersensitive ear. From listening to Stockhausen," mentions the narrator in a moment of high irony (104). Yet though they may hear her laugh literally, they surely do not hear what that laugh implies. Nor do they hear what she may have to say, for Olympe is not of their world, and the language that she speaks might just as well be Swahili, insofar as the tourists are concerned.

For the most part then, it is a question of people just not

listening; and that becomes extremely burdensome for the people who would try to speak their thoughts aloud. Often, the problem begins at home. The narrator of *La Déclaration* complains that his own mother doesn't listen to him when he tries to tell her that he is not well (38). Yet obviously his problem is more generalized than that: "Why is it that nobody listens to me, that people avoid my gaze and turn away from me?" (29). In "Famille I" the troubled son likewise seeks consolation from his mother, but she is too engrossed in a television series to listen to him (*Et que les vers mangent le boeuf mort* 9). Suzanne cannot make herself heard when she speaks with her daughter. When she says that she "abhors" her co-worker, her daughter thinks she heard "adores" instead, leaving Suzanne to conclude, "My daughter never listens to me" (*La Vie commune* 43). Deafness can be a virtue for some, too, a handy tool to use in a broader strategy of power. Among the many wise precepts that the bailiff offers to his students is the advice to close their ears to any suggestion that the profession they intend to exercise is a less than honorable one (*Quelques Conseils utiles aux élèves huissiers* 8), just as he closes his own when confronted with anything that sounds unpleasant.

More efficient still are the techniques used to silence voices that disturb, techniques that commonly involve the use of a voice that is stronger. Suzanne temporarily silences her detested co-worker by correcting her orthography, "in a cutting voice" (*La Vie commune* 10); and the narrator of *La Puissance des mouches* silences a group of disorderly rugbymen by calling them to order "in a terrible voice" (21). Patently, silencing another's voice demands that power be exercised—and the very exercise of that power is the proof of its legitimacy. Rose Mélie argues that the reason the Militiamen murdered her brother was because they were afraid he might utter something that would put their own power into question. "Nobody is powerful," she concludes, "if he doesn't silence the speech of the other by any means possible. Power consists in shutting others up" (*La Compagnie des spectres* 20).

Some of the most touching characters in Salvayre's writings are the mute ones, those who have no voice (or very little), the ones who have become definitively overpowered. One thinks of Mme. Piche, a member of the benighted audience in *La Conférence de Cintegabelle*, whose questions might be enriching ones, if only the lecturer would let her voice be heard. Or Henriette, in *La Déclaration*, whose very muteness is a source of exasperation for the narrator. Upon those rare occasions when she timidly proffers an utterance, the narrator hears nothing other than "whimpering," and raises his own voice to a howl in order to silence her (*La Déclaration* 76). Olympe is one of those mute figures, too: she speaks rarely, hesitantly and uncertainly. The narrator intervenes from time to time to amplify her voice for our benefit, providing it with a resonance that it would otherwise lack. Brigitte Louichon has suggested that the power of language is generally forbidden to impoverished people, and that one of Lydie Salvayre's goals is to give the power of speech to those who ordinarily do not enjoy it (322). I feel that Salvayre's strategy in that sense is a more nuanced one, however. In certain cases, like that of Mme. Piche and Henriette, people who seek to make their voice heard are silenced, oppressed by a discursive power vastly more formidable than their own. In other cases, like that of the workers in *La Médaille* [*The Award*], they speak in a language that is interrupted and questioned disadvantageously by another language, that of the bosses. The workers speak, but they speak haltingly, in awkwardness and discomfort, unused as they are to the rhetorical norms of the medal ceremony, norms which the people in power have set in place precisely in order to confirm their power. In still other cases, Salvayre does indeed afford a voice to people who normally are voiceless. It is not often that we hear, for instance, a convicted murderer speak in his own voice, nor someone interned in a psychiatric hospital;

it is rare that we hear the voice of a secretary in literature, or that of an adolescent from a ravaged suburb. Yet once again, the crucial question arises: who is listening to these voices? Within the fictional worlds themselves, the answer would seem to be clear: almost nobody. Many of Salvayre's characters do speak at some length, and some (Louisiane, the lecturer, Suzanne, the narrator of *La Déclaration*, for example) speak until the point of exhaustion. But their voices do not carry. Or not, at least, within the boundaries of their world. If they are to be heard at all, it must be on the other side of those boundaries, where Salvayre's reader enjoys the luxury of listening to those voices, or not. In other terms—and this is yet another example of Salvayre's tendency to suggest exemplary behavior through the force of counterexample—she calls upon us to perform the very gesture of interlocutive hospitality which the "others" in the world of her characters systematically refuse.

In ways that are quite explicit and deliberate, Salvayre stages voice as a problem for her characters; moreover, those characters often recognize that problem and try to take its measure. In most instances, the problem resides in the voices of other people. Suzanne, for example, cannot abide the sound of her co-worker's voice, which she interprets not as language but as pure noise: "A noise wrenches me out of my somber thoughts. SHE SPEAKS. I had forgotten that she speaks. Can one prevent a human being from speaking?" (*La Vie commune* 27). In other instances, it is a problem of their own voices. Toward the end of his story, the narrator of *La Déclaration* reflects upon his own voice: "My voice has changed. It has become slow and sad, with occasional misfires in articulation, then sudden accelerations during which my spirit awakens. Words come out of my mouth like limp, drifting masses" (105). He speaks of his voice as if it were that of another, and largely independent of his will, listening to it from the outside as it were. His alienation from those around him has clearly been doubled and compounded by an alienation from himself; and, like so often in Salvayre, the principal symptom of that affliction is voice.

In some of her texts, Salvayre deploys voice in a dynamic of struggle, an agonistic opposing multiple voices, or sets of voices. Such is the case of *La Compagnie des spectres*, where Rose Mélie's howls and Maître Echinard's hushed utterances, voiced in cruelly indifferent administrative terms, compete with each other. With her characteristic perspicacity, Louisiane understands the rules of that competition, and recognizes too that it is an unequal one, at least insofar as the immediate situation is concerned: "And in that cold, impersonal, and dull tone which seemed to me the height of distinction (undoubtedly because it was the opposite of our own, sometimes plaintive, often loud, always exaggerated and dramatic), 'How old is your television?' he asked, as he adjusted his gold-rimmed glasses" (46). But competitions are always unequal ones in Salvayre's world, where the deck is always stacked in favor of the privileged. The underprivileged enjoy only a moral authority, which counts for very little in their circumstances. It is only when one steps outside of the fictional frame that the odds against them begin to shorten, for Salvayre wagers that her reader will judge the competition somewhat differently.

In *La Médaille* the competition of voice is again apparent, but this time it is not so much a matter of tone as a matter of language. The workers speak a language that is very different from that of the bosses. Curiously enough, both languages seem highly artificial in their deviation from what we might consider as standard language. The workers speak in a version of "popular" language deliberately exaggerated by Salvayre for strategic purposes, while that of the bosses is an exhortative, prevaricative rhetoric full of cliché and thinly-disguised commonplace, something the French call a *langue de bois*, or "wooden tongue." Predictably enough, the bosses have the upper hand in this struggle. They hold the floor longer; they speak with more assurance in their capacity as "hosts" in the medal ceremony; they belong to a community which is sure of its discursive purpose; and, speaking both before and after the workers whom they gratify, they are in a position to gloss and reformulate any remarks the latter might hazard. After Auguste Donte's acceptance speech, for example, the Director of Human Resources takes the microphone to congratulate that worker upon his "simple and poignant language," in a voice dripping with noblesse oblige (35), effectively dismissing him. Obviously, what the workers might have to say is a matter of no importance to the bosses, and their acceptance speeches have only a phatic value, at best. The novel's narrator adds his or her voice to that of the bosses moreover, mentioning that Donte's own voice is unpleasantly loud, and that his efforts at humor were not successful (25, 27).

In a similar manner, *Les Belles Ames* puts in place an agonistic of voices; and once again it is a question of social class. On the one hand are the voices of privilege, those of the bourgeois tourists; on the other, the voices of Olympe, the tour guide, the bus driver, and Jason, the young "Ambience Agent." Those two vocal camps affront each other much as in *La Médaille*, and familiar ironies question the ideas, judgments, and prejudices that they emit. Yet Salvayre shifts the balance of power significantly here, since her narrator (an extradiegetic one, like in *La Médaille*) weighs in this time on the side of the underprivileged. Speaking in the first person, with an "I" that interrupts and interrogates the third-person narration, that narrator unequivocally affirms his or her sympathy for her disempowered characters—in particular, for Olympe[5]—and thereby encourages the reader to regard them in the same sympathetic light.

In Salvayre's monological texts, the competition of voices is more subtle and nuanced; but it is no less real. Maître Echinard, in *Quelques Conseils utiles aux élèves huissiers*, and the lecturer, in *La Conférence de Cintegabelle*, hold forth largely uncontested.

Both perorate with considerable eloquence and ease. Yet they are marked by that very eloquence, since speaking "well" in Salvayre always signals a flaw in character. As they layer flourish upon flourish, as their tone becomes more and more pedantic and their rhetoric more and more inflated in their efforts to convince, Echinard and the lecturer progressively squander what capital they initially may have enjoyed with the reader. We listen to them distractedly, bemused in a sense by another voice whispering behind their own (as Blanchot might put it), a voice calling them into question, and urging us to reject what they say, precisely because of how they say it. Not to put too fine a point on it, that muted voice may undoubtedly be taken as Salvayre's own. Her game is a dangerous one, though. As I mentioned, the space she occupies with regard to that of her characters is extremely exiguous, leaving very little room for maneuver. Moreover, all things being equal, that which is said—and said again—will generally be more persuasive than that which is merely implied. Loud voices tend to be heard over soft ones. For Salvayre, then, it is a matter of obliging us to listen in the negative mode, where a whisper can be more compelling than the most stentorian voice.

It is legitimate, I feel, to imagine Salvayre whispering to us from behind the more egregious among the characters she creates. And one may hear an echo of her voice around certain other corners of her texts as well. There are several thematic clusters that recur frequently in her fictions and that seem to hold particular pungency for her, granted what we know of her own experience. For example, there are the references to Spain, and most particularly the Spain of the Second Republic, the Civil War, and its aftermath. Like Salvayre herself, the narrator of *La Puissance des mouches* was born to Spanish Republican refugees.[6] His parents met in the notorious French internment camp at Argelès, and it was there that he was conceived (18–19). There is more than a suggestion in that novel that the legacy of the war's violence, shaping as it did the narrator's family dynamic, lies at the root of the violence that he himself will eventually commit within that family. From time to time, Salvayre invokes the kinds of prejudices that Spanish refugees had to bear in French society, often speaking through the very voice of prejudice. In *La Vie commune*, for instance, Suzanne opines, "I know someone who professes Communist ideas, an excessively vulgar woman: an incredibly ill-bred anti-Franquist Spaniard, and with such rustic manners!" (69).

Another thematic cluster of this sort revolves around Salvayre's own profession, psychiatry. She alludes to that profession in her novels on many occasions, and always in a voice heavily laden with irony, in a tone that is fundamentally oppositional in character. Several of her characters have consulted psychiatrists, and some of them—the narrator of *La Déclaration*, Rose Mélie, the son in "Famille I"—have been committed against their will to psychiatric hospitals. In no case have those therapeutics brought about significant, positive change in their situations. In *La Conférence de Cintegabelle*, the lecturer rails against the profession in general, and against his psychiatrist brother-in-law in particular. The opinions he voices are often dubious ones; yet it would seem that Salvayre is suggesting to us that, in this case at least, he may be less wrongheaded than usual. Enjoying a privileged place on the itinerary of the most sordid sites in Europe with which "Real Voyages" proposes to gratify its tourists in *Les Belles Ames*, right up there with an exceptionally impoverished public housing project in Paris and a building squatted by young heroin addicts in Milan, is a visit to a psychiatric hospital in Turin, "the city where Nietzsche threw himself on a horse's neck" (151). Most especially, Salvayre comments upon the abuses of a psychiatry that has abdicated its traditional critical, person-to-person dialogue in favor of a brutal, thoughtless pharmaceutical doping. Rose Mélie, for one, recognizes that practice for what it is; and in her indictment of it, one may perhaps hear an echo of Salvayre's own voice: "if that imbecile thinks that fifty drops of Haldol morning, noon, and night will reduce me to silence, he's mistaken!" (*La Compagnie des spectres* 124). Similarly, the son in "Famille I" lives in a haze of psychotropic drugs. That will not prevent him, however, from committing murder.

Brigitte Louichon has argued that the particular dynamic of psychiatry, where a subject's speech addresses itself to an interlocutor "whose presence is always more or less manifest, but always silent," is often in evidence in Lydie Salvayre's fictions (316). It should be noted, though, that the representation of the "talking cure" in Salvayre is always truncated. That is, no real dialogue—and thus no effective therapy—takes place here. Characters may speak to others, but in no case do those others speak back to them in ways that provide a critical interaction enabling the subject to come to terms with his or her problems. For the many souls who suffer in Salvayre, there is consequently no true prospect of a cure.

The third and final thematic cluster I would like to mention is organized around literature itself. The question of Salvayre's stance with regard to literature in general is a complex and extremely rich one, and it deserves a far broader analysis than I can afford here. For the moment, then, let me suggest that Salvayre's attitude toward her other profession is equally as fraught with ambivalence as is her attitude toward psychiatry—and perhaps still more so. A few examples of that ambivalent stance will perhaps suffice.

There are many readers among Salvayre's characters, and they are of very different kinds. The narrator of *La Puissance des mouches* knows Pascal by heart; Rose Mélie has a library composed of the classic texts of Greek and Roman antiquity; and the lecturer in *La Conférence de Cintegabelle* piques himself on having read almost everything of note in the history of literature. Yet their readings bring little real consolation to these people. All of Pascal's warnings about the vanity of human attachment cannot attenuate the loathing that the narrator of *La Puissance des mouches* feels for his father; the wisdom of classical philosophy serves little when power, in the person of Maître Echinard, comes knocking on the door of Rose Mélie's apartment; and, if the lecturer has indeed read many books, he has understood almost nothing of what they have to say.

When Salvayre offers us thumbnail sketches of writers, rather than readers, those sketches are always unflattering ones. Suzanne's co-worker's favorite writer is "Benoît Dussert," whom Suzanne views as "the most saccharine, idiotic, and arrogant novelist of his generation," (*La Vie commune* 71). The writers whom the lecturer encounters in Paris are preening, narcissistic, rude and reptilian beings, far more interested in the mandarin rituals of a literary cocktail party than in the life of the mind. Flauchet, in *Les Belles Ames*, distinguishes himself as an unsavory character even among the detestable tourists, whom he eventually drives to distraction: "Everyone by now avoids Flauchet, an elitist and a bore who walks around with a broomstick up his ass" (139).

One may indeed seek to hear Salvayre's voice in her intertextual practices. Yet that voice varies vertiginously in tone. She quotes Swift epigraphically in *La Médaille*, for instance, and the satirical character of that novel might well persuade us of the frankness of Salvayre's metaliterary gesture. When the lecturer in *La Conférence de Cintegabelle* proclaims his admiration for Cervantes, Sterne, and Melville (67), however, the question of Salvayre's position is somewhat thornier, granted the way Salvayre has cut the legs out from under her character, persuading us that his literary taste is uninformed and misguided. Rose Mélie's dismissal of the contemporary French novel is voiced by a character whom Salvayre encourages us to view sympathetically, yet the lecturer also denounces that form, in tones no less final than Rose Mélie's own. The ways in which

Salvayre represents literature, in short, are continually vexed by equivocation and outright contradiction. On the one hand, reading and writing are essential activities allowing the subject a margin of creative freedom that he or she might not enjoy in other areas of his or her life. On the other hand, literature is often cast as a luxury, a supplement with regard to other activities, very largely constrained thereby and without any real performative value in the world. Provisionally at least, one must conclude that Salvayre voices positions with regard to literature that are unresolved, significantly conflictive, and undoubtedly in process—which may help to explain why she returns to that question, again and again, in her books.

It is when Lydie Salvayre lays the mask of fiction aside that we may hear her own voice most clearly. In that regard, two recent texts are exemplary. In *Le Vif du vivant*, her meditation upon Picasso's 1964 sketchbooks, Salvayre speaks to her reader directly, without the mediation of fictional character. For her, Picasso stands as the very incarnation of the artist, working alone and in opposition to power, insisting upon a superb and radical freedom, producing astonishing works with the least of his gestures. The fact that he is an anti-Franquist Spaniard, moreover, is by no means indifferent to her. Salvayre celebrates the way Picasso renders the human body in his erotic sketches, encouraging her reader not only to see, but also to *hear*: "Alone, as he orgasmically traces bodies that take their pleasure. For to have an orgasm is to triumph over death, and over the time which contains it. To come, *joder* in Spanish, a word brutal to the ear, a word that sounds pure and naked" (12). In the same perspective, she invokes Picasso's laugh, "a laugh of a free man, and his laugh consoles the world, which echoes it infinitely" (36). Her own voice resounds in bold tones, as she mocks Picasso's critics and their small-mindedness, castigates the "salaried aesthetes" who find the summit of lyricism in Georges Rouault (6), and decries a cultural nomenklatura which attempts to silence any voice that might put its own hegemony into question. What intrigues her most about Picasso is the way he courageously flaunts the voices that oppose him, and the example he offers as an artist in a society whose dominant ideology he rejects. If Picasso succeeds finally in making himself heard, according to Salvayre, it is because "he is life itself, and force, and excess" (24).

In *Contre*, we hear Salvayre's voice more immediately still, in both the figurative and the literal sense. Figuratively, since she has cleared away most of the devices such as plot, character, and narrative distance that tend to filter and muffle authorial voice, choosing instead to speak in the first person about a social and cultural reality that is, without a doubt, our own. Literally, since her printed text is complemented by a compact disc recording in which Salvayre herself performs the piece, accompanied by two guitars and a male voice. What may surprise readers and listeners—though perhaps it shouldn't be much of a surprise at all, upon reflection—is that Salvayre's voice in *Contre* confirms, and amplifies as it were, the authorial "whisperings" in her other works. Suavely ironic and muted in tone as *Contre* begins, rising progressively to the exhortative, strident pitch of its final moments, Salvayre's voice indicts the pernicious conventions and trite protocols that constrain us, in her view, in a society that wagers strategically upon the alienation of its members. We live in a society, she suggests, dominated by commercialism and consumerism; where the most harmonious music is the music of stock market quotations; where minorities and marginal figures—and most especially the poor—are systematically demonized; where household pets are treated with more consideration than the women who clean those households; where incarceration is generalized and education is viewed in the first instance as a system of control; where sex must be safe above all and people make love by email; where war is the only satisfactory diversion. Opiated by romance novels and "safe" literature; stoned on wine, cheese, and buttered croissants; lobotomized by antidepressants, mood elevators, and tranquilizers, we collaborate enthusiastically, she argues, in our own oppression and in that of others.

Clearly, Lydie Salvayre's is not an easy voice to listen to. And it is harder still in *Contre*, since she is speaking here more loudly, directly, and inevitably than in her previous works. Salvayre is a naysayer, of course, and naysayers are always troubling figures. Yet her message is nonetheless a fundamentally humanistic one. Like Diogenes, she is looking for "a man" (as she puts it on several occasions in *Contre*), that is, a person who has awakened from this cultural coma with some fundamental human values intact. According to her, that person must be prepared to act. As her title suggests, that action must be radically oppositional in nature, and vital, and forceful, and excessive, an incendiary gesture that begins by saying *no*—in a voice that demands to be heard, and will not be hushed.

Tanguy Viel's American Novel

THESE DAYS, IT takes a Frenchman to write a great American novel. Such is the wager that the narrator of Tanguy Viel's *La Disparition de Jim Sullivan* [Jim Sullivan's disappearance] (2013) stakes, in any case. Whether Viel himself is equally sanguine is another matter however, for he is an accomplished writer who has been practicing his craft for long enough to have shed his first illusions. During that time, he has authored a handful of well-made novels[1] that have earned him considerable critical acclaim.[2] Yet none of those texts has been gratified with the kind of popular success that his narrator so patently covets. That narrator is a novelist by trade, like Viel, and the fact that he remains anonymous throughout this text is surely not fortuitous. Having reached an age where one is tempted to cast a glance backward in order to take stock of things, he remarks:

> Recently, as I was thinking about the books I have read in the last few years, I realized that there were now more American novels in my library than French novels. For a long while, however, I read mostly French literature. For a long while, I myself wrote books that took place in France, with French stories and French characters. But during the last few years, it's true, I finally recognized that I had come to the end of something, that after all, my stories could take place somewhere else, for instance in America, for instance in a cabin on the shore of a big lake, or in a motel on Route 75—anywhere, as long as something began to *move* a bit. (9)

It should be noted that his dissatisfaction plays out along two principal vectors, his readerly life and his writerly life. In both of those vectors, the problem is bound up in the notion of *Frenchness*. His own country, as he sees it, is "too static, too petrified in a certain sense" (9). He himself is feeling stifled, and he experiences an intense "need to breathe" that only American novels can satisfy (9–10).

I mentioned that the narrator's anonymity is not fortuitous, and neither is the fact that he should be both French and a novelist. Clearly, Tanguy Viel is exploiting his narrator's resemblance to himself for effect here; but whether he is using him as an amanuensis, a stalking-horse, a ventriloquist's dummy, or a punching bag cannot be decided immediately and definitively. For the relations between author and narrator are constantly shifting in *La Disparition de Jim Sullivan*. Sometimes the suggestion is that they are simple and unproblematic, verging upon identity; at other times there is a great deal of distance between those two figures, and considerable irony generated in that distance. Like most features in a good novel (whether that novel be French or American) this question is significantly mobile—and it demands that we readers be mobile in turn.

The theme of mobility is very much at issue in the first pages of this text, as the narrator considers the prospect of moving from the provincialism of the French novel to the cosmopolitanism of the American novel. The latter, in his view, is fundamentally and inevitably internationalist in scope, even when its setting is narrowly local: "On that level, the Americans have a distinct edge on us. Even when they situate the action in Kentucky, in the middle of henhouses and cornfields, they manage to write an international novel" (10). For it is perhaps not so much a question of production as one of reception, and of commercial success. American novels are thus ones "that are translated into every language in the world and that are sold in every bookstore [. . .] novels that people buy in Paris as much as in New York.

It's something that I just can't understand" (10).

He intends that it should not escape him for much longer, though, because he has by now a fairly precise idea of how American novels are made. They are peopled by characters named "Dwayne" and "Lee" and "Jim," "Susan" and "Milly" and "Daisy." In general, those people are divorced, if not at the moment when their story begins, then shortly thereafter. Because adultery is rampant in American novels: "Adultery is a very important feature in the American novel. It's even an obsession in the American novel" (106). In the few moments when they're not committing adultery, those people drive Buicks and Dodges and Chryslers and Cadillacs and Pontiacs and Mercurys and Thunderbirds. They drink veritable tsunamis of Jack Daniel's (often while driving their Buicks and Dodges and Chryslers, etc.). They read Melville and Thoreau and Whitman and Emerson and Faulkner and Burroughs and Kerouac and Pynchon and DeLillo. Whatever other jobs those people may hold, there is always a university professor among them, the narrator has remarked (19). And indeed when he comes to write his own American novel, he will put on stage a professor of literature, that is to say, a figure so innately and compellingly fascinating as to galvanize the attention of even the most hardened reader.

Being American, these people are prone to violence. That is undoubtedly a cultural characteristic, rather than a natural one, for the society in which they live is saturated with violence at every level. Little wonder then that such a phenomenon should leave its trace on the American novel, and in fact the narrator has noted that two events are always mentioned therein: the Kennedy assassination and the events of September 11, 2001. In recent years (and whatever else the American novel may take as its subject) evocation of the latter event has been *de rigueur*, "because all of their American brains seem to have frozen on that day, forever, or at least long enough for the doctors in

Northville to have dramatically increased the doses of fluoxetine, naltrexone, and alprazolam that they prescribe" (98).

Presumably, those pharmacological therapies are intended to reduce the incidence of disagreeable flashbacks in Americans; yet that very technique is unavoidable in their novel, according to the narrator: "insofar as the American novel is concerned, it is impossible to avoid flashbacks, including flashbacks that serve no purpose" (25). With admirable thoroughness, he has assembled a catalogue of other effects always found in American novels. For example, they are extremely rich in detail, as if the very amplitude of detail could guarantee the authenticity of the stories they tell: "I have noticed that nobody writes an American novel without a very sharp sense of detail" (23). They present, moreover, sheer cascades of events, one after the other, in a heady and unending procession only mildly inflected by narrative teleology (24). Importantly, that procession must not result in any sort of resolution, and nor should we expect to find the answers to the questions that we may have been tempted to ask, because "in America the lines one sketches never loop back on themselves" (147). The final and most important feature of the American novel, at least insofar as the narrator of *La Disparition de Jim Sullivan* is concerned, is that people *disappear* in them. Though the case of Jim Sullivan is admittedly exceptional in this regard, granted that he disappeared before making any sort of *appearance* whatever.

If the narrator has such a clear sense of what the American novel involves, it is surely because he has read a great many of them. Yet it is not only because of that, I think. In addition to soaking up everything he can through his readings, by osmosis as it were, the narrator has also informed himself about America and its culture in a more programmatic and analytic manner. Having chosen to situate his own American novel in Detroit, he has carefully researched his subject, learning a great deal about that great city and its life. "For example," he remarks, "in

Detroit, according to what I read on the Internet, a person can perceive in his field of vision up to three thousand two hundred windows at the same time" (11). Such a datum speaks eloquently about Detroit's particular character, he senses—though he is by no means certain how to interpret it. "I have never understood what that means, three thousand two hundred windows at the same time, but, I tell myself, if I write something like that in my novel, people will understand that my characters live in a big, complex, international city, a city filled with promises and glass surfaces" (11–12).

That moment is an emblematic one, insofar as the narrator's novelistic technique is concerned. For what the narrator adduces as evidence of his research is a pure factoid. It may or may not be true; but even if it is true, it is only trivially true. He confesses that he doesn't understand it; nevertheless, he is determined to deploy it in his novel. Undoubtedly, his readers will fail to understand it, too. Yet understanding is perhaps less important to him than seduction. He finds this bit of information richly alluring, suggestive of a world far beyond his ken, and he trusts that his readers will, too. The vision of a sleek and virtually infinite reflective surface that it conjures comments pungently upon the way that the narrator himself views America, and upon the image of America that he will attempt to put on offer in his novel, too. For the passage deals with the act of *seeing*, after all. Each of the three thousand two hundred windows that a citizen of Detroit can see at any one time constitutes an opportunity to discover what the life of the city actually involves; but clearly that opportunity is wasted here—and it is very likely to be wasted in any novel the narrator writes, as well.

The other infinite reflective surface that this passage limns is of course the Internet. And the narrator makes no bones about the fact that the Internet is his principal source of documentation (if it is indeed not his only one). He has come to know Detroit from afar, at a distance, but he feels confident that the Internet mediates that distance reliably, and that his virtual experience of Detroit is as good as real. For example, he has consulted the many photos of a devastated Detroit "floating around the Internet," and has concluded that Detroit is a kind of modern Pompeii (14). It should be pointed out that this is another kind of *reading*, one that stands in a supplementary relation to the narrator's readings of American novels. In fact, he often refers to his research explicitly as reading, for instance when he remarks that Detroit has become one of the poorest and most dangerous cities in America, "I read" (13), or when he introduces the suburb of Sterling Heights, describing it as the sixth safest city in the United States, "judging from what I've read" (30). The narrator has read a great deal thus, that at least seems indisputable. But on the one hand reading is not quite the same as lived experience, and the narrator is sadly lacking in the latter. On the other hand, reading ought to be complemented by interpretation, yet the narrator very rarely sees the need to interpret anything at all, contenting himself with the accretion of fact and incident. His efforts to come to grips with Detroit on the Internet are not likely to lead him to real understanding, and nor are they likely to furnish the material for a successful American novel; he might just as well be gazing at those three thousand two hundred empty windows. In other terms, the narrator's comments in the early pages of *La Disparition de Jim Sullivan* put on stage a parable of reading and writing gone badly awry, a feature that Tanguy Viel exploits for darkly comic effect, in a dynamic that demands a firm hand lest it turn back upon its author.

All of this certainly tells us a great deal about the narrator himself, and about the way that he approaches his project. As he grapples with the idea of the American novel, he comes to recognize how very tenuous and hypothetical his own relation to that form actually is. Wondering how he might present a character with the pleasingly American name of Ralph Amberson, the narrator remarks, "If I were a real American novelist, I would certainly have taken a moment to describe Ralph Amberson's life in detail" (101). In order to paint a portrait of Ralph Amberson that will eventually be received by his readers as a convincing one however, the narrator must first imagine Ralph Amberson in a manner sufficient to convince himself. Yet for the time being at least the narrator's image of that character is not very fully fleshed, hinging as it does on one point only: "the way that I imagine Americans like Ralph Amberson is that they spend much of their lives asleep in the belly of a whale" (102). That whale's belly is the American Middle West, a site that exercises a great fascination upon the narrator as long as it remains in the realm of the virtual. For insofar as he thinks of it as a tangible site, it is a place he would never dream of visiting, even if the opportunity to do so actually presented itself: "If I were to visit the United States one day, I would certainly not go to the Middle West" (102).

Once again, it is a question of distance here, a distance that may be conceived both literally and figuratively. First and most obviously, the narrator has never visited America, and the literal distance separating him therefrom is one of the principal factors that vex his efforts to write an American novel. Yet another of those factors devolves surely upon the narrator's lack of imagination, upon his inability to *imagine* the other and to make it his own. In both instances, it should be noted, one can think of the narrator's problem as a failure to bridge a gap between himself and the object of his curiosity. More than anything else, it is that which accounts for his inability to understand. One passage is especially interesting in that regard. It occurs when Dwayne Koster, the protagonist of the American novel that the narrator wishes to write, turns to Lee Matthews, a shady dealer in dubious international art, seeking his advice and counsel. They retreat into Matthews's office, closing the door behind them, and there a deal is struck. But the narrator—or rather a hastily and transparently constructed character who stands in for him, "a man strangely alone [. . .] who was wandering in the store" (111–12)—can make out only a few words of their conversation: "Iraq," "dollars," "cargo," "Baltimore" (112). In other terms, the narrator is not privy to this conversation, he is situated at a *distance* from this particular event. Readers may recall other scenes like this one, scenes that call our attention to the limits of narratorial knowledge, either explicitly or more subtly, framing them as a question of distance.[3]

I remarked a moment ago that a variable distance characterizes the relation between Tanguy Viel and his narrator, and that Viel plays upon that variability for effect. In the first instance, that distance is considerable: unlike his narrator, Tanguy Viel has visited America; he is well aware that not all American males are named "Dwayne" and "Lee" and "Jim"; he may even suspect that in those moments when Americans are not reading Melville and Thoreau they might turn to Flaubert and Stendhal—or even to Jean Echenoz (in English translation, naturally). Yet there are other moments in *La Disparition de Jim Sullivan* that tempt the reader to imagine less distance between author and narrator. Some of them are carefully constructed by Viel, and accompanied by a wink, as it were. Thus, for example, when the narrator remarks, "I learned that there's a hockey team, even in Brest" (50), the reader may see therein a mildly metaleptic allusion to the novel immediately preceding this one in the author's oeuvre, *Paris-Brest* (2009), or the reader may recall the fact that Viel himself was born in Brest. Other moments suggesting the analogy of Viel and his narrator are perhaps marginally less intentional. One wonders, for instance, if Viel is any more aware than his narrator that Americans spell "motherfucker" as one word, rather than as two (34).

In the context of the very local questions I have been raising here, the figure of the narrator is more interesting than that of the author. Another interesting figure is the narratee, yet his interest resides principally in the way he illuminates the strategies that the narrator deploys in an effort to write his American novel. From the outset, it is clear that the narrator is addressing his tale to someone who is French, just like him. That is abundantly confirmed when he uses the first person plural in order to create a sense of complicity between himself and his narratee: "We in France, of course, think it bizarre to put a hockey team in a book" (49–50). That phenomenon is also apparent in passages where the field of reference of that *we* is broader and less precisely targeted: "we have a country that is twice the size of Montana in terms of hunting and fishing, and yet we can't seem to write international novels" (11). Other moments testify to the manner in which the narrator cultivates his narratee, coaxing him toward this interpretation or that, playing upon his natural curiosity or upon the preconceptions he imagines him to possess, in a process that Umberto Eco has called "constructing the reader."[4] The narrator uses a classic technique when he intimates to his narratee that the level of knowledge they share is vastly superior to that of the characters. For example, when Dwayne wonders whether he is being spied upon, the narrator remarks, "Dwayne thought about that impression and concluded it was false. And we've known for a long time that it's true" (132), flattering his narratee's vanity while at the same time reinforcing his own authority as purveyor of narrative truth. He is moreover careful to parcel out that truth little by little, rather than in full spate, for instance when he explains what a home run in baseball entails, or when he outlines the rules of the poker game known as Texas Hold'em (49, 53).

Notably, the narrator does everything he can to make his interlocutor feel at home in the very strange world that is America. The fact that he has chosen to locate his story in Detroit, rather than in Denver, Dallas, or Dogpatch, suggests his desire to attenuate the foreignness of this place for the benefit of his narratee, just a bit, for the city was of course founded by French explorers, and its name comes from the French word *détroit.* In the same perspective, when the narrator mentions the names "Cadillac" and "Pontiac" (13, 14), his gesture is not entirely innocent of performative intent. When he notes that in America, unlike in France, hosts take their guests on tours of their homes (48), he is careful to frame that custom as a bizarre cultural quirk, much as an anthropologist might if he were called upon to describe the sexual mores of headhunters in the Upper Amazon to an audience of French nuns. It is legitimate to see in that moment a wry inscription of the narrator's broader technique with regard to his narratee, and indeed that of Tanguy Viel with regard to his reader, as well. For in a real sense, both of them are taking their guests on a guided tour of their homes in passages such as this one, conforming to a practice that is indisputably American in character.

I do not mean to wallow in this recursive, metaliterary dimension of the text; I merely wish to recognize it for what it is, and to identify some of the tropes that subtend it. The *mise en abyme* is clearly chief among the latter, for we are constantly confronted with embedded inscriptions of the acts of writing and reading in this novel.[5] Particularly interesting are the moments when the narrator speaks directly about his project and the way he has chosen to pursue it, and I would like briefly to examine three kinds of moments like that. First and most plainly apparent are the passages where the narrator ponders the template offered by the American novel, and thinks about the figure of the American novelist. "I have thought long and hard about what an American novelist might have done with that, a dinner in the White America of Michigan," he remarks, adding, "I have thought quite a bit about the sort of pages he would have written, that American novelist" (47). Setting himself to his task, the narrator feels that he must *imitate* that American novelist as closely as he can, that he must perceive, reason, and write just like an American novelist would, in order to produce a convincing American novel: "I had to approach things just like an American novelist, I had to describe the cocktails in their glasses precisely, and every object in the kitchen, too" (47).

In some sense, then, the process is not a particularly complicated one, since the narrator has decided to follow a path that has been clearly blazed by a number of strong precursor figures with whom he is intimately familiar. Nevertheless, his confidence wavers from time to time, and he wonders aloud whether his technique is effective or not. Those are the second kinds of moments that intrigue me, and I shall offer just one of them by way of example. Having interrupted an account of the family history of his protagonist, Dwayne Koster, in order to note that any American novel worth its salt necessarily mentions the assassination of John F. Kennedy, the narrator continues, "He, Dwayne, if I can tell this story here, was watching television when his favorite program was interrupted in order to inform America that President Kennedy had just died, there, in Dallas, at noon, from a bullet to the head that had killed him instantly" (42). The phrase "if I can tell this story here" serves as a shifter, putting us on notice that we are moving from one discursive register to another. Yet at the same time it testifies to the way the narrator seeks his narratee's approval for the writerly technique he is using, and for the effect he is trying to achieve thereby. Moreover, he is hoping that his narratee will excuse this lapse in diegetic continuity, this *interruption*, by putting the very notion of interruption on stage and causing it to perform. In that fashion, he suggests that interruptions can occasionally be just as important as the stories they interrupt. Patently, this is a man who has read his Blanchot.[6]

The third and final example of metacommentary that I would like to put in evidence involves moments when the narrator alludes overtly and in explicit terms to his own hesitation with regard to his task. Once again, I shall invoke one such passage that seems to me exemplary of the many others one finds in the novel: "I have often hesitated, trying to determine how to order the events in the story, because of the different characters who figure in it, and thus the different narrative paths that would necessarily cross each other more or less, but which would obviously demand the reader's patience" (59). Many things are going on in this passage, to be sure, but the most interesting one is the way the narrator offers up his own hesitation to the narratee, trusting that the latter will interpret it not as a sign of the narrator's incompetence, but rather as a sign of his good faith. Once again, we're in the presence of a seduction technique here. Yet the blarney in which he engages masks a real difficulty on the narrator's part. For he is on foreign ground in his efforts to write an American novel, and despite the maps he has consulted, from time to time it is hard for him to see his way forward.

In those moments of hesitation, the narrator tends to look toward the notion of event, because if there is one solid and non-negotiable principle in the American novel, it is that something must *happen*. At strategic moments in the text, we find comforting reassurances that something will indeed happen. A case in point is the hockey stick in the trunk of Dwayne Koster's car. It is mentioned several times in the text, and it clearly serves as the equivalent of Chekhov's shotgun on the wall. Any reader who may have missed the importance of the hockey stick in the early pages will recognize its function unmistakably when the narrator remarks, "I told myself that it might come in handy" (68). Yet by the time Dwayne Koster actually puts it to use, against an agent of the FBI (140), it is almost beside the point. In other words, the shotgun on the wall does eventually go off, but it doesn't make much noise.

That seems to be a general principle in *La Disparition de Jim Sullivan*, and it can be traced in a couple of other instances as well. It is unavoidable, for example, in a dimension of the novel's thematics wherein Americans are described as virtual time bombs. In apparently offhanded manner, the narrator remarks of Dwayne Koster, "like many Americans, there's a dormant volcano in his brain—the kind of volcano that can erupt at any time" (50). In similar fashion, the epithet that he applies to Milly Hartway is "a bomb likely to explode" (58). The affair that Dwayne and Milly engage in is likewise explosive, at least insofar as Dwayne is concerned, for he experiences it, the narrator informs us, as a "bomb he held, as if it were strapped to his body" (64). Immediately thereafter the narrator assures us that the event we're waiting for is inevitable. "And of course it would," he says. "Of course, of the bombs that Susan and Dwayne held in their hands, it was his, Dwayne's, that would explode" (65), and he launches thus a countdown intended to keep us on the edge of our seat. All of this is very promising, of course. Yet those promises are very largely unfulfilled in the novel, for they lead to anticlimax rather than climax.

The phenomenon is so widespread and so systematic that it leads one to suspect that the principle of event is being deliberately subverted here, and along with it the textual isotopy that Roland Barthes identified as the hermeneutic code.[7] That effect is especially apparent in those moments of the novel where Jim Sullivan comes into view. The title of the text encourages us to believe that he will be a paramount figure in this tale. Moreover it puts the notion of mystery on offer in a pleasingly canny fashion, granted that *disparition* in French can mean either "disappearance" or "death." Critics have noted that Tanguy Viel's texts often borrow structural elements from the detective novel, and Viel himself has acknowledged the advantages which that genre provides.[8] Here however he plays with that set of conventions more dramatically than in his previous novels, organizing his play around the very spectral figure of Jim Sullivan; and that is the other instance of unfulfilled promise that I would like to examine.

The first time that we hear of him is when the narrator mentions that the only thing that comforts Dwayne Koster is listening to "his favorite Jim Sullivan" (17), with no other introduction, as if his were a household name. Jim Sullivan comes right out of the blue, then—and yet we have been waiting for his appearance since first setting eyes on the title of this novel. The narrator exploits the power of that title, mentioning that, "it was a pity that the whole world didn't listen to such a singer; and a pity, too, that Jim Sullivan had disappeared in such strange circumstances" (18). He stokes the hermeneutic code repeatedly and unabashedly, once again insisting on the title: "I don't know if the time has come to speak about that, but it's a fact that many things surrounding Jim Sullivan's disappearance, almost forty years ago in the New Mexican desert, are still mysterious" (18). As he brings those remarks to a close, he casually informs us that he himself is writing a novel entitled *La Disparition de Jim Sullivan*. It is a gesture familiar to us at least since Gide's *Les Faux-monnayeurs* [*The Counterfeiters*], but it is no less arresting in the present case.

In short, things are set up in a way that leads us to believe that Jim Sullivan and the mystery surrounding him will be absolutely central in the novel that bears his name—whether it be a question of Tanguy Viel's novel or that of the narrator. Yet things do not play out that way. We are told, as if grudgingly, that Jim Sullivan had set out for Nashville in 1975 and that he had been arrested in by the police in New Mexico, and subsequently released. "After that, we don't know. We do know that in that part of the country, more extraterrestrial phenomena are reported than anywhere else in the United States. And after all, it's America: we don't know what happened, his body was never found" (84). In other terms, Chekhov's shotgun has once again misfired, for there is no explosion of truth here, no resolution of the kind we might have anticipated, of the kind we have been *encouraged* to anticipate. Diehard, committed readers may infer that the focus of narrative significance has shifted in the course of this story from Jim Sullivan to Dwayne Koster, and they may look for resolution in the latter moments of Dwayne's story. Yet there they will realize that this particular serpent has bitten its own tail, as the narrator describes Dwayne driving into the west: "toward New Mexico, because it's amply clear by now that the reason for this book is Jim Sullivan" (148).

Well, *no*, one is tempted to reply, that is *not* the case. At best, his role is pretextual, rather than textual. Something else is afoot here, and one suspects that it involves literature itself, and its uses. Throughout this novel, literature is often called into question. One will recall that Dwayne Koster is—or *had been*, until recent events overtook him—a professor of literature. The literature that he professes is not just any literature moreover, but American literature; the genre in which he specializes is the novel; and the period that interests him is our own. Here is how the narrator sets the scene:

> What I immediately imagined, in Ann Arbor, was Dwayne Koster's large office, with books lining all the walls, with a view of the manicured lawns of the campus and the groups of students who came to sit in the lecture halls, dressed like Americans, with checked shirts and Converses on their feet, who after the course was over came to ask Dwayne questions about literature, because I haven't told you yet, but Dwayne taught literature. American literature, of course. He had even written a well-received dissertation dealing with the influence of *Moby Dick* on the contemporary novel, though I never developed that much, for fear of being boring. (20)

What better hero of an American novel might one imagine than this one, a professional critic of that form, one who works in a distinguished American university, who has labored to acquire a great deal of knowledge about American literature, who has distilled that knowledge in a thesis, and who dispenses that knowledge liberally to eager, attentive American students? And what better setting than this one to demonstrate the uses of literature? For in academia the value of literature is absolutely unquestioned, a matter of fundamental, unshakable faith. Such may not be the case outside of the academy however, as the narrator clearly recognizes. In the civilian world, literature—and more particularly the criticism of literature—must be approached with a great deal of circumspection, carefully bearing in mind that if literature has its uses, it also has its *abuses*. The narrator recognizes that there exists a threshold effect when discussing literature, and that beyond that threshold lies the worst nemesis of any storyteller, boredom.

It is far more prudent, undoubtedly, to speak of literature in general terms. One can safely point out, for instance, that literature provides those who embrace it with a source of cultural capital. Thus, Milly Hartway is described as "brazen enough to have a pierced navel, cultured enough to read novelists as sophisticated as Thomas Pynchon or Don DeLillo" (62–63). Thus too, the work of contemporary writers like Burroughs and Kerouac is "cooler than *Moby Dick*" (34). Yet there too it is wise to be circumspect in one's approach, for anyone frequenting literature in a manner especially close and sustained risks too much of a good thing. The narrator underscores that point on several occasions, and notably when he remarks that much of what Dwayne has learned about the world has come from his readings: "all of these things that Dwayne had read a thousand times in a thousand novels tired him a bit, he said, campfires and bears rummaging in trash bins, in novels, yes, it was a bit tiring" (80). He is tired, then, that much is clear. It is the American novel that has tired him out. One wonders moreover if the American novel, as a cultural form, is not a bit tired, too.

Perhaps that is one of the factors involved in the narrator's decision to write his own American novel. Yet just as the narrator has opted for prudence when discussing literature in general terms, so too has he chosen to be relatively guarded about his own literary project. Once again, it is useful to think of this matter in terms of space and *distance*. For the narrator behaves as if literature were somehow perilous, something to be kept at arm's length. From time to time, it's true, he offers brief glimpses of his novel, often accompanied by the epithet "I wrote." He begins the second chapter, for instance, by noting, "In Detroit, in 1805, I wrote, a huge fire devastated the city" (13); and further along he remarks, "In Romeo Street, I wrote in my novel, the only thing out of place, the only thing that would never be in its place according to Dwayne, was Alex Dennis" (44).[9] At other times when he speaks about his project, the terms that he uses are less precise. Invoking the murky dealings of the antiquarian Lee Matthews, the narrator mentions briefly how objects seem to find their way into his possession from the attics of Maine or South Carolina, or, more recently, from Kabul or Baghdad. For the benefit of anyone wishing more information on that subject, the narrator adds, "things that I have developed at length in my novel" (74).

Yet the narrator is also capable of pointing out certain things that he *did not* develop in his novel. Musing that Lee Matthews might have had an affair with Dwayne Koster's mother, and that in fact it might have been Matthews whom Dwayne had glimpsed in his mother's bed on the day of the Kennedy assassination, the narrator remarks, "ultimately, I didn't develop that. It remained a possibility, of course, but I didn't develop it" (71). We are squarely in the domain of the non-narrated here, and in that of possible worlds, too. More interesting than that, perhaps, is the way the passage comments upon the narrator's project and his own relation thereto. There is a moment further along that comments still more pungently upon that project, and in more explicit terms. Discussing how an FBI man labors to find his way in the increasingly baroque twists of Dwayne Koster's story, the narrator intimates that the task is by no means easy, for that story involves interests as various as those of General Motors, of the Republican Party, and even those of local politics in the state of Illinois, where a young man who would one day become the first African-American president of the United States was just beginning to make himself known (119). In yet another gesture of metanarrative, he adds:

> I didn't insist on that too much in my novel, because I didn't want to write a political thriller with complicated stories mixing real people and fictional characters, like American writers often do, it's true. After all, even if I was gazing toward America the whole time I worked, I nevertheless remained a French writer. And we French are not used to mixing real people with fictional characters. That's why I didn't mention Barack Obama's name in my novel. (120)

Among the features of this passage one might choose to remark (the way the FBI agent's hermeneutic efforts mirror our own, for instance, or what it has to say about the principle of literary hybridity, or about nation and culture), one consideration is abundantly clear and preeminent: the novel we are holding in our hands is *not* the one the narrator has written. We knew that, of course, theoretically, but a variety of effects have been deployed in this text in a campaign to distract us from that fact. Here, in a moment of brutal romantic irony, we are reminded that Tanguy Viel's *La Disparition de Jim Sullivan* and the narrator's *La Disparition de Jim Sullivan* are two different novels, the former taking its place in the phenomenal world, the latter a mere figment.

Across that ontological abyss however, the two novels comment upon each other and call each other into question incessantly. That dynamic is a virtual one, to be sure, but virtuality is after all fiction's most privileged discursive register. In a game of narrative misdirection, Tanguy Viel coaxes us away from the tangible novel toward a hypothetical novel whose obvious flaws encourage us to rethink the very idea of the novel.

In other words, what we have in *La Disparition de Jim Sullivan* is not so much a real American novel executed by a real French writer as the fiction of an American novel executed by a fictional French writer. Not an American novel, but an "American novel." And that fiction in turn serves to limn another kind of text, a purely notional one this time, imagined by a writer savvy enough to know that it is unwise to wager all of one's chips on the turn of a single card. Especially when the stakes are so high. For what is really at issue here is an "American novel" truly and finally worthy of the name—and heaven knows we "Americans" are just dying for a novel like that, these days.

Pierre Bayard's Wormholes

Pierre Bayard, a professor of literature at the University of Paris-VIII and a practicing psychoanalyst, occupies a rare position as a critic and a theorist, because he speaks to specialists and general readers alike. His recent work is trenchant, original, and deeply engaging. From *Qui a tué Roger Ackroyd?* [*Who Killed Roger Ackroyd? The Mystery Behind the Agatha Christie Mystery*] (1998) onward, Bayard's books have piqued the interest of readers well beyond the limited circle of those who habitually consume French criticism and literary theory, and have served thus to expand the horizon of possibility of critical writing in significant ways. One might attempt to explain that phenomenon in a variety of manners, focusing upon issues of style, of subject, of interpretive strategy, or of legibility and accessibility. Chief among the many things that may keep one coming back to Bayard, the stance that he takes with regard to his own work is particularly refreshing. He writes in a conditional, hypothetical mode, rather than a declarative one, keenly aware of how very mobile literary objects are, at their best. Bayard is not afraid to take risks, and he searches for new forms through a process of bold experimentation. He seeks moreover to enlist his reader in that quest, proposing a contract to him or her, one whose principal clauses are articulative and ludic. In short, in terms of mood and general approach, Bayard's books display clear affinities with a certain strain of contemporary fiction. For practical purposes, one might call the latter the *critical novel*, that is, a novel that puts its own principles of construction on display; a novel that is aware of its own literary heritage; a novel that thematizes its own structure; a novel that invites its readers to take a critical position with regard to the material that it presents.

The similarities that prevail between Pierre Bayard's essays and the contemporary critical novel are more than merely coincidental, I believe, for his work verges toward the novel in certain key ways. That such a phenomenon is largely intentional on Bayard's part is confirmed in a recent remark of his: "What I have tried to do in my books, and what I continue to dream about, is to shift one of the fundamental boundaries of writing, that is, the line separating theory and fiction" ("Comment j'ai fait régresser la critique" 34). Bayard's essays are more obviously narrative than most critical writing, and indeed he puts very considerable talents as a storyteller on offer in each of his books. Furthermore, just like the novel, Bayard's writing is animated by the technique of character. The protagonist in each case is a version of Bayard himself in a hermeneut's costume, and each text also elaborates a character loosely defined as the "reader" (a role the actual reader may choose to play as scripted, or not). Literary texts from Agatha Christie to Shakespeare to Conan Doyle themselves become characters under Bayard's pen, and take their place in a process of mutual interrogation whose fundamental nature may seem, even to a casual reader, patently fictional.

Working through Pierre Bayard's recent work, I would like to examine the phenomenon I have just described, in order to understand more clearly what may account for it and, more broadly speaking, what may be involved in the wagers it stakes. A good place to begin is with a consideration of Bayard's conception of fictional worlds, and of the way that we may come to satisfactory terms with the latter. In his view, imaginary worlds are incomplete, a feature that becomes glaringly obvious when they are compared to the referential world, as they inevitably must be. Developing that point in *Qui a tué Roger Ackroyd?*, Bayard insists that this incompletion is necessary and structural, rather than anecdotal:

> But most importantly *the world that the text produces is an incomplete world*, even if certain works propose worlds that are more complete than others. It would be more accurate to speak of *fragments of worlds*, constituted by pieces of characters and dialogues, where whole sections of reality are missing. It is essential to note that these gaps in the fictional world do not result from a lack of information that historical research might eventually hope to repair, but from a *structural flaw, that is, the fictional world does not suffer from a lost completeness, since it has never been complete.* Consequently, the text is illegible unless the reader gives it final form, for instance by imagining, consciously or unconsciously, innumerable details that are not directly provided. (127)

Two crucial—and related—issues are involved here. First, the problem of representation: any mimetic gesture is inevitably impoverished with regard to what it represents; no constructed artifact can compete with the plenitude and abundance of the real world. The second issue is bound up in what Gerald Prince calls "narrativity,"[1] and more precisely the relative degree of narrativity that a given text displays. Prince suggests that the latter textual feature "depends partly on the extent to which that narrative fulfills a receiver's desire by representing oriented temporal wholes [. . .] involving a conflict, consisting of discrete, specific, and positive situations and events, and meaningful in terms of a human(ized) project and world" (*Dictionary* 65). Thus, it might be claimed that Balzac or Tolstoy offers a higher degree of narrativity than does, say, Jean-Philippe Toussaint or Nicholson Baker.[2]

Yet the wild card here is undoubtedly the notion of "a receiver's desire." It is well nigh impossible to theorize in a cogent manner; nevertheless we are all aware that literary texts play upon readerly desire—upon *us* in fact, not to put too fine a point on it. Pierre Bayard, for his part, never loses sight of that truth, and indeed it is one of the cornerstones of the theoretical edifice he has constructed over the last several years. Thus, his insistence that the reader is called upon to address the incompletion of narrative by imagining certain things that the text has not furnished. Common narratological wisdom holds that one cannot ask what Achilles's name was when he hid among the women, because Homer doesn't provide that datum. Bayard would be tempted to ask that question nonetheless, I think, for at least two reasons. In the first instance, because readerly *desire* is, to his way of thinking, an integral part of the way texts work, and it must consequently be accounted for in some way. Secondly, he would be tempted to pose the question because the incompletion of fictional worlds might be marginally less radical and definitive than it seems on the surface.

I shall return to that latter point in a moment. For the time being, let me underscore Bayard's notion that a reader must *act* in some fashion when he or she is faced with the incompleteness of a fictional world. He returns to that activist model of reading again and again in his work, arguing that textual incompletion must be repaired, as if prosthetically, and characterizing that process as the first duty of criticism:

> A literary work is never complete, or rather it never constitutes a complete world, in the sense that our world, despite its imperfections, is complete. If the work borrows elements from already existing worlds, our own for instance, it does not construct a whole universe for us to see and live in; instead, it offers a series of fragmentary data which would not be adequate without our intervention. In characterizing that insufficient literary space, it would be more precise to speak of *pieces of worlds*.
>
> In that perspective, *the activities of reading and criticism are obliged to complete such a world.* (*Enquête sur Hamlet* 48)

It's a tall order, let us agree. Yet by the same token it is one that provides the reader with broad room for maneuver, enfranchising him or her significantly in the production of literary meaning. Philippe Lejeune once remarked about George Perec's work, "In each of his texts, there is a place for me, for me to do something. An invitation to a partner, an accomplice, I must take my turn" (*La Mémoire et l'oblique* 41); clearly enough, Bayard feels much the same way about literature in general. This interventionist model is one that Bayard deploys, in different ways, in each of his books. In *Qui a tué Roger Ackroyd?*, for instance, Bayard intervenes from his position in the real world—that is to say, as a reader of Agatha Christie's detective novel—to redress a judicial scandal in the fictional world. "If Dr. Sheppard turned out not to be the killer," he argues, "Hercule Poirot would have caused a miscarriage of justice, and, after him, everyone who accepted his solution without protest" (14–15). In order to make sense of Bayard's approach, it is important to realize that in his view the scandal of injustice is not limited to the fictional world where it first occurs; it ramifies in the real world too, by contagion as it were, through the mediation of "everyone who accepted his solution without protest." Thus it is not only the fictional world that must be set right, but the real world as well—and indeed perhaps especially.

This is a pattern that Bayard will follow in each of the books subsequent to *Qui a tué Roger Ackroyd?*, that interventionist gesture being either more obvious (*Comment améliorer les oeuvres ratées?*, *Enquête sur Hamlet*, *L'Affaire du chien des Baskerville*) or more subtle (*Peut-on appliquer la littérature à la psychanalyse?*, *Demain est écrit*, *Comment parler des livres que l'on n'a pas lus?*, *Le Plagiat par anticipation*) in any given instance. The aspect of his work that Bayard has called "detective criticism," and which includes to date *Qui a tué Roger Ackroyd?*, *Enquête sur Hamlet*, and *L'Affaire du chien des Baskerville*, puts the interventionist gesture on stage in an almost theatrical way; and indeed there is a strong dimension of performance in each of those texts.

They serve to exemplify Bayard's notion that readers have an important role to play in literature, one that is more ample than they may have suspected. More broadly speaking, they put into play the principles of an activist literary criticism, a position that Bayard occupies indefatigably, and which he defends with a great deal of vigor. In his detective criticism, that defense is mounted not only through showing, but also through telling:

> Indeed, that is the principal difference which distinguishes detective criticism, non only from other work based on inquiry, but from all of literary criticism: its *interventionism*. Whereas other approaches are content to comment upon texts passively, no matter what kind of scandals those texts may include, detective criticism intervenes actively, refusing to accept those scandals. It does not merely register the weaknesses of the texts and cast doubt on presumed killers, it dares to pursue its consequences to the end, as it seeks the real killers. (*L'Affaire du chien des Baskerville* 62–63)

Intervention is omnipresent and inescapable in Bayard's detective criticism, where it serves as both motive and outcome. Elsewhere in his work, he puts that same principle forward in other ways. In *Comment améliorer les oeuvres ratées?* [How can one make unsuccessful works better?] (2000), for example, Bayard invites his reader to imagine that the infelicities one may encounter in canonical literary works can be palliated or indeed remedied, that one can in effect *rewrite* those texts in strategic fashions. In *Peut-on appliquer la littérature à la psychanalyse?* [Can literature be applied to psychoanalysis?] (2004), he proposes his interventionist model in terms that have still vaster implications for literature and the ways we view it, when he argues that, "most of the time in literature we are faced with something that is theoretically incomplete, and whose richness springs from that very incompletion" (144). Once again, just as in the case of fictional worlds, Bayard invokes the idea of incompletion, but this time he situates it on a more abstract plane. Our readerly desire to address that incompletion on the theoretical level, as well as any material steps we may take in that direction, figure inevitably and centrally, for Bayard, in the dynamics of literature. Intervention and readerly activism are for him imperatives, and the cumulative force that they eventually assume in his writing is, more than anything else, moral in character—at least insofar as the first layer of Bayard's multiple irony is concerned. It is an astonishing stance for a literary critic; but it is also a most bracing one.

The vehicle of the interventionist model as Bayard sketches it is of course interpretation; and indeed each of Bayard's books, whatever other stories it may tell, is fundamentally a fable of interpretation. He conceives of interpretation in a highly idiosyncratic manner, as one might well expect. In *Qui a tué Roger Ackroyd?*, he speaks of "the delirium of interpretation" (15), offering the latter as one of the objects of investigation in that book. If interpretation for Bayard has a pathological aspect to it, flirting with hallucination, intoxication, and delusion, it is also—and by the same token, as it were—significantly unfettered, unbounded, and free to play over the field that it surveys. Most importantly perhaps, in terms of Bayard's own view of things, interpretation is an intensely personal phenomenon.

Bayard holds dear to that idea throughout his work, and he advances it on a variety of fronts, in a variety of voices, sometimes stridently polemical, sometimes more sober in tone. He is candid about the subjective quality of his own approach certainly, but his interpretive gesture is not the only one at issue. To Bayard's way of thinking, any interpretation is indelibly stamped by the consciousness that imagined it, and it must consequently be read as such. This leads him to propose a couple of reflections on reading that may be taken as axiomatic in his theory of literature. On the one hand, "Neutral reading does not exist"; on the other hand, "reading is no longer a matter of a *we*, but of an *I*" (*Peut-on appliquer la littérature à la psychanalyse?* 32, 172). In that fashion, Bayard sets the terms of reading and interpretation in a manner that will allow him to make a still more vertiginous leap of theoretical faith. If those activities are necessarily and fundamentally subjective ones, and if reading and interpretation are intimately bound up in what we call textuality, then it follows that textuality itself is necessarily colored by the subjectivity that apprehends it: "there is no literary text that is independent of the subjectivity of the reader" (*Qui a tué Roger Ackroyd?* 128).

Stretching a point predicated upon an expanded notion of what a "text" may be, many people will accept Bayard's thesis on commonsense grounds, as indeed they accept the idea that no reading is "neutral," that is to say, innocent of the subjectivity which produces it. But Bayard is not content to stop there in his brief for subjectivity. Having suggested that no literary text can exist altogether apart from the consciousness that grapples with it, he further contends that literary texts contain something of us, even prior to that encounter: "Now, *every literary work represents us unconsciously*, or, if you prefer, speaks essentially about us" (*Comment améliorer les oeuvres ratées?* 117). Indeed, as Bayard sees it, the critic's principal task is to ferret out and make explicit the manner in which the text represents the reading subject, through a process that is fundamentally introspective:

> For the founding principle of the idea of the interior paradigm is to think of the critical gesture as a *stroll through the work*, put into the service of a critic's reflection on himself. As spoken about by the work—reconfigured in function of his fantasies and personal language—, having become one of its characters, the critic may come to terms, above and beyond the forgotten textual object, with the major referent of his research: himself. (*Enquête sur Hamlet* 144–45)

In all of this, Bayard is playing on at least two fronts. Clearly enough, there is a substantial element of wryness, irony, and indeed self-mockery in the most extreme positions Bayard takes in his discussion of interpretive subjectivity. But at the same time, he is arguing quite seriously for a more unconstrained vision of the critical act, one that is not altogether innocent of the delirium of interpretation. He is unapologetic about the idiosyncratic character of his own readings, most obviously so in *Comment parler des livres que l'on n'a pas lus?* [*How to Talk About Books You Haven't Read*] (2007):

> Undoubtedly I might be accused, like an aesthete with gold-rimmed glasses, of speaking about books I haven't read, or of recounting incidents which, strictly speaking, do not occur in them. However, I don't believe that I have lied about them; rather, on every occasion I have articulated a subjective truth, describing with the greatest possible accuracy what I saw in them, faithful to myself, and remaining attentive to the moment and the circumstances in which I felt obliged to invoke them. (143–44)

I have argued that Bayard's books resemble novels in certain of their key aspects; yet Bayard himself sees them—and in fact any other critical gesture at all, insofar as it recognizes its own biases—as verging toward another literary genre, precisely by virtue of their subjectivity: "Thus criticism, breaking away from the work that constrained and handicapped it, finally comes to resemble the literary genre that puts the subject on stage most clearly, that is, autobiography" (*Comment parler des livres que l'on n'a pas lus?* 152). And thus we arrive where we suspected we might be headed all along, to a vision of text-as-pretext wherein the interpreting consciousness becomes the "fundamental object" of criticism; where introspection is what legitimates interpretation, and indeed elevates it "to the level of art"; and where any reading at all becomes an exercise in narcissism:

"the main thing is to speak of oneself, and not about books" (*Comment parler des livres que l'on n'a pas lus?* 152, 153, 154).

Let us recapitulate, then. According to Bayard, fictional worlds are incomplete, and we readers must intervene in them in order to palliate that incompletion. We do so through our interpretations. Those latter are necessarily subjective, constructed out of our readerly desire, and geared to making the text render up its truth about *us*. The question of the site of our intervention remains, however, and it is a most intriguing one. Even if we accept the interventionist model that Bayard proposes, and if we accept, too, the ego-driven nature of any intervention, we may still be at a loss to see how to get from the real world to a fictional one—and hopefully back again. In *Qui a tué Roger Ackroyd?* Bayard alludes tantalizingly to "the immense intermediate world between the world of the work and our own" (129), suggesting that readers habitually shy away from imagining such a world because conventional, rationalist reading contracts dissuade them from doing so. A couple of years later, in *Comment améliorer les oeuvres ratées?*, he postulates the existence of intertextual alleyways connecting different fictional worlds:

> It thus becomes clear, through these several examples, that secret passages exist between the most apparently distant texts, allowing one to cross from one to the other. In a sentence, in the corners of a novelistic structure, in the unexplained gesture of a character, lie openings that one may take to sneak into another work, or to import therefrom into the one where one is elements that might enrich it.
>
> No work, in such a light, is alone. As vast as it may be, it is merely a limited part of a still vaster whole, a simple piece lost in the immense world of universal texts. By virtue of that, the work is in multiple correspondence with many other hidden pieces, whose

> existence and whose means of access the attentive and rigorous critic must reveal. (160–61)

We might call these passages *wormholes*, for the sake of convenience. I borrow that term from the lexicon of science fiction, where it designates a kind of tunnel connecting different regions in the vast expanse of space/time—regions hitherto thought to be utterly separate—and enabling passage from one to another.

At a first glance, it would seem that the phenomenon which Bayard describes is limited to the mutual relations of fictional worlds. More closely considered however, it becomes clear that what he is talking about is precisely the kind of intermediary site that his interventionist model calls for. That is, when he invokes "passages" between texts allowing one to cross from one to the other, that vision is predicated upon another kind of migration, one more dramatic still, from the real world to the fictional one. That site of passage can likewise be thought of as a wormhole, connecting topologically as it does places notionally unconnected. It is in just such a perspective, furthermore, that the incompletion of fictional worlds can be imagined as less definitive than it seems, for to the degree that those worlds communicate with each other *and* with the referential world, actively and constantly through the agency of readers, the degree of their incompletion diminishes.

Bayard's vision is a powerful one, and powerfully invigorating of literary experience. Firmly based in a synchronic, Eliotic view of literature, it serves to amplify the notion of textuality in important ways, and to expand the boundaries of what we think of as a literary work. The incessant backing-and-forthing that it hypothesizes underscores the dynamic character of literature. Bayard's model coaxes production and reception into mutual articulation, such that each enriches the other. The franchise that it offers the reader is a truly exceptional one, it should be noted. Any reader willing to take Bayard at his word cannot fail to be moved as he or she surveys the newly configured horizon of readerly possibility that he describes. Imagine that one might actually inhabit a fictional world—however temporarily—and act in it, too. Imagine that one might pull Anna Karenina back from the train's path, or suggest to Pierre Menard that he read Cervantes. Imagine that one might bring about a meeting between Lancelot du Lac and Humbert Humbert. Imagine that one might prompt Oblomov to abandon his couch, Ahab his obsession with the white whale, or the Consul his drunken ways. Imagine that. . . .

There is one obstacle in the path of anyone who would take Bayard at his word, however, and that is the fact that, as he limns his wormholes, Bayard is patently—and indeed happily—wallowing in the delirium of interpretation. Consequently, those literalists among his readers will undoubtedly bridle just a bit when asked to accept his view of things. For the latter is principally intuitive rather than rational; and indeed intuition plays a key role for Bayard in any encounter with literature, be that encounter on the ground of production or on that of reception. In *Peut-on appliquer la littérature à la psychanalyse?*, for example, he speaks of writerly intuition, comparing it to endopsychic knowledge: "I mean a particular kind of intuition that Freud also ascribes to paranoiacs, primitive people, and superstitious people, and which affords to the people who possess it a direct access to phenomena which scientists may come to know only by long and roundabout research" (24). Here once again, we are in the presence of a wormhole, one that affords a "direct access" from one site to another one far removed. And once again, we are in full delirium, swept into an interpretive flood in full spate. In short, whether we recognize it or not, we ourselves have emigrated from one world to another, for the world that Bayard has created here—and which we now inhabit, largely unsuspecting—is clearly a fictional one. And those wormholes are the most characteristic figures of that fiction, as well as the surest guarantors of the very passage that they themselves enable.

Turning for the moment to an approach that is marginally more rationalist, one way to think about wormholes is through the notion of metalepsis. That trope is demonstrably and explicitly on Bayard's mind in *Demain est écrit* [Tomorrow is written] (2005), when he discusses Poe's tale, "The Oval Portrait." Pondering the relation between the death of a female character in that text and the fate of Poe's wife Virginia, Bayard remarks: "A strange murder, one might say by metalepsis, to borrow a narrative figure described at length by Gérard Genette, and which allows one to slip from one narrative level into another" (87).[3] What Bayard is adumbrating here is another sort of wormhole, one which allows the writer, or more properly an inhabitant of the writer's real world, to enter the fictional world of the tale.[4] Yet that sort of emigration is not the exclusive prerogative of people on the production side of things. Bayard makes it clear that people on the reception side of the literary dynamic are apt to emigrate in that fashion, as well. Certainly such is true of the critic, according to Bayard. Speaking of the way the critic slowly approaches the "object of his or her anxiety" in a reading, Bayard describes an uncanny moment: "Its exact locus in the text cannot be situated, and the critic can only rely upon what he feels: the sense that the words he is reading have become strange or, on the contrary, too familiar; the impression that it is no longer the other who is at issue, but himself; the presence of an unreal atmosphere, as if he were no longer on the usual side of the mirror, as if he had broken through the barrier of the page" (*Demain est écrit* 140). That crossing over to the other side of the mirror or through the page is clearly metaleptic in character, and it constitutes a key clause in the kind of reading contract that Pierre Bayard proposes.

It is useful to take a look at how Gérard Genette conceives

that trope—as indeed Bayard invites us to do—in order to understand what specific purposes it may serve for Bayard himself. Genette first invokes it in a passage of *Figures III* (1972) entitled "Metalepsis": "The passage from one narrative level to another can by effected only by the narration, in principle, an act that consists precisely of introducing into a given situation, through discourse, the knowledge of another situation. Any other kind of transit is, if not impossible, always transgressive" (243–44). The notion of transgression is very important indeed, and it will come to color, in one way or another, many other subsequent constructions of the trope. That feature becomes very clear indeed when Genette describes the way that metalepsis puts conventional—and even hallowed—boundaries into question: "All these games display by the intensity of their effects the importance of the boundary that they labor to cross, against all credibility, *and which is precisely narration (or representation) itself*, a mobile but sacred frontier between two worlds: the one where one tells and the one that is told" (245). Let us note in passing that Genette sees metalepsis as a kind of game, and thus, granted his particular worldview, as something a bit apart from real-world concerns. Finally, insofar as this initial formulation is concerned, Genette alludes to the way that metalepsis disturbs us by intimating that our readerly metaphysics are not quite as stable as we might have imagined: "The most troubling thing about metalepsis resides in this inacceptable yet insistent hypothesis which suggests that the extradiegetic is perhaps always already diegetic, and that the narrator and his or her narratees—that is to say, you and me—belong perhaps to some story" (245). The idea of transgression, along with the figures that attend it (unacceptability, marginality, illegitimacy, uncanniness, and so forth), is absolutely central in Genette's formulation of the trope of metalepsis; and try as he might, when he returns to that figure, he cannot shake it.

For he does return to metalepsis, thirty years after *Figures III*, and this time in a sustained manner, keynoting a colloquium organized around it,[5] and subsequently devoting an entire book to it.[6] It is thus legitimate to suppose that there is something about metalepsis which continues to fascinate Genette, something rather more compelling than what may be displayed in certain other figures to which he has turned his agile mind. In *Métalepse: De la figure à la fiction* (2004), Genette tries for all he is worth to restrain the trope, which threatens to ramify in disturbing ways: "I think it is reasonable to restrict the term *metalepsis* from now on to a manipulation [. . .] of the particular causal relation that links the author to the work, or more broadly the producer of a representation to that representation itself" (13-14). Restricting metalepsis in this fashion leaves the reader safely out of the picture, of course. Yet Genette continues to fret about the way that metalepsis, through its intrusive quality, can call the reader so dramatically into question: "This ability to intrude into diegesis, which the author uses as he or she wishes, can also be extended to the other inhabitant of the extradiegetic universe, the reader" (94). The most disquieting feature of all—and undoubtedly one of the reasons that the trope grips him so—is that, when Genette takes a step back from it, he sees metalepsis all around him, a fully integrated element of the landscape, rather than a marginal one:

> Actually, fiction is nourished and peopled throughout by elements taken from material or spiritual reality: Harpagon's avarice or Rastignac's ambition can only be identified as such through the idea of avarice or ambition that the author and his or her readership have constructed in contact with the real world—and with other dramatic or novelistic works. This perpetual and reciprocal transfusion of real diegesis to fictional diegesis, and from one fiction to another, is the very soul of fiction in general, and of each fiction in particular. Every fiction is created out of metalepses. And every

> reality, when it recognizes itself in a fiction, and when it recognizes a fiction in its own universe: "That man over there is a real Don Juan." (131)

It is in such a perspective that he returns to the trope, by now inevitably as it were, in *Bardadrac* [Tote bag] (2006) and then *Codicille* [Codicil] (2009). In the former, he takes the opportunity to adduce a few telling examples of the figure that he had hitherto neglected to mention (279); in the latter, he speaks of the transgressive quality of metalepsis once again, and more particularly about the way that it questions the distinction between dream and reality (176–80). Along the way, he offers an apology for his fascination with metalepsis, one based in his dawning awareness of the figure's omnipresence:

> It will perhaps be thought that I am making too much of, and bringing to bear too many things, or speaking too often and too long about, a simple figure of style or a funny twist of fiction. Yet our society happens to rely in large measure—and in fact more and more so—on the fascination that the passage from the pixelated image to lived reality exerts on everyone, or almost everyone, from the "seen on TV" to the "seen in real life," and vice versa of course. (*Codicille* 179)

There, in a nutshell, is how Genette's conception of metalepsis evolves. From a dangerously transgressive and fundamentally illegitimate figure, he comes to see it as one that enables a dynamic both interactive and reciprocal, a dynamic moreover that is intimately bound up in the fabric of our daily lives, for better or for worse. From the exceptional, metalepsis has itself migrated in Genette's poetics to a site that is far more normative—despite his lingering suspicion that there is something about it which is very disturbing indeed.

The notion that metalepsis is a transgressive figure is an exceptionally persistent one, however. Evidence of its stamina becomes apparent in almost every other effort to describe the trope. Gerald Prince speaks of its intrusive quality, for instance[7]; Sophie Rabau invokes the transgressive way that it abolishes discursive boundaries[8]; Klaus Meyer-Minnemann describes an effect of *bizarrerie* produced by metalepsis, as it plays among different orders of narrative space and time[9]; Jan Christoph Meister talks about the aporetic function of metalepsis, and the way it abolishes differences among ontological levels and communicative contracts[10]; John Pier speaks about the way metalepsis subverts normative narrative hierarchies[11]; Jean-Marie Schaeffer argues that metalepsis serves as a constant reminder of the divided mental state that fiction fosters—and indeed demands.[12]

Among all of these critics and theoreticians, Pierre Bayard is undoubtedly closest to Genette in the way he conceives of metalepsis. Or, more accurately, to the Genette who gradually came to view metalepsis as a phenomenon broadly distributed in the everyday world, and thus rather less anomalous than he had once imagined it to be. Yet Bayard's stance seems to me more radical than Genette's, insofar as his wormholes cannot be reduced to mere tropes. While the figure of metalepsis is undoubtedly involved in the way that Bayard conceives them, and while some of the gestures that they describe are certainly metaleptic in character, his wormholes are more complex than that, both in their conception and in the maneuvers that they enable. In fact, they are nothing less than the pathways of a fully integrationist vision of literature.

Though that vision is implicit in Pierre Bayard's work from *Qui a tué Roger Ackroyd?* onward, it is in *L'Affaire du chien des Baskerville* that he puts it explicitly and materially on offer. In the early pages of that book he argues a brief for the autonomy of fictional characters: "Contrary to popular belief, they are not mere paper figures, but living beings who lead an autonomous existence, sometimes going so far as to commit murder unbeknownst to the author" (18–19). Further along, Bayard invokes once again the idea of the incompletion of fictional worlds, noting that many of the details concerning the lives of characters are not communicated to us, leaving us thus largely in the dark about them:

> This uncertainty is related to an essential point that I will study a bit later, the particular mode of existence of literary characters, who, I am persuaded, are far more autonomous than we normally imagine, and who can consequently take certain initiatives, unbeknownst to the writer or the reader. This strong inclination toward autonomy on the part of the characters increases still more the incompleteness of the literary world by boosting its interior mobility, and it reinforces the difficulty of limiting it. (68)

In an effort to understand aspects of *The Hound of the Baskervilles* that have escaped previous critics, "often too rational" in his view (99), Bayard outlines his integrationist position, relying in the first instance on Thomas Pavel's *Fictional Worlds*. Therein, discussing different philosophical attitudes concerning the relations of real world and fictional ones, Pavel writes: "Some theoreticians promote a segregationist view of these relations, characterizing the content of fictional texts as pure imagination without truth value; their opponents adopt a tolerant, integrationist outlook, claiming that no genuine ontological difference can be found between fictional and nonfictional descriptions of the actual world" (11). Pavel's own position with regard to those opposing stances is a moderate, relativist, and rationalist one. "Texts, media, are not just referential paths leading to worlds," he asserts, "to read a text or to look at a painting means already to inhabit their worlds" (74); yet he uses the verb "inhabit" in a figural sense, rather than a literal one. In a similar perspective, he views the reader's participation in the events of fictional worlds as a heavily mediated form of psychological projection: "We are moved by the fate of fictional characters, since, as Kendall Walton argues, when caught up in a story, we participate in fictional happenings by projecting a fictional ego who attends the imaginary events as a kind of nonvoting member" (85). In short, Pavel tends more toward segregationism than toward integrationism.

Quite the opposite is true of Bayard, for whom fictional worlds and the real interpenetrate incessantly and as it were naturally, in view of the fact that both are very largely constructed—and by that I mean *imagined*—through language: "We must conclude that one cannot distinguish real people and imaginary characters through language, and that consequently the integration of those figures is inevitable, whether one be open-minded or not" (*L'Affaire du chien des Baskerville* 104).[13] Indeed, the position that Bayard stakes out is one that he describes—with a good deal of glee, one might note—as more radical and uncompromising still than that of mainstream integrationism:

> As you may have guessed, the author of these lines places himself without the least hesitation in the integrationist camp, and moreover in that part of the camp which is the most tolerant of and open to the special kind of existence that literary characters incarnate.
>
> I am tolerant toward fictional creatures for two principal reasons. The first is the conviction that there is a vast permeability between fiction and the real. It is thus useless to try to police the frontiers between those worlds, because many passages traverse them, in both directions. Not only, as we shall see, do we inhabit a fictional world for a certain length of time, but the inhabitants of that world come to live, from time to time, in our own.
>
> The second reason—which would not be approved, I fear, by integrationists, even the most open-minded ones—is my deep belief that literary characters enjoy a certain autonomy, both within the world that they inhabit and in their wanderings between that world and

> our own. Or if you prefer, that we (the author no more than the readers) do not completely control their acts and gestures. (106–07)

Stepping back from this heady and vertiginous position just for a moment, in an attempt to see it in perspective, it becomes clear that what Bayard is calling for is nothing other than an abolition of the boundaries we habitually postulate between fictional and real life. "In literature as in life," he writes at one point in *L'Affaire du chien des Baskerville* (63), and that phrase could well be taken as a motto for his theoretical enterprise as a whole.

Granted that, is it really so surprising that Pierre Bayard's books should resemble novels? That resemblance is quite obvious and deliberate in Bayard's detective criticism. Indeed, in those texts, there is something ostentatious about it, as if Bayard were challenging his reader in some fashion with his transgeneric play. "Devoted to the reading of a detective novel," says Bayard in the early pages of *Qui a tué Roger Ackroyd?*, "this book finds itself out of necessity adopting the form of a detective novel" (15). And in point of fact the rest of that text bears him out. It puts on stage a detective (Bayard), hot on the trail of a criminal (the individual who *really* killed Roger Ackroyd), intent also on proving a wronged man's innocence (Dr. Sheppard), and thus to correct a judicial error and make justice prevail. There is even an "explosion of truth" at the end, in the best tradition of the detective novel.

"'But our book is not merely a detective novel about a detective novel," warns Bayard. "It also has a second, more theoretical object that concerns delirium, and more particularly the delirium of interpretation" (15). It is precisely in this perspective, I think, that *Qui a tué Roger Ackroyd?* becomes a model for all of Bayard's books thereafter. That is, rather than the way it adopts so patently and neatly the form of a certain kind of novel, the real novelistic quality of Bayard's book is bound up in the way that it plays out a highly fictionalized drama of interpretation. It is difficult not to become engaged in that drama, but that's just the point, of course. Each of Bayard's books scripts a role the reader may play within the broader fiction that it describes. Bayard has every reason to anticipate that we will accept the contract he tenders, for he wagers heavily upon our readerly desire, and more precisely still upon our wish to make a difference in the fictional worlds that we may encounter. Encouraging us to put that wish into action, Bayard provides a space wherein the fiction of intervention subtly but ineluctably comes to the fore, and whatever else may have been at issue—the legacy of the Baskervilles; or how fictional events can seem to anticipate events in the real world; or the way we claim to possess certain books we have read, though we may have forgotten almost everything about them—recedes into the background while we migrate to another world, characters in a fiction whose principal stake is our own readerly experience.

More than anything else, that fluid and in a sense *unthinking* migration is what interests Bayard, and he has constructed his books quite deliberately in order to enable it. They are best read "flat out on one's bed," as Georges Perec said about *La Vie mode d'emploi* [*Life, A User's Manual*] ("Notes sur ce que je cherche" 10), that is, in a leisurely and even dreamy manner. That is how novels are best read, I would submit, if by "best" we can agree to mean "most pleasurable." I know that such an assertion will seem like heresy to many of my colleagues in the world of literary criticism. Nevertheless, I am persuaded of its fundamental truth—and all the more so after once again reading Pierre Bayard, who exhorts us so insistently to reconsider the way that we read fiction, and thereby, too, vitally and inevitably, the way that we read critical writing. For such is the curious role that Bayard scripts for us in the worlds that he imagines: we are constantly reading ourselves reading (and vice versa, as it were) when we inhabit those worlds, miles away from everything else, and at the same time squarely in the middle of things.

Notes

Marie NDiaye's Greening

[1] See Lydie Moudileno, "Délits, détours et affabulation: L'écriture de l'anathème dans *En famille* de Marie Ndiaye," especially 451.

[2] See Warren Motte, "Marie NDiaye's Sorcery," in *Fables of the Novel: French Fiction Since 1990*, especially 115-16.

[3] Marie-Claire Barnet speaks of "this special way she has of shaking up the rules of reading" (154).

[4] See Jordan 65: "Elusive, undecidable, ghostly: key epithets for characterizing Marie NDiaye's work. Whether it be the dull worry that stalks both characters and readers, and whose origin can never be clearly determined, or the subtle play between the real and the oneiric, or the extraordinary way her writing resists interpretation, all the while amassing a proliferation of mysteries that demand to be interpreted, this literary universe is created under the sign of opacity."

[5] See for instance Barnet, who characterizes it as a "hybrid diary" (157), and Jordan, who speaks of a "hybrid text [. . .]. Both album and personal diary" (75).

[6] Shirley Jordan points out that while the narrator of the text and Marie NDiaye seem to share certain traits—"both of them are writers; both are the mothers of small children at the moment of writing; both are married to a 'Jean-Yves' (NDiaye's husband is the writer Jean-Yves Cendrey, of course); both are the daughters of an African father and a French mother; both live on the banks of the Garonne"—the autobiographical pact in the text nonetheless remains "elusive" (75). Rather than an

autobiography, Jordan thinks of the text as a "ludic autofiction" (66).

[7] The woman standing next to the banana tree will eventually be named, but we shall see that NDiaye shrouds that process of nomination in a great deal of skepticism.

[8] "Feminine figures resemble each other more than superficially: they are the key to an unyielding mystery and myth, and they point toward the river, designated as feminine and greenish-brown, the Garonne, in the Gironde, so aptly named for an inquiry into the echoes of the feminine" (Barnet 158).

[9] "The network of 'women in green' to which the author/narrator belongs constitutes, as I have suggested, a second-order family, a chosen family, which guarantees, as she remarks, '[its] own originality' (AV, 77)" (Jordan 79).

[10] See Shirley Jordan, for example, who speaks of "NDiaye's panoply of generators of instability" (75).

[11] See See K. Ambroise Teko-Agbo's reading of the principle of alterity in NDiaye's *En famille*, especially 163: "Here is where Marie NDiaye's fiction stands out. She valorizes by revealing the problem of the strange and invites us to reflect on the place of the strange and the stranger in our societies. With what eyes do we look upon the stranger?"

[12] Roland Barthes defines the hermeneutic code as "the different (formal) terms, according to which a puzzle arises, comes into focus, defines itself, holds itself back, and finally unveils itself" (*S/Z* 26).

[13] See also Barnet 165: "Doesn't the literary universe of *Autoportrait en vert* propose a world at the edge of psychosis, very close to the utterly unreasonable?"

[14] See Jordan 68-69: "More radically, one detects in NDiaye the recurrent theme of a failure to see (one can't see clearly; one can't believe one's eyes) that confuses the protagonist, making her lose her bearings—and also the reader, who is trying to find his or her own bearings."

Jean Rolin's Explosion

[1] In *Le Dénouement*, Lionel Ruffel suggests that contemporary literature stages a ritual of mourning for modernity that involves a conscious transformation of inherited tradition (88-89).

[2] I have noted Jean Rolin's major works in my bibliography.

[3] Rolin mentions Sebald several times, invoking particularly the section of *The Rings of Saturn* that deals with Conrad and the Congo. See *L'Explosion de la durite* 105-06, 155, 171, 191.

[4] See *Loiterature* 9: "Loiterature distracts attention from what it's up to, and in that it's a bit like a street conjuror whose patter diverts us from what's really going on."

[5] See Montalbetti and Piégay-Gros 29: "Digression doesn't correspond to a real improvisation; rather, it is a feigned slippage in the discourse, one which tries to restitute to writing the freedom of manner that is proper to speech."

[6] See "The Critical Novel in France, Today" 50-53, and *Fiction Now* 10-12.

[7] Like his brother Olivier, Jean Rolin was an active member of the Gauche Prolétarienne, a militant Maoist group in the years immediately after May 1968.

[8] See Lionel Ruffel 103: "As one sees, if there exists a discourse that seeks to reduce the 20th century to nothing, many critical works and many novels agree on the necessity of inscribing themselves within history."

[9] See Bayard, *L'Affaire du chien des Baskerville* 114-15: "Thus, the hypothesis invoked previously is confirmed, to wit, that there exists, between fictional worlds and the 'real' world, an *intermediary world* proper to each, more or less invested depending on the subjects, and which exerts a function of transition between illusion and reality. This world is neither completely imaginary nor completely real, granted that figures from both universes mix and cohabitate therein."

[10] See Beaujour, "The Game of Poetics," especially 61-63.

[11] See for example 9, 25, 76, 104, 194.

Christine Montalbetti's Engaging Narrations

[1] Christine Montalbetti, *La Fiction* 225.

[2] See Genette 262: "To the orientation toward the narrator, to the desire to establish or maintain with him or her a contact, or even a dialogue (whether real, like in *La Maison Nucingen*, or fictive, like in *Tristram Shandy*) corresponds a function that recalls both the 'phatic function' (confirming contact) and the 'conative' function (acting on the addressee) that Jakobson defines. Rodgers calls these narrators, the Shandy types who are always facing their addressees, and often more interested in their relations with the latter than in the story itself, 'raconteurs.' Instead of that, we might call them 'talkers,' and perhaps we ought to call the function they tend to privilege the *communicative function*."

[3] See Warhol 816: "Every engaging address to 'you' simultaneously reminds the narratee (and the reader) that the story is only a fiction and encourages the reader to apply to nonfictional, real life the feelings the fiction may have inspired."

[4] *Maître de conférences* at the Université Paris VIII, Montalbetti is also a distinguished literary theorist, specializing in narratology. Her principal critical works are noted in my bibliography.

[5] In an interview in *L'Humanité* in 2002, Montalbetti remarks that she conceives her theoretical work and her practice of fiction as "two absolutely distinct activities," conceding that certain contradictions between the two may prevail ("Entretien").

[6] See Montalbetti, *La Fiction* 24: "The fact that I recognize a text as fictional implies a particular kind of reading, which contemporary poeticians, borrowing an expression from the English poet Coleridge, call 'willing suspension of disbelief.'"

[7] See for instance *Sa fable* 95: "I am seated [*assise*]"; or *Western* 139: "I am certain [*sûre*]."

[8] See *Sa fable* 63: "our Simon"; *L'Origine* 21: "Our man"; *Western* 10: "our thirty-something man"; *Expérience* 60: "our four birds"; or *Nouvelles* 75: "our two characters."

[9] On the hermeneutic code, see Barthes 25-27.

[10] In "Introduction à l'étude du narrataire," Gerald Prince calls these effects *surjustifications*, adding that "These always provide interesting details about the personality of a narratee, if often very indirectly; for, while they allay his resistance, conquer his prejudices, calm his fears, they reveal him" (185).

[11] See *Sa fable* 19: "But you know about that"; *L'Origine* 78: "let yourself be swept away in a vortex of vocabulary"; *Western* 26: "You know the tired pace of morning thoughts"; *Expérience* 26: "Have you ever noticed that sometimes nothing can be taken for granted"; *Nouvelles* 29: "You know how these things happen most of the time." See also Warhol 813: "Whereas a distancing narrator, such as Fielding's, often refers to 'the Reader' or 'my reader,' an engaging narrator, very much like an evangelical preacher, more frequently speaks to 'you.'"

[12] See also for example *Sa fable* 43: "go right ahead, Mister Hanz, come right in, because it's time for you to appear on the stage. Ding-dong."

[13] See Warhol 814: "an engaging narrator sometimes does imply imperfections in the narratee's ability to comprehend, or sympathize with, the contents of the text, even while expressing confidence that the narratee will rise to the challenge."

[14] On the way in which such anticipation of questions may illuminate the relations of narrator and narrateee, see Gerald Prince, "Introduction à l'étude du narrataire" 184, and Piwowarczyk 175.

[15] See Warhol 814: "Although engaging narrators tend to inscribe their narratees through overjustifying their own assertions, they usually do so in the spirit of sympathetically and earnestly attempting to convert the narratees to their own point of view."

[16] See also 29: "Digression doesn't correspond to a real

improvisation; instead, it's a feigned infelicity of discourse, which attempts to provide writing with the same appearance of freedom that characterizes speech."

[17] See 21: "The first function of digression is to create a diversion: constituting a pause in the story, it plays the double role of diversion and deferral technique."

[18] See *Loiterature* 8-9: "A reason I'm interested in loiterly literature, then, is that it has this characteristic of the trivial: It blurs categories, and in particular it blurs those of innocent pleasure taking and harmless relaxation and not-so-innocent 'intent'—a certain recalcitrance to the laws that maintain 'good order.' In so doing, it carries an implied social criticism. It casts serious doubt on the values good citizens hold dear—values like discipline, method, organization, rationality, productivity, and, above all, work—but it does so in the guise of innocent and. more particularly, insignificant or frivolous entertainment: a mere passing of the time in idle observations or witty remarks, now this, now that, like the philosopher pursuing his ideas as he sits daydreaming on his bench. Or like the poet mooching along, his idleness a contrast to the busy street, going to the bank and the bookstore, doing this, then that."

[19] See *Loiterature* 9: "Loiterature distracts attention from what it's up to, and in that it's a bit like a street conjuror whose patter diverts us from what's really going on."

[20] See Genette 264: "this 'auctorial' discourse, to borrow from German critics a term indicating both the presence of the author (real or fictional) and the sovereign authority of that presence in his work."

[21] See also, for example, *L'Origine* 30-31: "that could be the conceit of the novel, my hero killed by a bandit in the third chapter, with no flashbacks, after that we would go on to something else entirely, to the bandit's story for instance, or his mother's story, or any other story at all."

[22] See also *L'Origine* 47: "It's something I must explain, and I think that you'll quickly understand it if you look into your

own memories"; *Expérience* 70: "You continue in that same vein, you yourself have memories of the farm"; and *Nouvelles* 42: "You yourself have a few memories of aquariums."

[23] See *Narrative as Theme* 30: "I am thinking of all of the frontal and lateral ellipses found in narrative and either explicitly underlined by the narrator [. . .] or inferable from a significant lacuna in the chronology or through a retrospective filling-in."

[24] See Warhol 813: "Engaging narrators [. . .] usually assume that their narratees are in perfect sympathy with them."

Antoine Volodine's Crossings

[1] I am not the only critic to be so embarrassed. Frédéric Briot, for example, imagines Volodine's first seven novels together, as a "vast field of ruins" ("Les Chimères" 206); Jean-Louis Hippolyte calls Volodine's first Minuit book, *Lisbonne dernière marge*, "as postexotic as the previous ones" (*Fuzzy Fiction* 169); and Anne Roche comes to a startling conclusion about *Biographie comparée de Jorian Murgrave* and *Dondog*: "Looking at them together, one realizes a striking fact: they are the same" ("Clarity" 54).

[2] See Hippolyte 168: "Reluctant to have his novels bowdlerized into normality under a 'safe' label (sci-fi, space opera, *le fantastique*, horror, fantasy), Volodine coined the term *fantastique post-exotique*, which in time simply became *post-exotisme*. Like *shaggås* and *romånces*, postexoticism was—at first—a dead sign that pointed to his ideological heterogeneity and aesthetic fractiousness. Of course this alien and idiosyncratic terminology only added to the preexisting ontological malaise. Critics were unsatisfied, and while the quarrel was forgotten, it was never settled."

[3] On the notion of indeterminacy, see Hippolyte 149: "every facet of the Volodinian text actively incorporates some degree of vagueness."

[4] See Jean-Didier Wagneur: "Volodine has erected a pluricultural universe where myths and epics take part in the most archaic forms of world literature" ("Introduction" 9).

[5] Volodine imagines these figures as absolutely essential ones:

"The entire post-exotic novelistic edifice is conceived, constructed, and told by men and women exiled from the world until their death, whereas before their exile they did whatever they could to change the world radically" ("On recommence" 255). Pascale Casanova, for her part, describes the metanarrator as "a pure poet of subversion" ("A Fragmentary History" 46).

[6] See Marie-Pascale Huglo: "The narrative voice makes disparate accounts consonant without losing its capacity for circulation and metamorphosis. It brings about the passage between times, spaces, and consciousnesses, without ceasing to pass" ("The Post-Exotic Connection" 102-03).

[7] See Frédéric Briot: "In Volodine, the story is that people are telling stories, in every sense of the word, with a savory principle of uncertainty and incompleteness" ("Les Chimères d'Antoine Volodine" 209).

[8] See Mélanie Lamarre: "Antoine Volodine's novels multiply mise-en-abymes of literary production and reception" ("Ici Breughel" 151).

[9] See Volodine's remark to Jean-Didier Wagneur: "The traditional lovers of post-exoticism are separated by prison, by war, or by eternity; and they meet in dreams" ("On recommence" 246).

[10] "Those are crazy people's dreams," Maleeya comments, when Mevlido asks her what she thinks of his dreams (28).

[11] See Jean-Louis Hippolyte: "Both the prison and the psychiatric ward function as coercive spaces where narrating only occurs under the ominous gaze of others, at their prompting, because and despite of them" (*Fuzzy Fiction* 184).

[12] "A total institution may be described as a place of residence and work where a large number of like-situated individuals, cut off from the wider society for an appreciable period of time, together lead an enclosed, formally administered round of life. Prisons serve as a clear example, providing we appreciate that what is prison-like about prisons is found in institutions whose members have broken no laws" (*Asylums* xiii). See also *Asylums* 3-12.

[13] See Anne Roche: "The catastrophe has always already happened, before the first page of the book. The revolution, the revolutions, have failed" ("The Clarity of Secrets" 54).

[14] "In spite of the global revolution," remarks Deeplane, "they have sunk to a level of barbarity that astonishes even the specialists. It has become an unfathomable species. They have undergone several wars of extermination, but even now a new conflict is approaching. The population has been reduced a hundredfold, and perhaps more. Whole continents are currently uninhabitable. Those who have survived are socially organized, but no longer believe either in themselves or in society. They have inherited political systems whose meanings are forgotten; for them, ideology is a senseless prayer. The ruling classes have been gangsterized, the poor obey. People behave as if they were already dead, and as if moreover they didn't give a damn about that" (199-200).

[15] See 390: "Mevlido's fate had mimicked that of the global revolution, fraught with bad choices, stupid crimes, psychotic distortions, monstrous stagnations and treachery."

[16] Anne Roche points out that in Volodine's world, "death is not immediate, and is multiple" ("The Clarity of Secrets" 56).

[17] "For forty years, you train for reincarnation and travel" (224).

Marie Cosnay's Roman-Fleuve

[1] See *Introduction à l'étude des textes* 138: "Now, in practice, precisely, in the process of reading, the text is not a static object that you can perceive in one glance; instead it's a parade of utterances whose boundaries are fluid, the continuous passing, in variable rhythms, with sometimes random pauses, of a series of objects that incessantly overlap. There is a dynamic in that process, and it is that of reading."

[2] See "L'Interruption: Comme sur une surface de Riemann," in *L'Entretien infini*, and especially this crucial insight: "Interruption is necessary to any sequence of words;

intermittency enables becoming; discontinuity enables continuity of understanding" (107).

[3] See for example "Concerning Marthe Arnaud, it was said that she squatted down in art galleries, shouting out loud" (27); "Marthe was enthusiastic. She squatted down, shocked gallery owners" (33); "I didn't know what to do with Marthe, she was enthusiastic, childish, squatting, painful, combative" (46); "Maybe Marthe laid down, squatted down" (63).

[4] See *L'Ecriture du désastre* 10: "Disaster is on the side of forgetting; forgetting without memory, the unmoving withdrawal of something that hasn't been traced—the immemorial perhaps; remembering through forgetting, once again the outside."

[5] For a typology of mirror scenes in literature, see Motte, *Mirror Gazing*.

[6] In Beckett, *Disjecta* 133-37."

[7] See for instance "La Peinture des van Velde ou le Monde et le Pantalon" (*Disjecta* 118-32), "Three Dialogues (*Disjecta* 138-45, especially 142-45), "Bram van Velde" (*Disjecta* 151), and "Geer van Velde" (*Disjecta* 117).

[8] The passage that Cosnay quotes appears in "Peintres de l'empêchement," *Disjecta* 136.

[9] Cosnay borrows that passage, once again, from "Peintres de l'empêchement," *Disjecta* 136.

[10] The catalogue of the Bibliothèque Nationale de France gives that title as *Manière de blanc*, with both substantives in the singular.

[11] See also *Villa Chagrin* 55: "She's got a manuscript under her arm. She arrives in Paris. End of the second period. She falls under a car, so blind has she become. She dies."

[12] See Blanchot, *L'Ecriture du désastre* 98: "Fragmentary writing would be risk itself. It isn't based in any theory, it doesn't give rise to any practice that might be defined by *interruption*. Interrupted, it proceeds."

[13] See for example "November 1, I'm sick, with frightening dreams of separation, then victory which, finally, encourage me.

The precise question concerns the better quality, the surer certainty of things we don't see" (9); "The body's sap is no longer, Ovid would say. The image remains to be taken from that, the lines to be seen behind what we don't see" (38); and "On each of Marthe's letters, Bram sketches what we don't see" (73).

[14] See *La Chambre claire* 135: "Any photograph is a certificate of presence. That certificate is the new gene that its invention has grafted onto the family of images."

Patrick Deville's Novelty

[1] See for instance Fieke Schoots, "*Passer en douce à la douane*": *L'écriture minimaliste de Minuit*; Pierre Hyppolite, "Hyperréalisme et représentation minimaliste dans *La Femme parfaite* de Patrick Deville"; Sophie Bertho, "L'Attente postmoderne: A propos de la littérature contemporaine en France"; and William Cloonan, "Homage to Jérôme Lindon: The Novel in 2001."

[2] After this essay was written, the Editions du Seuil brought out an omnibus volume entitled *Sic transit*, in which those three texts are grouped as a trilogy, with a French translation of this essay as an afterword.

[3] For another discussion of *Kampuchéa*, see Pierre Schoentjes, "Les 'beaux hasards' de Patrick Deville: *Kampuchéa* et la terreur," forthcoming in *Carnets de Chaminadour*.

[4] Strictly speaking, it is the narrator who addresses us in *Kampuchéa*, but in light of Deville's efforts to erase the distinction between author and narrator, and for simplicity's sake, I shall say "Deville" from here onward.

[5] See Jean-François Hamel's discussion of the politics of Deville's *Pura Vida* and *La Tentation des armes à feu*, in "Le Pistolet *passé* sous la ceinture."

[6] See his remarks in "La Fabrique du héros" 22: "I found the form of the book in the very first draft, in 1999; it consisted in taking two newspapers published a week apart in two border

capitals, and using the play of the two newspapers, *Diario* and *Tiempo*, to write about the two consecutive Fridays that the narrator spends in Managua (Nicaragua) and then in Tegucigalpa (Honduras)." See also "Plus formaliste peut-être que minimaliste. . ." 326-27: "I shall nonetheless say a few words about the very long project that I mentioned. . . . It is based in the reading of two daily newspapers published on two consecutive Fridays. I read those newspapers from first page to last, including the classified ads, the supplements, etc. And I tried to trace each article, each advertisement, and so forth, as far back as possible."

[7] See for example 52: "One might regret that the executioner Ta Mok lacked Coppola's talent, hadn't seen *Apocalypse Now*, nor read Conrad"; and 77: "But it's Coppola who collects them all in a deadly bouquet, in his Colonel Walter Kurtz, who collects Conrad's hero and Marie Ier and Pol Pot in the very image of horror and madness."

[8] *La Voie royale* 16, *Kampuchéa* 118.

[9] On page 158 of *Kampuchéa* Deville remarks, "I told him I had written the account of a train trip between Baku and Tbilisi," an account that figures prominently in *La Tentation des armes à feu*.

[10] Deville clearly recognizes that trait. See for example "Plus formaliste" 323-24: "Anything can be called a *novel*, even if nothing is utterly made up therein. The very act of inventing a narrator already makes the text a novel. The major literary exercise, except writing poetry, is always called—and its pretty logical—a *novel*. There exists no definition of it. *Novel* means that it's a literary text."

[11] See Fieke Schoots 92: "*Le Feu d'artifice* is a novel about the writing of a novel, about its construction and representation. It's a novel that speaks, both in its diegetic dimension and on the thematic and stylistic level, about the search for order, and at the same time about the subversion of all order."

Gérard Gavarry's Ceremony

[1] Gérard Gavarry's major works include *La Barbacane* (1968, with Michel Bézard), *Jojo* (1982 and 1993), *Le Genre des dames* (1984), *La Ville de Paris* (1987), *Quarantaine* (1990), *Allada* (1993), *Hop là! un deux trois* [*Hoppla! 1 2 3*] (2001), *Façon d'un roman, ou Comment d'après le Livre de Judith j'ai inventé une histoire de banlieue, et à l'aide du cocotier, du cargo, du Centaure, écrit trois fois* Hop là! [*Making a Novel, Or How, Following the Book of Judith, I Devised a Story of the Suburbs, and with the Help of the Coconut Palm, Cargo Ship, and Centaur, Thrice Wrote* Hoppla!] (2003), *Eros acharné* (2007), and *Expérience d'Edward Lee, Versailles* (2009).

[2] Sustained considerations of Gavarry's work may be found in Harri Veivo, "Strange Things on the Edge of the City"; and in Warren Motte, "Gérard Gavarry's Hops" and "Reading Gérard Gavarry."

[3] See Barthes, *S/Z*, especially 25-27.

[4] See *Façon d'un roman* 13-14: "The triptych, with its three panels, satisfied my old desire to marry the principle of variation to that of complementarity. I had a model for that, in a volume of the Adventures of Tintin. One may recall the three parchments of *The Secret of the Unicorn*, and how they must be superimposed against the light in order finally to read the complete message that reveals where the treasure of the pirate Rackham the Red is to be found. That structure suited me—not very different from that of the four Christian Gospels, moreover related to the tales of oral tradition and to all myths, where several versions succeed each other from age to age or coexist simultaneously, at once confirming each other, completing each other, and competing with each other."

[5] For a discussion of the way that idea takes shape in the rest of Bayard's writing, see Motte, "Pierre Bayard's Wormholes."

[6] Gavarry remarks, "Of the thirteen portraits that comprise the series as Rudolf Schäfer conceived it, the *Journal Littéraire*

published nine, including three full-page portraits of a man, a woman, and a young boy." It is tempting to presume that these photos are the same ones that Schäfer published in book form in *Der Ewige Schlaf: Visages de Mort* (1989).

[7] See for example the passage where the Director, having until then only seen the photographs upside down, commands the apprentice to give him the magazine. "This time how will he react?" asks Gavarry (47), playing upon our readerly curiosity.

Lydie Salvayre's Voices

[1] See Ann Smock's interesting discussion of Blanchot's argument, in *What Is There to Say?*, 114-18.

[2] Lydie Salvayre earned her medical degree at the University of Toulouse, and practiced psychiatry, first in Marseille, then in the near suburbs of Paris, until her recent retirement.

[3] See *Fictions of Authority* 18-19: "I use the term *personal voice* to refer to narrators who are self-consciously telling their own histories. I do not intend this term to designate all 'homodiegetic' or 'first-person' narratives—that is, all those in which the voice that speaks is a participant in the fictional world—but only those Genette calls 'autodiegetic,' in which the 'I' who tells the story is also the story's protagonist (or an older version of the protagonist)."

[4] *La Declaration*, *La Vie commune*, *La Puissance des mouches*, *La Compagnie des spectres*, *Quelques Conseils utiles aux élèves huissiers*, and *La Conférence de Cintegabelle* are all structured as monologues, voiced by what Gérard Genette calls an intradiegetic-homodiegetic narrator, that is, a character who tells his or her own story. In *Le Vif du vivant* and *Contre*, Salvayre seems to speak to us in her own voice—and likewise monologically. The exceptions to the monological rule are *La Médaille*, where many voices are heard, sometimes mediated by a narrator; *Les Belles Ames*, narrated by a figure who is not one of the characters; and three of the briefer texts in *Et que les vers mangent le boeuf mort*,

"Famille I," "Tanguer," and "Famille II."

[5] See for example *Les Belles Ames* 16: "Immediately upon seeing her, the guide feels an immense tenderness for her. And me too, I feel right away that same tenderness."

[6] Salvayre's parents were both Republican militants; her mother was an Anarchist, her father a Communist. They arrived in France as refugees in 1939.

Tanguy Viel's American Novel

[1] Tanguy Viel's previous novels include *Le Black Note* (1998), *Cinéma* (1999), *L'Absolue Perfection du crime* (2001), *Insoupçonnable* [Above suspicion] (2006), and *Paris-Brest* (2009).

[2] Sjef Houppermans, for instance, praises Viel as a "precious writer," and mentions that "he has published a small number of highly refined texts" (37). Ari Blatt sketches his career in this manner: "For the past decade Tanguy Viel has been crafting stories indebted in various ways to the classic thriller genre. His novels, rife with murderous machinations, dubious get-rich-quick schemes, ornery gangsters, and climactic double crosses, pay tribute to past and present masters, from the tales of Agatha Christie and Patricia Highsmith to the films of Alfred Hitchcock, Martin Scorcese, and Brian De Palma" ("Manic Fictions" 373). See also Blatt's discussion of recycling and reinvention in Viel's *Cinéma* ("Remake" 379).

[3] Think, for example, of the moments in *Eugénie Grandet* when Grandet *père* goes into his counting house, escaping completely from the narrator's gaze, a gaze that is otherwise all-encompassing and omniscient. See *Eugénie Grandet* 67-68: "Nobody, not even Madame Grandet, was allowed to enter, the man wanted to remain alone there like an alchemist at his kiln. There, undoubtedly, some hiding place had been artfully crafted, there were stored the property deeds, the scales to weigh the gold coins, there every night the bills, the receipts, and the balances were calculated"; and 166: "Early each morning, he had himself

pushed from his bedroom to the door of his den, undoubtedly full of gold."

[4] See *Postscript to* The Name of the Rose, especially 47-53.

[5] Frank Wagner has remarked that "Viel's work embeds it own (explicit or implicit) commentary in its very own fabric, presenting thus a very pronounced *metatextual* dimension" (218).

[6] See Maurice Blanchot's "L'Interruption: Comme sur une surface de Riemann," in *L'Entretien infini* 106-12, especially 107: "Interruption is necessary to any sequence of words; intermittency enables becoming; discontinuity enables continuity of understanding."

[7] See *S/Z* 26: "The hermeneutic code's inventory consists in distinguishing the different (formal) terms according to which a puzzle comes into focus, declares itself, formulates itself, defers itself, and finally divulges itself."

[8] See his conversation with Roger-Michel Allemand, especially 302-03.

[9] For other examples of the same phenomenon, see 61, 69, 70, 74, 80, 122, 135.

Pierre Bayard's Wormholes

[1] Prince defines that term as "The set of properties characterizing narrative and distinguishing it from nonnarrative; the formal and contextual features making a (narrative) text more or less narrative, as it were" (Dictionary 65).

[2] See Bayard, *L'Affaire du chien des Baskerville* 67: "And, especially, the world that the literary text produces is an incomplete world, even if certain works propose world that are more complete than others."

[3] See also *Demain est écrit* 87: "A famous example of metalepsis occurs in Woody Allen's *The Purple Rose of Cairo*, when the actor in a film, observing a seductive spectator during the projection, steps out of the screen to meet her."

[4] "The same thing happens to Poe's Virginia and to his

painter's Virginia: they migrate from the artist's life into his work, a crossing that transfigures them aesthetically, but at the same time condemns them to death" (*Demain est écrit* 87).

[5] That meeting, entitled "Metalepsis, Today," was held at the Institut Goethe de Paris in November 2002. The proceedings appear in John Pier and Jean-Marie Schaeffer, eds., *Métalepses: Entorses au pacte de la représentation.*

[6] *Métalepse: De la figure à la fiction* (2004) expands considerably upon Genette's contribution to the 2002 colloquium, "De la figure à la fiction."

[7] See his definition of the term "metalepsis" in *A Dictionary of Narratology*: "The intrusion into one diegesis (diégèse) of a being from another diegesis; the mingling of two distinct diegetic levels. Should an extradiegetic narrator suddenly enter the world of the situations and events recounted, for instance, a metalepsis obtains" (50-51). Elsewhere, he suggests that metalepsis involves "contamination" ("Disturbing Frames" 626).

[8] "Constructing a world wherein author, characters, and readers rub elbows and speak to each other would amount in other terms to imagining a kind of utopia which would push the process of interpretation of any literary text to its extreme limit" ("Ulysse à côté d'Homère: Interprétation et transgression des frontières énonciatives" 61).

[9] See "Un procédé narratif qui 'produit un effet de bizarrerie': La métalepse littéraire," especially 135.

[10] See "Le *Metalepticon*: Une étude informatique de la métalepse," particularly 232.

[11] See "Métalepse et hiérarchies narratives" 248: "metalepsis, through the permutations and substitutions that it puts into play, weakens distinctions, implicitly or explicitly opening up a space or a site of negotiation between levels, and voicing thereby the intrinsically paradoxical character of narrative representation."

[12] Invoking the transgressive aspect of metalepsis, he argues: "this transgression, far from being an anomaly, is merely a particularly explicit illustration of that which constitutes the central definitional trait of fictional immersion, that is, the manner in which it implies a divided mental state" ("Métalepse et immersion fictionnelle" 325).

[13] See also *L'Affaire du chien des Baskerville* 105: "language is a permanent factor in the interference of worlds."

Bibliography

Allemand, Roger-Michel. "Tanguy Viel: Imaginaires d'un romancier." *Analyses* 3.3 (2008): 297-314

Asibong, Andrew, and Shirley Jordan. "Rencontre avec Marie NDiaye." *Revue des Sciences Humaines* 293 (2009): 187-99.

Balzac, Honoré de. *Eugenie Grandet.* Paris: Garnier-Flammarion, 1964.

Barnet, Marie-Claire. "Déroute d'un *Autoportrait en vert* (mère): Vers l'errance de Marie NDiaye." *Revue des Sciences Humaines* 293 (2009): 153-70.

Barthes, Roland. *La Chambre Claire: Note sur la photographie.* Paris: Gallimard/Seuil, 1980.

---. *S/Z.* Paris: Le Seuil, 1970.

Bassman, Lutz. *Les aigles puent.* Lagrasse: Verdier, 2010.

---. *Avec les moines-soldats.* Lagrasse: Verdier, 2008.

---. *Danse avec Nathan Golshem*. Lagrasse: Verdier, 2012.

---. *Haikus de prison.* Lagrasse: Verdier, 2008.

Bayard, Pierre. *L'Affaire du chien des Baskerville*. Paris: Minuit, 2008.

---. *Aurais-je été résistant ou bourreau?* Paris: Minuit, 2013.

---. *Aurais-je sauvé Geneviève Dixmer?* Paris: Minuit, 2015.

---. *Balzac et le troc de l'imaginaire: Lecture de La Peau de chagrin*. Paris: Lettres Modernes-Minard, 1978.

---. *Comment améliorer les oeuvres ratées?* Paris: Minuit, 2000.

---. "Comment j'ai fait régresser la critique." In Laurent Zimmerman, ed. *Pour une critique décalée: Autour des travaux de Pierre Bayard*. Nantes: Editions Cécile Defaut, 2010. 19-37.

---. *Comment parler des lieux où l'on n'a pas été?* Paris: Minuit, 2012.

---. *Comment parler des livres que l'on n'a pas lus?* Paris: Minuit, 2007.

---. *Demain est écrit*. Paris: Minuit, 2005.

---. *Enquête sur Hamlet: Le dialogue de sourds*. Paris: Minuit, 2002.

---. *Et si les oeuvres changaient d'auteur?* Paris: Minuit, 2010.

---. *Le Hors-sujet: Proust et la digression*. Paris: Minuit, 1996.

---. *How to Talk About Books You Haven't Read*. Trans. Jeffrey Mehlman. New York: Bloomsbury, 2007.

---. *Il était deux fois Romain Gary.* Paris: Presses Universitaires de France, 1990.

---. *Il existe d'autres mondes.* Paris: Minuit, 2014.

---, ed. *Lire avec Freud: Pour Jean-Bellemin-Noel.* Paris: Presses Universitaires de France, 1998.

---. *Maupassant, juste avant Freud.* Paris: Minuit, 1994.

---. *Le Paradoxe du menteur: Sur Laclos.* Paris: Minuit, 1993.

---. *Peut-on appliquer la littérature à la psychanalyse?* Paris: Minuit, 2004.

---. *Le Plagiat par anticipation.* Paris: Minuit, 2009.

---, ed. *Pour Eric Chevillard.* Paris: Minuit, 2014.

---. *Qui a tué Roger Akroyd?* Paris: Minuit, 1998.

---. *Sherlock Holmes Was Wrong: Reopening the Case of* The Hound of the Baskervilles. Trans. Charlotte Mandell. New York: Bloomsbury, 2008.

---. *Symptôme de Stendhal:* Armance *et l'aveu.* Paris: Lettres Modernes-Minard, 1980.

---. *Who Killed Roger Akroyd? The Mystery Behind the Agatha Christie Mystery.* Trans. Carol Cosman. New York: New Press, 2000.

Beaujour, Michel. "The Game of Poetics." In Jacques Ehrmann, ed. *Game, Play, Literature.* Boston: Beacon, 1971. 58-67.

Beckett, Samuel. *Disjecta: Miscellaneous Writings and a Dramatic Fragment*. Ed. Ruby Cohn. New York: Grove, 1984.

Bertho, Sophie. "L'Attente postmoderne: A propos de la littérature contemporaine en France." *Revue d'Histoire Littéraire de la France*. 91.4-5 (1991): 735-43.

Blanchot, Maurice. *L'Ecriture du désastre*. Paris: Gallimard, 1980.

---. *L'Entretien infini*. Paris: Gallimard, 1969.

Blatt, Ari. "Remake: Appropriating Film in Tanguy Viel's *Cinéma*." *Contemporary French and Francophone Studies* 9.4 (2005): 379-86.

---. "Tanguy Viel's Manic Fictions." *Contemorary French and Francophone Studies* 14.4 (2010): 373-80.

Booth, Wayne. *The Rhetoric of Fiction*. Chicago: University of Chicago Press, 1961.

Briot, Frédéric. "Les Chimères d'Antoine Volodine." *Roman 20-50* 19 (1995): 205-214.

Casanova, Pascale. "A Fragmentary History of Trashcan Literature." Trans. Roxanne Lapidus. *SubStance* 101 (2003): 44-51.

Chambers, Ross. *Loiterature*. Lincoln: University of Nebraska Press, 1999.

---. *Story and Situation: Narrative Seduction and the Power of Fiction*. Minneapolis: University of Minnesota Press, 1984.

Charles, Michel. *Introduction à l'étude des textes.* Paris: Le Seuil, 1995.

Cloonan, William. "Homage to Jérôme Lindon: The Novel in 2001." *French Review* 76.1 (2002): 45-59.

Conrad, Joseph. *Lord Jim*. New York: Bantam, 1965.

Cosnay, Marie. *Adèle, la scène perdue.* Le Chambon-sur-Lignon: Cheyne, 2005.

---. *L'Allée du bout du monde.* Toulouse: Publie.net, 2010.

---. *André des Ombres.* Paris: Laurence Teper, 2008.

---. *A notre humanité.* Meudon: Quidam, 2012.

---. *La Bataille d'Anghiari*. Las Couti: L'Or des Fous, 2013.

---. *Le Chemin des amoureux.* Limoges: Le Bruit des Autres, 2007.

---. *Comment on expulse, responsabilités en miettes*. Vulaines-sur-Seine: Le Croquant, 2011.

---. *Cordelia la Guerre*. Paris: L'Ogre, 2015.

---. *Déplacements*. Paris: Laurence Teper, 2007.

---. *Des métamorphoses*. Le Chambon-sur-Lignon: Cheyne, 2012.

---. *Entre chagrin et néant.* Paris: Laurence Teper, 2009.

---. *Le Fils de Judith.* Le Chambon-sur-Lignon: Cheyne, 2014.

---. *La Langue maternelle.* Le Chambon-sur-Lignon: Cheyne, 2010.

---. *Noces de Mantoue.* Paris: Laurence Teper, 2009.

---. *Où vont les vaisseux maudits?* Serres-Morlaas: Atelier in 8, 2011.

---. *Ovide: D'Orphée à Achille.* Caen: NOUS: 2011.

---. *Quand les mots du récit.* Toulouse: Publie.net, 2010.

---. *Que s'est-il passé?* Le Chambon-sur-Lignon: Cheyne, 2003.

---. *Les Temps filiaux.* Serres-Morlaas: Atelier in 8, 2008.

---. *Trois Meurtres.* Le Chambon-sur-Lignon: Cheyne, 2008.

---. *Villa Chagrin.* Lagrasse: Verdier, 2006.

Derrida, Jacques. *Otobiographies: L'enseignement de Nietzsche et la politique du nom propre.* Paris: Galilée, 1984.

---. *La Voix et le phénomène: Introduction au problème du signe dans la phénoménologie de Husserl.* Paris: Presses Universitaires de France, 1967.

Deville, Patrick. *Ces deux-là.* Paris: Minuit, 2000.

---. *Cordon-bleu.* Paris: Minuit, 1987.

---. *Equatoria.* Paris: Le Seuil, 2009.

---, and Thierry Guichard. "La Fabrique du héros." *La Matricule des Anges* 49 (2004): 18-22.

---. *La Femme parfaite*. Paris: Minuit, 1995.

---. *Le Feu d'artifice*. Paris: Minuit, 1992.

---. *Kampuchéa*. Paris: Le Seuil, 2011.

---. *Longue Vue*. Paris: Minuit, 1988.

---. *Peste & choléra*. Paris: Le Seuil, 2012.

---. *Plague and Cholera*. Trans. J.A. Underwood. London: Little, Brown, 2014.

---. "Plus formaliste peut-être que minimaliste…" In Marc Dambre and Bruno Blanckeman, eds. *Romanciers minimalistes 1979-2003*. Paris: Presses Sorbonne Nouvelle, 201. 311-30.

---. *Pura Vida: Vie & mort de William Walker*. Paris: Le Seuil, 2004.

---. *Sic transit*. Paris: Le Seuil, 2014.

---. *La Tentation des armes à feu*. Paris: Le Seuil, 2006.

---. *Vie & mort de sainte Tina l'Exilée*. Tours: Publie.net, 2011.

---. *Viva*. Paris: Le Seuil, 2014.

Draeger, Manuela. *L'Arrestation de la grande Mimille*. Paris: L'Ecole des Loisirs, 2007.

---. *Au nord des gloutons*. Paris: L'Ecole des Loisirs, 200.

---. *Belle-Méduse*. Paris: L'Ecole de Loisirs, 2008.

---. *La Course au kwak*. Paris: L'Ecole des Loisirs, 2004.

---. *Le Deuxième Mickey*. Paris: L'Ecole des Loisirs, 2003.

---. *Herbes et golems*. Paris: L'Olivier, 2012.

---. *Moi, les mammouths*. Paris: L'Ecole des Loisirs, 2015.

---. *Nos bébés-pélicans*. Paris: L'Ecole des Loiris, 2003.

---. *La Nuit des mis bémols*. Paris: L'Ecole des Loisirs, 2011.

---. *Un oeuf dans la foule*. Paris: L'Ecole des Loisirs, 2009.

---. *Onze Rêves de suie*. Paris: L'Olivier, 2010.

---. *Pendant la boule bleue*. Paris: L'Ecole des Loisirs, 2002.

---. *Le Radeau de la sardine*. Paris: L'Ecole des Loisirs 2010.

Eco, Umberto. *Postscript to* The Name of the Rose. Trans. William Weaver. New York: Harcourt Brace, 1984.

Freud, Sigmund. "Mourning and Melancholia." In *The Standard Edition of the Complete Psychological Works of Sigmund Freud.* Ed. and trans. James Strachey. Vol. 14. London: Hogarth Press and the Institute of Psycho-Analysis, 1957. 237-58.

Gavarry, Gérard. *Allada.* P.O.L, 1993.

---, and Michel Bézard. *La Barbacane.* Paris: Gallimard, 1968.

---. *Eros acharné*. Paris: P.O.L, 2007.

---. *Expérience d'Edward Lee, Versailles*. Paris: P.O.L, 2009.

---. *Façon d'un roman, ou Comment d'après le Livre de Judith j'ai inventé une histoire de banlieue, et à l'aide du cocotier, du cargo, du Centaure, écrit trois fois* Hoplà! Paris: P.O.L, 2003.

---. *Le Genre des dames*. Paris: P.O.L, 1984.

---. *Hop là! Un deux trois*. Paris: P.O.L, 2001.

---. *Hoppla! 1 2 3*. Trans. Jane Kuntz. Champaign: Dalkey Archive Press, 2009.

---. *Jojo*. Paris: Hachette, 1982; Paris: P.O.L, 1993.

---. *Making a Novel, Or How, Following the Book of Judith, I Devised a Story of the Suburbs, and with the Help of the Coconut Palm, Cargo Ship, and Centaur, Thrice Wrote* Hoppla! Trans. Jane Kuntz. Champaign: Dalkey Archive Press, 2011.

---. *Quarantaine.* Paris: P.O.L, 1990.

---. *La Ville de Paris*. Paris: P.O.L, 1987.

Genette, Gérard. *Bardadrac.* Paris: Le Seuil, 2006.

---. *Codicille*. Paris: Le Seuil, 2009.

---. "De la figure à la fiction." In Pier and Schaeffer 21-35.

---. *Figures III*. Paris: Le Seuil, 1972.

---. *Métalepse: De la figure à la fiction*. Paris: Le Seuil, 2004.

Goffman, Erving. *Asylums*. New York: Anchor, 1961.

Hamel, Jean-Francois. "Le Pistolet *passé* sous la ceinture." *Critique* 719 (2007): 263-78.

Hippolyte, Jean-Louis. *Fuzzy Fiction*. Lincoln: University of Nebraska Press, 2006.

Houppermans, Sjef. "Tanguy Viel: From Word to Image." Trans. Donald Nicholson-Smith. *Yale French Studies* 114 (2008): 37-50.

Huglo, Marie-Pascale. "The Post-Exotic Connection: Passage to Utopia." Trans. Roxanne Lapidus. *SubStance* 101 (2003): 95-108.

---. "La Pythie de Créteil: Voix et spectacle dans *La Compagnie des spectres* de Lydie Salvayre." *Etudes Françaises* 39.1 (2003): 39-55.

Hyppolite, Pierre. "Hyperréalisme et représentation minimaliste dans *La Femme parfaite* de Patrick Deville." In Marc Dambre and Bruno Blanckeman, eds. *Romanciers minimalistes 1979-2003.* Paris: Presses Sorbonne Nouvelle, 2012. 55-69.

Jordan, Shirley. "Marie NDiaye: Enigmes photographiques albums éclatés." *Revue des Sciences Humaines* 293 (2009): 65-82.

Kristeva, Julia. *Black Sun: Depression and Melancholia*. Trans. Leon Roudiez. New York: Columbia University Press, 1989.

Kronauer, Elli. *Aliocha Popovitch et la rivière Saphrate*. Paris: L'Ecole des Loisirs, 2000.

---. *Ilia Mouromietz et le rossignol brigand*. Paris: L'Ecole des Loisirs, 1999.

---. *Mikhailo Potyk et Mariya la très-blanche mouette*. Paris: L'Ecole des Loisirs, 2001.

---. *Sadko et le tsar de toutes les mers océanes*. Paris: L'Ecole des Loisirs, 2000.

---. *Soukmane fils de Soukmane et les fleurs écarlates*. Paris: L'Ecole des Loisirs, 2000.

Lamarre, Mélanie. "'Ici Breughel, il fait très noir: répondez': Figures de la communication dans l'oeuvre d'Antoine Volodine." *Roman 20-50* 46 (2008): 149-61.

Lanser, Susan Sniader. *Fictions of Authority: Women Writers and Narrative Voice*. Ithaca: Cornell University Press, 1992.

Lejeune, Philippe. *La Mémoire et l'oblique: Georges Perec autobiographe*. Paris: P.O.L, 1991.

Louichon, Brigitte. "Lydie Salvayre: 'Parler au nom d'Olympe.'" In Nathalie Morello and Catherine Rodgers, eds. *Nouvelles Ecrivaines: Nouvelles voix?* Amsterdam: Rodopi, 2002. 309-25.

Lyotard, Jean-François. *La Condition postmoderne: Rapport sur le savoir.* Paris: Minuit, 1979.

Majdalani, Charif. "Post-Exoticism, or Internal Literatures." Trans. Roxanne Lapidus. *SubStance* 101 (2003): 64-66.

Malraux, André. *The Royal Way.* Trans Stuart Gilbert. New York: H. Smith and R. Haas, 1935.

---. *La Voie royale.* Paris: Grasset, 1930.

Meister, Jan Christoph. "Le *Metalepticon*: Une étude informatique de la métalepse." Trans. Ioana Vultur. In Pier and Schaeffer 225-46.

Meyer-Minnemann, Klaus. "Un procédé narratif qui 'produit un effet de bizarrerie': La Métalepse littéraire." In Pier and Schaeffer 133-50.

Montalbetti, Christine, and Jacques Neefs, eds. *Le Bonheur de la littérature: Variations critiques pour Béatrice Didier.* Paris: Presses Universitaires de France, 2005.

Montalbetti, Christine. *Le Cas Jekyll.* Paris: P.O.L, 2010.

---. *Chateaubriand: La fabrique du texte.* Presses Universitaires de Rennes, 1999.

---, and Nathalie Piégay-Gros. *La Digression dans le récit.* Paris: Bertrand-Lacoste, 2000.

---. *En écrivant* Journée américaine. Paris: Biro/P.O.L, 2009.

---. "Entretien." *L'Humanité* 21 Nov. 2002 <http://www.humanite.presse.fr/popup_print.php3?id_article=127125>.

---. *L'Evaporation de l'oncle*. Paris: P.O.L, 2011.

---. *Expérience de la campagne*. Paris: P.O.L, 2005.

---. *La Fiction*. Paris: Flammarion, 2001.

---. *Gérard Genette: Une poétique ouverte*. Paris: Bertrand-Lacoste, 1998.

---. *Images du lecteur dans les textes romanesques*. Paris: Bertrand-Lacoste, 1992.

---. *Journée américaine*. Paris: P.O.L, 2009.

---. *Love Hotel*. Paris: P.O.L, 2013.

---. "Narrataire et lecteur: Deux instances autonomes." *Cahiers de Narratologie* 11 (2005). <http://revel.unice.fr/cnarra/document.html?id=13>.

---. *Nouvelles sur le sentiment amoureux*. Paris: P.O.L, 2007.

---. *L'Origine de l'homme*. Paris: P.O.L, 2002.

---. *The Origins of Man*. Trans. Betsy Wing. Champaign: Dalkey Archive Press, 2012.

---. *Paradoxe sur le comédien: Diderot*. Paris: Bertrand-Lacoste, 2000.

---. *Le Personnage*. Paris: Flammarion, 2003.

---. *Petits Déjeuners avec quelques écrivains célèbres*. Paris: P.O.L, 2008.

---. *Plus rien que les vagues et le vent*. Paris: P.O.L, 2014.

---. *Sa fable achevée, Simon sort dans la bruine*. Paris: P.O.L, 2001.

---. *Le Voyage, le monde et la bibliothèque*. Paris: Presses Universitaires de France, 1997.

---. *Western*. Paris: P.O.L, 2005.

---. *Western*. Trans. Betsy Wing. Champaign: Dalkey Archive Press, 2009.

Motte, Warren. "The Critical Novel in France, Today." *World Literature Today* 81.6 (2007): 50-53.

---. *Fiction Now: The French Novel in the Twenty-First Century*. Champaign: Dalkey Archive Press, 2008.

---. "Gérard Gavarry's Hops." *SubStance* 111 (2006): 64-82.

---. "Marie NDiaye's Sorcery." In *Fables of the Novel: French Fiction Since 1990*. Normal: Dalkey Archive Press, 2003. 113-33.

---. *Mirror Gazing*. Champaign: Dalkey Archive Press, 2014.

---. "Pierre Bayard's Wormholes." *Studies in Twentieth and Twenty-First Century Literature*. 35.2 (2011): 268-94.

---. "Reading Gérard Gavarry." *Context* 21 (2008): 1-3.

---. "Voices in Her Head." *SubStance* 104 (2004): 13-29.

Moudileno, Lydie. "Délits, détours et affabulation: L'écriture de l'anthème dans *En famille* de Marie NDiaye." *French Review* 71.3 (1998): 442-53.

---. "L'Excellent Français de Marie NDiaye." *Revue des Sciences Humaines* 293 (2009): 25-38.

NDiaye, Marie. *All My Friends*. Trans. Jordan Stump. San Francisco: Two Lines Press, 2014.

---. *Among Family*. Trans. Heather Doyal. Tunbridge Wells: Angela Royal, 1997.

---. *Autoportrait en vert*. Paris: Mercure de France, 2005.

---. *Comédie classique*. Paris: Minuit, 1987.

---. *La Diablesse et son enfant*. Paris: L'Ecole des Loisirs, 2000.

---. *En famille*. Paris: Minuit, 1990.

---. *La Femme changée en bûche*. Paris: Minuit, 1989.

---. *Hilda*. Paris: Minuit, 1999.

---. *Ladivine*. Paris: Gallimard, 2013.

---. *Mon Coeur à l'étroit*. Paris: Gallimard, 2007.

---. *La Naufragée*: J.M.W. Turner. Charenton: Flohic, 1999.

---. *Papa doit manger*. Paris: Minuit, 2003.

---. *Les Paradis de Prunelle*. Paris: Albin Michel, 2002.

---, and Jean-Yves Cendrey. *Puzzle*. Paris: Gallimard, 2007.

---. *Quant au riche avenir*. Paris: Minuit, 1985.

---. *Rosie Carpe*. Paris: Minuit, 2001.

---. *Rosie Carpe*. Trans. Tamsin Black. Lincoln: University of Nebraska Press, 2004.

---. *Self-Portrait in Green*. Trans. Jordan Stump. San Francisco: Two Lines Press, 2014.

---. *Les Serpents*. Paris: Minuit, 2004.

---. *La Sorcière*. Paris: Minuit, 1996.

---. *Le Souhait*. Paris: L'Ecole des Loisirs, 2005.

---. *Un temps de saison*. Paris: Minuit, 1994.

---. *Three Strong Women*. Trans. John Fletcher. London: MacLehose Press, 2012.

---. *Tous mes amis*. Paris: Minuit, 2004.

---. *Trois Femmes puissantes*. Paris: Gallimard, 2009.

O'Brien, John. "An Interview with John O'Brien." <http://www.dalkeyarchive.com/interview>.

Pavel, Thomas. *Fictional Worlds*. Cambridge: Harvard University Press, 1996.

Perec, Georges. "Notes sur ce que je cherche." In *Penser/Classer*. Paris: Hachette, 1985. 9-12.

---. *La Vie mode d'emploi*. Paris: Hachette, 1978.

---. *Life A User's Manual.* Trans. David Bellos. Boston: Godine, 1987.

Pier, John. "Métalepse et hiérarchies narratives." In Pier and Schaeffer 247-61.

---, and Jean-Marie Schaeffer, eds. *Métalepses: Entorses au pacte de la représentation*. Paris: Ecole des Hautes Etudes en Sciences Sociales, 2005.

Piwowarczyk, Mary Ann. "The Narratee and the Situation of Enunciation: A Reconsideration of Prince's Theory." *Genre* 9.2 (1976): 161-77.

Prieto, Eric. *Listening In: Music, Mind, and the Modernist Narrative*. Lincoln: University of Nebraska Press, 2003.

Prince, Gerald. *A Dictionary of Narratoloygy*. 1987. Rev. ed. Lincoln: University of Nebraska Press, 2003.

---. "Disturbing Frames." *Poetics Today* 27.3 (2006): 625-30.

---. "Introduction à l'étude du narrataire." *Poétique* 14 (1973): 178-96.

---. *Narrative as Theme: Studies in French Fiction*. Lincoln: University of Nebraska Press, 1992.

Rabau, Sophie. "Ulysse à côté d'Homère: Interprétation et transgression des frontières énonciatives." In Pier and Schaeffer, 59-72.

Roche, Anne. "The Clarity of Secrets." Trans. Roxanne Lapidus. *SubStance* 101 (2003): 52-63.

Rolin, Jean. *Campagnes*. Paris: Gallimard, 2000.

---. *C'était juste cinq heures du soir*. With Jean-Christian Bourcart. Cherbourg-Octeville: Le Point du Jour, 1998.

---. *Christians in Palestine*. Trans. Marjolijn de Jager. Brooklyn: Ig, 2006.

---. *La Clôture*. Paris: P.O.L, 2002.

---. *Cyrille et Méthode*. Paris: Gallimard, 1994.

---. *Dingos, suivi de Cherbourg-Est/Cherbourg-Ouest*. Monaco: Editions du Patrimoine, 2002.

---. *Les Evénements*. Paris: P.O.L, 2015.

---. *L'Explosion de la durite*. Paris: P.O.L, 2007.

---. *The Explosion of the Radiator Hose*. Trans Louise Rogers Lalaurie. Champaign: Dalkey Archive Press, 2011.

---. *La Frontière belge*. Paris: Lattès, 1989.

---. *L'Homme qui a vu l'ours: Reportages et autres articles 1980-2005*. Paris: P.O.L, 2006.

---. *Joséphine*. Paris: Gallimard, 1994.

---. *Journal de Gand aux Aléoutiennes*. Paris: Lattès, 1982.

---. *La Ligne de front*. Paris: Quai Voltaire, 1988.

---. *L'Or du scaphandrier*. Paris: Lattès, 1983.

---. *L'Organisation*. Paris: Gallimard, 1996.

---. *Ormuz*. Paris: P.O.L, 2013.

---. *Le Ravissement de Britney Spears*. Paris: P.O.L, 2011.

---. *Terminal Frigo*. Paris: P.O.L, 2005.

---. *Traverses*. Paris: NIL, 1999.

---. *Un chien mort après lui*. Paris: P.O.L, 2009.

---. *Vu sur la mer*. Strasbourg: Bueb et Reumaux, 1986.

---. *Zones*. Paris: Gallimard, 1995.

Rousset, Jean. *Dernier Regard sur le Baroque*. Paris: Corti, 1998.

Ruffel, Lionel. *Le Dénouement*. Lagrasse: Verdier, 2005.

---. "Interrogation: A Post-Exotic Device." Trans. Roxanne Lapidus. *SubStance* 101 (2003): 79-94.

Saint-Gelais, Richard. "Faction Antoine Volodine." *Tangence* 52 (1996): 89-104.

Salvayre, Lydie. *7 Femmes*. Paris: Perrin, 2013.

---. *The Award.* Trans. Jane Davey. New York: Four Walls Eight Windows, 1997.

---. *Les Belles Ames*. Paris: Le Seuil, 2000.

---. *BW*. Paris: Le Seuil, 2009.

---. *La Compagnie de spectres*. Paris: Le Seuil, 1997.

---. *The Company of Ghosts, Followed by Some Useful Advice for Apprentice Process-Servers*. Trans. Christopher Woodall. Normal: Dalkey Archive Press, 2006.

---. *La Conférence de Cintegabelle*. Paris: Le Seuil/Verticales, 1999.

---. *Contre*. Paris: Le Seuil/Verticales, 2002.

---. *La Déclaration*. Paris: Julliard, 1990. Paris: Verticales, 1997.

---. *Dis pas ça*. Paris: Le Seuil/Verticales, 2006.

---. *Everyday Life*. Trans. Jane Kuntz. Normal: Dalkey Archive Press, 2006.

---. *Hymne*. Paris: Le Seuil, 2011.

---. *The Lecture*. Trans. Linda Coverdale. Normal: Dalkey Archive Press, 2005.

---. *Et que les vers mangent le boeuf mort*. Paris: Le Seuil/Verticales, 2002.

---. *La Médaille*. Paris: Le Seuil, 1993.

---. *La Méthode Mila*. Paris: Le Seuil, 2005.

---. *Pas pleurer*. Paris: Le Seuil, 2014.

---. *Passage à l'ennemie*. Paris: Le Seuil, 2003.

---. *Portrait de l'écrivain en animal domestique*. Paris: Le Seuil, 2007.

---. *Portrait of the Writer as a Domesticated Animal*. Trans. William Pedersen. Champaign: Dalkey Archive Press, 2010.

---. *The Power of Flies*. Trans. Jane Kuntz. Champaign: Dalkey Archive Press, 2007.

---. *La Puissance des mouches*. Paris: Le Seuil, 1995.

---. *Quelques Conseils utiles aux élèves huissiers*. Paris: Verticales, 1997.

---. *La Vie commune*. Paris: Julliard, 1991. Paris: Verticales, 1999.

---. *Le Vif du vivant*. Paris: Editions Cercle d'Art, 2001.

Schaeffer, Jean-Marie. "Métalepse et immersion fictionelle." In Pier and Schaeffer 323-24.

Schafer, Rudolf. *Der Ewige Schlaf: Visages des Morts*. Hamburg: Kellner, 1989.

Schoentjes, Pierre. "Les 'beaux hasards' de Patrick Deville: *Kampuchéa* et la terreur." *Carnets de Chaminadour*, forthcoming.

---. "L'Ironie contemporaine de la fugue à la fantaisie: Chevillard au risque de l'ironie." In Didier Alexandre et Pierre Schoentjes, eds. *L'Ironie: Formes et enjeux d'un écrivain contemporain.* Paris: Classiques Garnier, 2013. 223-46.

Schoots, Fieke. "*Passer en douce à la douane*": *L'écriture minimaliste de Minuit.* Amsterdam and Atlanta: Rodopi, 1997.

Smock, Ann. *What Is There to Say? Blanchot, Melville, des Forêts, Beckett.* Lincoln: University of Nebraska Press, 2003.

Teko-Agbo, K. Ambroise. "*En famille* or the Problem of Alterity." Trans. Ruthmarie H. Mitsch. *Research in African Literatures* 26.2 (1995): 158-68.

Toussaint, Jean-Philippe. *The Bathroom.* Trans. Nancy Amphoux and Paul De Angelis. Champaign: Dalkey Archive Press, 2008.

---. *La Salle de bain.* Paris: Minuit, 1985.

Veivo, Harri. "Strange Things on the Edge of the City: Writing Strategies in Contemporary French Suburban Literature." *Semiotica: Journal of the International Association for Semiotic Studies/Revue de l'Association Internationale de Sémiotique* 150 1-4 (2004): 283-305.

Viel, Tanguy. *L'Absolue Perfection du crime.* Paris: Minuit, 2001.

---. *The Absolute Perfection of Crime.* Trans. Linda Coverdale. New York: New Press, 2003.

---. *Beyond Suspicion.* Trans. Linda Coverdale. New York: New Press, 2008.

---. *Le Black Note*. Paris: Minuit, 1998.

---. *Cet homme-là*. Paris: Desclée de Brouwer, 2009.

---. *Cinéma*. Paris: Minuit, 1999.

---. *La Disparition de Jim Sullivan*. Paris: Minuit, 2013.

---. *Insoupçonnable*. Paris: Minuit, 2006.

---. *Paris-Brest*. Paris: Minuit, 2009.

---, and Amandine Riant, Marie-Thérèse Roinet. *Tanguy Viel parle des Editions de Minuit*. Paris: Université de Paris X, Pôle des Métiers du Livre, 2002.

---. Volodine, Antoine. *Alto solo*. Paris: Minuit, 1991.

---. *Bardo or not Bardo*. Paris: Le Seuil, 2004.

---. *Biographie comparée de Jorian Murgrave*. Paris: Denoël, 1985.

---. *Dondog*. Paris: Le Seuil, 2002.

---. *Des anges mineurs*. Paris: Le Seuil, 1999.

---. *Des enfers fabuleux*. Paris: Denoël, 1998.

---. "Ecrire en français une littérature étrangère." *Chaoïd* 6 (2002): 52-58.

---. *Ecrivains*. Paris: Le Seuil, 2010.

---. *Lisbonne, dernière marge*. Paris: Minuit, 1990.

---. *Macau*. Paris: Le Seuil, 2010.

---. *Minor Angels*. Trans. Jordan Stump. Lincoln: University of Nebraska Press, 2004.

---. *Naming the Jungle*. Trans. Linda Coverdale. New York: New Press, 1995.

---. *Un navire de nulle part*. Paris: Denoël, 1986.

---. *Le Nom des singes*. Paris: Minuit, 1994.

---. *Nos animaux préférés*. Paris: Le Seuil, 2006.

---. *Nuit blanche en Balkhyrie*. Paris: Gallimard, 1997.

---, and Jean-Didier Wagneur. "On recommence depuis le début." In Anne Roche and Dominique Viart, eds. *Antoine Volodine: Fictions du politique*. Caen: Minard, 2007. 227-77.

---. *Le Port intérieur*. Paris: Minuit, 1996.

---. *Le Post-exotisme en dix leçons, leçon onze*. Paris: Gallimard, 1998.

---. *Post-Exoticism in Ten Lessons, Lesson Eleven*. Trans. J.T. Mahany. Rochester: Open Letter, 2015.

---. *Rituel du mépris*. Paris: Denoel, 1986.

---. *Songes de Mevlido*. Paris: Le Seuil, 2007.

---. *Terminus radieux*. Paris: Le Seuil, 2014.

---. *Vue sur l'ossuaire*. Paris: Gallimard, 1998.

---. *Writers*. Trans Katina Rogers. Champaign: Dalkey Archive Press, 2014.

Wagner, Frank. "'C'est à moi que tu parles?' (Allocutaires et auditeurs dans *Le Black Note* de Tanguy Viel)." In Christine Bosman Delzons, Sjef Houppermans, and Daniele du Ruyter-Tognotti eds. *Territoires et terres d'histoires: Perspectives, horizons, jardins secrets dans la littérature française d'aujourd'hui.* Amsterdam: Rodopi, 2005. 217-44.

Wagneur, Jean-Didier. "Introduction." Trans. Roxanne Lapidus. *SubStance* 101 (2003): 3-11.

Warhol, Robyn. "Toward a Theory of the Engaging Narrator: Earnest Interventions in Gaskell, Stowe, and Eliot." *PMLA* 101.5 (1986): 811-18.

WARREN MOTTE is College Professor of Distinction at the University of Colorado and a Chevalier in the Order of Academic Palms. He specializes in contemporary French literature, with particular focus upon experimentalist works that put accepted notions of literary form into question. His recent books include *Fables of the Novel: French Fiction since 1990* (2003), *Fiction Now: The French Novel in the Twenty-First Century* (2008), and *Mirror Gazing* (2014).

MICHAL AJVAZ, *The Golden Age.*
The Other City.

PIERRE ALBERT-BIROT, *Grabinoulor.*

YUZ ALESHKOVSKY, *Kangaroo.*

FELIPE ALFAU, *Chromos.*
Locos.

JOE AMATO, *Samuel Taylor's Last Night.*

IVAN ÂNGELO, *The Celebration.*
The Tower of Glass.

ANTÓNIO LOBO ANTUNES, *Knowledge of Hell.*
The Splendor of Portugal.

ALAIN ARIAS-MISSON, *Theatre of Incest.*

JOHN ASHBERY & JAMES SCHUYLER, *A Nest of Ninnies.*

ROBERT ASHLEY, *Perfect Lives.*

GABRIELA AVIGUR-ROTEM, *Heatwave and Crazy Birds.*

DJUNA BARNES, *Ladies Almanack.*
Ryder.

JOHN BARTH, *Letters.*
Sabbatical.

DONALD BARTHELME, *The King.*
Paradise.

SVETISLAV BASARA, *Chinese Letter.*

MIQUEL BAUÇÀ, *The Siege in the Room.*

RENÉ BELLETTO, *Dying.*

MAREK BIENCZYK, *Transparency.*

ANDREI BITOV, *Pushkin House.*

ANDREJ BLATNIK, *You Do Understand.*
Law of Desire.

LOUIS PAUL BOON, *Chapel Road.*
My Little War.
Summer in Termuren.

ROGER BOYLAN, *Killoyle.*

IGNÁCIO DE LOYOLA BRANDÃO, *Anonymous Celebrity.*
Zero.

BONNIE BREMSER, *Troia: Mexican Memoirs.*

CHRISTINE BROOKE-ROSE, *Amalgamemnon.*

BRIGID BROPHY, *In Transit.*
The Prancing Novelist.

GERALD L. BRUNS, *Modern Poetry and the Idea of Language.*

GABRIELLE BURTON, *Heartbreak Hotel.*

MICHEL BUTOR, *Degrees.*
Mobile.

G. CABRERA INFANTE, *Infante's Inferno.*
Three Trapped Tigers.

JULIETA CAMPOS, *The Fear of Losing Eurydice.*

ANNE CARSON, *Eros the Bittersweet.*

ORLY CASTEL-BLOOM, *Dolly City.*

LOUIS-FERDINAND CÉLINE, *North.*
Conversations with Professor Y.
London Bridge.

MARIE CHAIX, *The Laurels of Lake Constance.*

HUGO CHARTERIS, *The Tide Is Right.*

ERIC CHEVILLARD, *Demolishing Nisard.*
The Author and Me.

MARC CHOLODENKO, *Mordechai Schamz.*

JOSHUA COHEN, *Witz.*

EMILY HOLMES COLEMAN, *The Shutter of Snow.*

ERIC CHEVILLARD, *The Author and Me.*

ROBERT COOVER, *A Night at the Movies.*

STANLEY CRAWFORD, *Log of the S.S. The Mrs Unguentine.*
Some Instructions to My Wife.

RENÉ CREVEL, *Putting My Foot in It.*

RALPH CUSACK, *Cadenza.*

NICHOLAS DELBANCO, *Sherbrookes.*
The Count of Concord.

NIGEL DENNIS, *Cards of Identity.*

PETER DIMOCK, *A Short Rhetoric for Leaving the Family.*

ARIEL DORFMAN, *Konfidenz.*

COLEMAN DOWELL, *Island People.*
Too Much Flesh and Jabez.

ARKADII DRAGOMOSHCHENKO, *Dust.*

RIKKI DUCORNET, *Phosphor in Dreamland.*
The Complete Butcher's Tales.

RIKKI DUCORNET (cont.), *The Jade Cabinet.*
The Fountains of Neptune.

WILLIAM EASTLAKE, *The Bamboo Bed.*
Castle Keep.
Lyric of the Circle Heart.

JEAN ECHENOZ, *Chopin's Move.*

STANLEY ELKIN, *A Bad Man.*
Criers and Kibitzers, Kibitzers and Criers.
The Dick Gibson Show.
The Franchiser.
The Living End.
Mrs. Ted Bliss.

FRANÇOIS EMMANUEL, *Invitation to a Voyage.*

PAUL EMOND, *The Dance of a Sham.*

SALVADOR ESPRIU, *Ariadne in the Grotesque Labyrinth.*

LESLIE A. FIEDLER, *Love and Death in the American Novel.*

JUAN FILLOY, *Op Oloop.*

ANDY FITCH, *Pop Poetics.*

GUSTAVE FLAUBERT, *Bouvard and Pécuchet.*

KASS FLEISHER, *Talking out of School.*

JON FOSSE, *Aliss at the Fire.*
Melancholy.

FORD MADOX FORD, *The March of Literature.*

MAX FRISCH, *I'm Not Stiller.*
Man in the Holocene.

CARLOS FUENTES, *Christopher Unborn.*
Distant Relations.
Terra Nostra.
Where the Air Is Clear.

TAKEHIKO FUKUNAGA, *Flowers of Grass.*

WILLIAM GADDIS, JR., *The Recognitions.*

JANICE GALLOWAY, *Foreign Parts.*
The Trick Is to Keep Breathing.

WILLIAM H. GASS, *Life Sentences.*
The Tunnel.
The World Within the Word.
Willie Masters' Lonesome Wife.

GÉRARD GAVARRY, *Hoppla! 1 2 3.*

ETIENNE GILSON, *The Arts of the Beautiful.*
Forms and Substances in the Arts.

C. S. GISCOMBE, *Giscome Road.*
Here.

DOUGLAS GLOVER, *Bad News of the Heart.*

WITOLD GOMBROWICZ, *A Kind of Testament.*

PAULO EMÍLIO SALES GOMES, *P's Three Women.*

GEORGI GOSPODINOV, *Natural Novel.*

JUAN GOYTISOLO, *Count Julian.*
Juan the Landless.
Makbara.
Marks of Identity.

HENRY GREEN, *Blindness.*
Concluding.
Doting.
Nothing.

JACK GREEN, *Fire the Bastards!*

JIŘÍ GRUŠA, *The Questionnaire.*

MELA HARTWIG, *Am I a Redundant Human Being?*

JOHN HAWKES, *The Passion Artist.*
Whistlejacket.

ELIZABETH HEIGHWAY, ED., *Contemporary Georgian Fiction.*

AIDAN HIGGINS, *Balcony of Europe.*
Blind Man's Bluff.
Bornholm Night-Ferry.
Langrishe, Go Down.
Scenes from a Receding Past.

KEIZO HINO, *Isle of Dreams.*

KAZUSHI HOSAKA, *Plainsong.*

ALDOUS HUXLEY, *Antic Hay.*
Point Counter Point.
Those Barren Leaves.
Time Must Have a Stop.

NAOYUKI II, *The Shadow of a Blue Cat.*

DRAGO JANČAR, *The Tree with No Name.*

MIKHEIL JAVAKHISHVILI, *Kvachi.*

GERT JONKE, *The Distant Sound.*
Homage to Czerny.
The System of Vienna.

JACQUES JOUET, *Mountain R.*
Savage.
Upstaged.

MIEKO KANAI, *The Word Book.*

YORAM KANIUK, *Life on Sandpaper.*

ZURAB KARUMIDZE, *Dagny.*

JOHN KELLY, *From Out of the City.*

HUGH KENNER, *Flaubert, Joyce and Beckett: The Stoic Comedians.*
Joyce's Voices.

DANILO KIŠ, *The Attic.*
The Lute and the Scars.
Psalm 44.
A Tomb for Boris Davidovich.

ANITA KONKKA, *A Fool's Paradise.*

GEORGE KONRÁD, *The City Builder.*

TADEUSZ KONWICKI, *A Minor Apocalypse.*
The Polish Complex.

ANNA KORDZAIA-SAMADASHVILI, *Me, Margarita.*

MENIS KOUMANDAREAS, *Koula.*

ELAINE KRAF, *The Princess of 72nd Street.*

JIM KRUSOE, *Iceland.*

AYSE KULIN, *Farewell: A Mansion in Occupied Istanbul.*

EMILIO LASCANO TEGUI, *On Elegance While Sleeping.*

ERIC LAURRENT, *Do Not Touch.*

VIOLETTE LEDUC, *La Bâtarde.*

EDOUARD LEVÉ, *Autoportrait.*
Newspaper.
Suicide.
Works.

MARIO LEVI, *Istanbul Was a Fairy Tale.*

DEBORAH LEVY, *Billy and Girl.*

JOSÉ LEZAMA LIMA, *Paradiso.*

ROSA LIKSOM, *Dark Paradise.*

OSMAN LINS, *Avalovara.*
The Queen of the Prisons of Greece.

FLORIAN LIPUŠ, *The Errors of Young Tjaž.*

GORDON LISH, *Peru.*

ALF MACLOCHLAINN, *Out of Focus.*
Past Habitual.
The Corpus in the Library.

RON LOEWINSOHN, *Magnetic Field(s).*

YURI LOTMAN, *Non-Memoirs.*

D. KEITH MANO, *Take Five.*

MINA LOY, *Stories and Essays of Mina Loy.*

MICHELINE AHARONIAN MARCOM, *A Brief History of Yes.*
The Mirror in the Well.

BEN MARCUS, *The Age of Wire and String.*

WALLACE MARKFIELD, *Teitlebaum's Window.*

DAVID MARKSON, *Reader's Block.*
Wittgenstein's Mistress.

CAROLE MASO, *AVA.*

HISAKI MATSUURA, *Triangle.*

LADISLAV MATEJKA & KRYSTYNA POMORSKA, EDS., *Readings in Russian Poetics: Formalist & Structuralist Views.*

HARRY MATHEWS, *Cigarettes.*
The Conversions.
The Human Country.
The Journalist.
My Life in CIA.
Singular Pleasures.
The Sinking of the Odradek.
Stadium.
Tlooth.

HISAKI MATSUURA, *Triangle.*

DONAL MCLAUGHLIN, *beheading the virgin mary, and other stories.*

JOSEPH MCELROY, *Night Soul and Other Stories.*

ABDELWAHAB MEDDEB, *Talismano.*

GERHARD MEIER, *Isle of the Dead.*

HERMAN MELVILLE, *The Confidence-Man.*

AMANDA MICHALOPOULOU, *I'd Like.*

STEVEN MILLHAUSER, *The Barnum Museum.*
In the Penny Arcade.

RALPH J. MILLS, JR., *Essays on Poetry.*

MOMUS, *The Book of Jokes.*

CHRISTINE MONTALBETTI, *The Origin of Man.*
Western.

NICHOLAS MOSLEY, *Accident.*
Assassins.
Catastrophe Practice.
A Garden of Trees.
Hopeful Monsters.
Imago Bird.
Inventing God.
Look at the Dark.
Metamorphosis.
Natalie Natalia.
Serpent.

WARREN MOTTE, *Fables of the Novel: French Fiction since 1990.*
Fiction Now: The French Novel in the 21st Century.
Mirror Gazing.
Oulipo: A Primer of Potential Literature.

GERALD MURNANE, *Barley Patch.*
Inland.

YVES NAVARRE, *Our Share of Time.*
Sweet Tooth.

DOROTHY NELSON, *In Night's City.*
Tar and Feathers.

ESHKOL NEVO, *Homesick.*

WILFRIDO D. NOLLEDO, *But for the Lovers.*

BORIS A. NOVAK, *The Master of Insomnia.*

FLANN O'BRIEN, *At Swim-Two-Birds.*
The Best of Myles.
The Dalkey Archive.
The Hard Life.
The Poor Mouth.
The Third Policeman.

CLAUDE OLLIER, *The Mise-en-Scène.*
Wert and the Life Without End.

PATRIK OUŘEDNÍK, *Europeana.*
The Opportune Moment, 1855.

BORIS PAHOR, *Necropolis.*

FERNANDO DEL PASO, *News from the Empire.*
Palinuro of Mexico.

ROBERT PINGET, *The Inquisitory.*
Mahu or The Material.
Trio.

MANUEL PUIG, *Betrayed by Rita Hayworth.*
The Buenos Aires Affair.
Heartbreak Tango.

RAYMOND QUENEAU, *The Last Days.*
Odile.
Pierrot Mon Ami.
Saint Glinglin.

ANN QUIN, *Berg.*
Passages.
Three.
Tripticks.

ISHMAEL REED, *The Free-Lance Pallbearers.*
The Last Days of Louisiana Red.
Ishmael Reed: The Plays.
Juice!
The Terrible Threes.
The Terrible Twos.
Yellow Back Radio Broke-Down.

JASIA REICHARDT, *15 Journeys Warsaw to London.*

JOÃO UBALDO RIBEIRO, *House of the Fortunate Buddhas.*

JEAN RICARDOU, *Place Names.*

RAINER MARIA RILKE,
The Notebooks of Malte Laurids Brigge.

JULIÁN RÍOS, *The House of Ulysses.*
Larva: A Midsummer Night's Babel.
Poundemonium.

ALAIN ROBBE-GRILLET, *Project for a Revolution in New York.*
A Sentimental Novel.

AUGUSTO ROA BASTOS, *I the Supreme.*

DANIËL ROBBERECHTS, *Arriving in Avignon.*

JEAN ROLIN, *The Explosion of the Radiator Hose.*

OLIVIER ROLIN, *Hotel Crystal.*

ALIX CLEO ROUBAUD, *Alix's Journal.*

JACQUES ROUBAUD, *The Form of a City Changes Faster, Alas, Than the Human Heart.*
The Great Fire of London.
Hortense in Exile.
Hortense Is Abducted.
Mathematics: The Plurality of Worlds of Lewis.
Some Thing Black.

RAYMOND ROUSSEL, *Impressions of Africa.*

VEDRANA RUDAN, *Night.*

PABLO M. RUIZ, *Four Cold Chapters on the Possibility of Literature.*

GERMAN SADULAEV, *The Maya Pill.*

TOMAŽ ŠALAMUN, *Soy Realidad.*

LYDIE SALVAYRE, *The Company of Ghosts.*
The Lecture.
The Power of Flies.

LUIS RAFAEL SÁNCHEZ, *Macho Camacho's Beat.*

SEVERO SARDUY, *Cobra & Maitreya.*

NATHALIE SARRAUTE, *Do You Hear Them?*
Martereau.
The Planetarium.

STIG SÆTERBAKKEN, *Siamese.*
Self-Control.
Through the Night.

ARNO SCHMIDT, *Collected Novellas.*
Collected Stories.
Nobodaddy's Children.
Two Novels.

ASAF SCHURR, *Motti.*

GAIL SCOTT, *My Paris.*

DAMION SEARLS, *What We Were Doing and Where We Were Going.*

JUNE AKERS SEESE, *Is This What Other Women Feel Too?*

BERNARD SHARE, *Inish.*
Transit.

VIKTOR SHKLOVSKY, *Bowstring.*
Literature and Cinematography.
Theory of Prose.
Third Factory.
Zoo, or Letters Not about Love.

PIERRE SINIAC, *The Collaborators.*

KJERSTI A. SKOMSVOLD, *The Faster I Walk, the Smaller I Am.*

JOSEF ŠKVORECKÝ, *The Engineer of Human Souls.*

GILBERT SORRENTINO, *Aberration of Starlight.*
Blue Pastoral.
Crystal Vision.
Imaginative Qualities of Actual Things.
Mulligan Stew. Red the Fiend.
Steelwork.
Under the Shadow.

MARKO SOSIČ, *Ballerina, Ballerina.*

ANDRZEJ STASIUK, *Dukla.*
Fado.

GERTRUDE STEIN, *The Making of Americans.*
A Novel of Thank You.

LARS SVENDSEN, *A Philosophy of Evil.*

PIOTR SZEWC, *Annihilation.*

GONÇALO M. TAVARES, *A Man: Klaus Klump.*
Jerusalem.
Learning to Pray in the Age of Technique.

LUCIAN DAN TEODOROVICI, *Our Circus Presents . . .*

NIKANOR TERATOLOGEN, *Assisted Living.*

STEFAN THEMERSON, *Hobson's Island.*
The Mystery of the Sardine.
Tom Harris.

TAEKO TOMIOKA, *Building Waves.*

JOHN TOOMEY, *Sleepwalker.*

DUMITRU TSEPENEAG, *Hotel Europa.*
The Necessary Marriage.
Pigeon Post.
Vain Art of the Fugue.

ESTHER TUSQUETS, *Stranded.*

DUBRAVKA UGRESIC, *Lend Me Your Character.*
Thank You for Not Reading.

TOR ULVEN, *Replacement.*

MATI UNT, *Brecht at Night.*
Diary of a Blood Donor.
Things in the Night.

ÁLVARO URIBE & OLIVIA SEARS, EDS., *Best of Contemporary Mexican Fiction.*

ELOY URROZ, *Friction.*
The Obstacles.

LUISA VALENZUELA, *Dark Desires and the Others.*
He Who Searches.

PAUL VERHAEGHEN, *Omega Minor.*

BORIS VIAN, *Heartsnatcher.*